The Book Rat's Daughter

The Book Rat's Daughter

A Memoir

CAROLYN MICHAELS KERR

Foreword by Marshall Bruce Gentry

RESOURCE *Publications* · Eugene, Oregon

THE BOOK RAT'S DAUGHTER
A Memoir

Copyright © 2025 Carolyn Michaels Kerr. All rights reserved. Except for brief quotations in critical publications or reviews, no part of this book may be reproduced in any manner without prior written permission from the publisher. Write: Permissions, Wipf and Stock Publishers, 199 W. 8th Ave., Suite 3, Eugene, OR 97401.

Resource Publications
An Imprint of Wipf and Stock Publishers
199 W. 8th Ave., Suite 3
Eugene, OR 97401

www.wipfandstock.com

PAPERBACK ISBN: 979-8-3852-5103-2
HARDCOVER ISBN: 979-8-3852-5104-9
EBOOK ISBN: 979-8-3852-5105-6
VERSION NUMBER 11/12/25

Scripture quotations taken from The Holy Bible, New International Version®, NIV®. Copyright © 1973, 1978, 1984, 2011 by Biblica, Inc. Used with permission of Zondervan. All rights reserved worldwide. www.zondervan.com

Cover art: "Departure" by Melora Kuhn, courtesy of the artist and Galerie Eigen + Art Liepzig/Berlin

In memory of my father,

J. Ramsey Michaels

Contents

Foreword by Marshall Bruce Gentry | ix

1 When I Croak | 1
2 Mormon Hymnal | 4
3 Geneva Bible | 7
4 Memoir (His) | 10
5 Collector | 16
6 Beginnings | 19
7 Museum | 23
8 Turnbull Legacy | 26
9 Early Years | 32
10 Devils | 39
11 High School | 42
12 Princeton and Beyond | 44
13 Getting Canned | 48
14 (Re)catching the Virus | 53
15 The Good Book | 57
16 Oldest English Byble | 59
17 King James Version | 63
18 The Mushroom Effect | 66
19 Companions | 70
20 Lunches | 76
21 Common Ground | 82
22 Decisions, Decisions | 85
23 The Move | 89
24 Organization | 92
25 Courtly Lover | 97
26 Carnal Lover | 100

Contents

27 Books He Wrote | 104
28 More Bibles | 107
29 The Competition | 117
30 Concordance | 123
31 The Christian's Dictionary | 125
32 My Father's Wild Enthusiast | 127
33 More Enthusiasm | 136
34 The Bethlehem Moravians | 141
35 Apocalypse | 147
36 Bunyan | 155
37 The Baptists | 160
38 Mary Abigail Dodge, aka Gail Hamilton | 168
39 Flannery | 173
40 Something Bad | 184
41 Ramsey! Ramsey! Stay with Me! | 191
42 Postscript | 195
43 PPS | 199

Appendix: Selections from My Father's Anthology | 203
Bibliography | 209

Foreword

READING THIS CHARMING MEMOIR about a book rat and his daughter, I find myself thinking, as always, about literary studies. In one of Flannery O'Connor's stories, "The River," there is a minor character named George who has been generally criticized, and harshly, by O'Connor scholars. We meet George when the story's young protagonist, Harry/Bevel Ashfield, the child of George's friends, arrives back home after stealing from his babysitter a volume dated 1832, *The Life of Jesus Christ for Readers Under Twelve*,[1] a book marked with the name of the babysitter's grandmother. George pronounces the book "valuable," "a collector's item," and his girlfriend warns everyone, "Don't let George go off with that."[2] The usual critical take on George, who, wearing "a thick pair of glasses,"[3] might be one of those pompous intellectuals that O'Connor always loved to satirize, is that George sees only the book's monetary value, not its spiritual value.

Carolyn Michaels Kerr's memoir about her father, J. Ramsey Michaels, shows O'Connor scholars that we may have been too quick to judge people like George. Professor Michaels deeply valued all sorts of books about theology, especially the old and rare ones, and perhaps even more especially the ones with monetary value. Often it is the case that the more enthusiastic and eccentric and questionable the author of a religious book was, the more Ramsey liked it. He loved marginalia. He loved alternative editions and printings. He loved researching the ownership history of a book. The theological contents fascinated him, even though they often presented ideas with which Ramsey would disagree. And still he could be quite pleased when he sold one of his great many books—as was his wife, Betty—especially when he could get a good price. J. Ramsey Michaels knew and cared

1. O'Connor, *Collected Works*, 167.
2. O'Connor, *Collected Works*, 167.
3. O'Connor, *Collected Works*, 167.

Foreword

about the fine points of theology—enough so that he could once be forced to retire from a religious academic institution because of one of those fine points—but he ended up teaching happily for years at what is now called Missouri State University, in Springfield.

Carolyn Kerr, a trained creative writer, has tastes that differ from those of her father. She identifies as a fan of Joyce Carol Oates and Jean Paul Sartre. But the daughter and father shared a deep and productive interest in the study of Flannery O'Connor. It was that interest that led me to become acquainted with them. They worked together well on O'Connor, and I have been delighted to publish work by both of them in the *Flannery O'Connor Review*. O'Connor is not responsible for bringing together Ramsey and Carolyn—they seem always to have had a strong bond—but O'Connor expanded and enriched the familial love.

The care with which Carolyn Kerr has followed and reconstructed and detailed her father's life—as an intense reader so committed to collecting that he deserves as an honorific the label "book rat"—makes clear that his memoir is truly the product of a labor of love. And the love goes beyond this particular father and this particular daughter. As we watch Carolyn demonstrate her father's love of books, watch her reconstruct the great tangle of texts and variants and scribblings on edges as volumes pass from one owner to the next, we see how books contribute to a history, to—dare I say it?—a civilization.

Perhaps that claim may seem a bit too grandiose. Part of what I enjoy about this book is its attention to detail. Inspired by Anne Fadiman, Carolyn accurately describes Ramsey as a "courtly lover of . . . carnal book lovers," by which she means that his admiration for books was increased, not decreased, by firm evidence that a text was thoroughly, even roughly, used by a prior owner, leaving behind detailed evidence of that usage. All books wish to be cherished the way Ramsey and Carolyn cherish them.

This memoir never quite reaches its end—there are always more books to be sorted, handled, enjoyed, and eventually gifted or sold—but this memoir is quite effectively attentive to our mortal end. Carolyn examines the details of dying and death within her family as carefully as she and her father have examined books. The memoir as a whole, on top of being a heartfelt tribute to the affection between a father and a daughter, is a spirited plea that we should all pay close attention to each other at every period of life, as well as to the books that work to bind us.

Marshall Bruce Gentry

1

When I Croak

IN THE WEEKS AND months following the death of my mother in July 2014, two weeks shy of my parents' sixtieth wedding anniversary, I can't say I was surprised at my father's newfound preoccupation with his own eventual end. It made sense. At eighty-three, he'd exceeded the average life expectancy of a white American male by six years, and Moses' three score and ten by a whopping thirteen. Our numerous end-of-life conversations, however, would undoubtedly—to an outsider—have seemed unusual, marked as they were by a persistent and unwavering refrain. Usually apropos of nothing.

In the check-out line at Trader Joe's, inching his cart (containing eight frozen dinners, five bottles of cheap Riesling, three limes, and a bar of shampoo soap I had aggressively recommended) dangerously close to the heels of a very large woman in front of us:

"When I croak, don't give the books to the sem [Gordon-Conwell Theological Seminary] like Nigel's family [my in-laws] did."

On Route 4, during the forty-five minute drive to the granite company where for some reason we're required to be physically present to approve the design (on a hard copy Xerox from the looks of it) for their joint headstone:

"When I croak, get in touch with Scott [DeWolfe] up in Alfred about the books. He'll be interested in some of the Shaker and Millerite material. He'll be able to direct you as to who to contact about the more valuable books, too."

Seated side by side in the industrial-looking albeit comfortable-enough chairs in the beige-and-brown waiting room of his tattooed urologist whom neither one of us much care for, and where he keeps patting the catheter bag strapped to his right leg as if it's a toddler or a pet:

"When I croak, if you don't want the books, get as much money for them as you can."

In an aisle of the State Street Discount appliance store, where we go to replace his refrigerator, which the week before had begun to make an ungainly if not ungodly noise:

"If I croak before Lynne Crocker has finished rebacking that 1824 Spanish Bible published in New York—did I tell you I found a similar one listed on ABE Books for $7900?—don't forget to pick it up. Call first though; she keeps irregular hours."

Five years later, he was living with us. Sipping from our glasses of wine one night (white for him, red for me), he settled into the maroon swivel chair and I in the brown rocking one, both of which had come from his house, surrounded on all sides of my former pottery studio by mostly floor-to-ceiling bookshelves, filled now with his books in the room he'd christened the "library," he looked around, deeply satisfied, raised his glass, and chirped:

"When I croak, you should think about turning this place into a used and rare bookstore. You know. By appointment only. You're a quick study."

I groaned. Hopefully to myself.

And how could I forget his repeated reminder: "When I croak, don't forget the books file on my computer. I try to keep it updated."

The file, titled "Ramsey Michaels' Books 2001–2019" is a compendium of detailed descriptions of items he found for sale online that corresponded to 604 of those books he considered the most noteworthy (i.e., rare and/or valuable) in his collection, including thirty-nine books listed under the grandiose title "Ramsey's Gold Room: Some of My Most Valuable Books." Included at the back of that file is "Books Not Priced or Sold" listing two "No copies for sale online" and seven "Already Sold." By way of a preamble, he began the file:

> Current listings of books I have in my personal library (culled mostly from Advanced Book Exchange). This list will give some idea of what the books are selling for. I make some comments on prices in italics. No comment usually means it sounds about right. Remember, these are the sellers' prices. Doesn't mean they will pay that much for the item. Half maybe. Probably less.

The online descriptions are cut and pasted in bold, his parenthetical italicized notes added beneath each entry. Like this:

(Mine is an earlier edition, 1559. Paid $200.)

(Mine is later, 1841 edition, with appendix and chart at the end. Paid $175.)

(Mine is just the same, except that it lacks the frontispiece portrait. One currently online without portrait, $1463. I paid about $150 at a London book fair.)

(This seems high. My title pages are all intact, two torn pages internally. Paid $75 in Greer, SC.)

(Mine is just the same except the Old Testament is dated 1583 instead of 1614. It is in a beautiful binding that looks 20th century. I paid $225.)

(Mine is similar except that it is Herbert #226 and all title pages are present. The Sternhold & Hopkins Metrical Psalms are 1594. Last page of Metrical Psalms, Evening Prayers, is missing. Mine has also the Book of Common Prayer (1614). It is rebound, late 19th or early 20th century. Paid $3000 in Hallowell, Maine.)

This last entry refers to his beloved 1595 Geneva Bible my father purchased with what he referred to as "Mormon money."

Which is as good a story as any to begin with.

2

Mormon Hymnal

In 2008, at the height of the recession, my father, always on the lookout for something of interest, stumbled upon one of his more remarkable (i.e., profitable) finds: at the Rockland, Maine, antiquarian mall, on a decidedly unremarkable shelf lined with dusty old books and random ephemera. A small book with the words "Saints Prayers" printed on the spine caught his attention. The title page announced "*A Collection of Sacred Hymns adapted to the faith and views of the Church of Jesus Christ of Latter Day Saints*, compiled by John Hardy. Boston: Jackson & Dow's Press, 1843." Like many people, he knew that "Latter Day Saints" was what Mormons called themselves. Like fewer people, he knew that 1843 was a little more than a decade after Joseph Smith published the Book of Mormon[1] in 1830. Like almost no one, he knew that this hymnal, if all the pages were intact, was worth a lot more than the lightly penciled $35 on the inside flyleaf. A dealer friend of his had recently sold a Mormon hymnal of comparable date and condition for $2500. Nevertheless, my father negotiated a 10-percent discount, something about which he felt a "twinge of guilt," he later admitted.

The little hymnal was compelling. It had some traditional Christian hymns found in many Protestant hymnals: "Come Thou Fount of Every Blessing," "Glorious Things of Thee Are Spoken," "How Firm a Foundation" among them, but more of them displayed unmistakable Mormon doctrines, as did the hymnal's chapter divisions. In addition to such standard

---

1. Full title: *The Book of Mormon: An Account Written by the Hand of Mormon upon Plates Taken from the Plates of Nephi*.

categories as "Public Worship," "Funeral," "Prayer Meetings," "Baptism," "Sacrament," "Resurrection," the "Second Coming of Christ," and "Promiscuous" (!) (an archaic term for "Miscellaneous"), there were some categories specific to Mormon doctrine such as "Gathering of Israel," "Stick of Joseph," and "Baptism for the Dead." "Stick of Joseph" is derived from a Mormon interpretation of Ezek 37:16–17:[2]

> Son of man, take a stick of wood and write on it, "Belonging to Judah and the Israelites associated with him." Then take another stick of wood, and write on it, "Ephraim's stick, belonging to Joseph and all the house of Israel associated with him." Join them together into one stick so that they will become one in your hand.

To the Latter Day Saints, the stick of Judah is the ancient Christian church and the stick of Joseph the Latter Day Saints, the two destined to be joined together at the second coming of Christ. Many of the hymns in the hymnal celebrated the history and experiences of the Latter Day Saints themselves, the "seed of Joseph" through his son Ephraim, "the record" revealed, referring presumably to the golden plates found by Smith in the Hill Cumorah as directed by an angel named Moroni. One of the hymns had as its refrain, "Adam-ondi-Ahman," the name of a historic site in Daviess County, Missouri. My father notes:

> Even cradle Latter Day Saints are uncertain what the words (other than "Adam") actually mean ("Adam in the presence of God" is one possibility), but they know it as the place where Adam and Eve and their children went first after being expelled from the garden of Eden (the way back to the garden being blocked by the cherubim and a flaming sword according to Gen 3:24). Accordingly, it is the place where Christ will come first to meet his priests and prophets and claim back his world. They locate it at Spring Hill, overlooking the Grand River in northwest Missouri, about seventy miles above Kansas City.

"Baptism for the dead," a doctrine the Latter Day Saints have been practicing since 1840, refers to the practice of baptizing a living person on behalf of a dead one in order that the deceased might have the opportunity to enter the kingdom of God. The dead person may choose (not sure how

---

2. Unless otherwise noted, all Scripture quotations are taken from the New International Version (NIV) Bible.

that works) to either accept or reject the baptism. Meanwhile the surrogate remains in the dark as to the dead person's choice, i.e., salvation.[3]

Despite its allure and my father's interest in early American religious groups, he had never specialized in Mormon material if only because "it was too large and too expensive a field to interest me."[4] After a month or two of sitting on his find, he began to contact a few dealers he knew of who specialized in all things Mormon, including one "high-powered Mormon bookseller" who promised to pay "top dollar" for early Latter Day Saints material. After this dead end, and several others, he found an interested party in LaFayette in upstate New York, fifteen miles east of Skaneateles, the town in which he'd grown up and to which he and my mother returned at least once a year. When they made contact and my father described the hymnal, the dealer replied that if it was complete and in "reasonably good" shape, it would bring in the "low five figures." This got my father's attention. That gas was well over four dollars a gallon that summer made little difference when compared with "low five figures!" They arranged to meet. In person, after carefully inspecting the hymnal, and apologizing ("Well, the market is not as good as it was when I emailed you"), Rick Grunder, an "amiable" ex-Mormon, said, "I'm afraid I can only offer you $12,000." My father writes, "Betty and I looked at each other." I can only imagine *that* look before he said, "I'll think about it," and five seconds later, "All right, I've thought about it! $12,000 will be just fine," whereupon the three of them went to a local bank where Mr. Grunder issued him a certified check. This would have been, as my father said, the "highlight of my career as a book rat" adding thoughtfully, "if money was the only factor."

---

3. This is not strictly a Mormon practice. In 1 Cor 15:29, Paul asks, "Now if there is no resurrection, what will those do who are baptized for the dead? If the dead are not raised at all, why are people baptized for them?" According to the NIV notes, this practice appears to be controversial: "Paul mentions this custom almost in passing, using it in his arguments substantiating the resurrection of the dead, but without necessarily approving the practice. The passage will likely remain obscure." Despite my Scripture-heavy Baptist upbringing, I had never registered this verse.

4. He was fascinated, however, with the Mormon tradition. We both were. One of the many books we read at the same time was Simon Worrall's account of the literary forger, Mark Hofmann, in *The Poet and the Murderer* (2002). After my father died, I read *Under the Banner of Heaven* by Jon Krakauer (2003) and lamented the fact that he was no longer around to discuss it with.

3

Geneva Bible

HE PROMPTLY BOUGHT THE coveted 1595 Geneva Bible he'd happened upon just weeks before his Mormon find in a second-floor bookshop in Hallowell, Maine, for $3000, a sum "way out of my league even in the best of times." Actually, including the sales tax the sum was $3150, exactly one hundred times the amount he had paid for the hymnal in a satisfying symmetry that wasn't lost on my father. He notes:

> It was in excellent condition with Theodore Beza's copious notes, maps of the Tigris-Euphrates territory surrounding the garden of Eden, Solomon's Temple, the land of Israel and the Mediterranean world, bound together (in a nineteenth- or early-twentieth-century binding) with a 1614 Book of Common Prayer, and a 1594 Sternhold and Hopkins Psalter, with the biblical psalms in English meter and even extensive musical notations. Still one of my treasures. The Latter Day Saints "been berry berry good to me!"

I had to look this last quote up. It is circa 1970s *Saturday Night Live* where Chico Escuela, portrayed by Garrett Morris, says "Baseball been berry, berry good to me." I'm pretty sure you can't say that anymore.

New Testament and Greek scholar, seminary professor, writer, ordained minister, Baptist congregant in good standing, and self-proclaimed book rat—among many other things—my father had a strong Calvinistic streak; his draw to an early Geneva Bible comes as no surprise. First printed in 1560, it preceded the now ubiquitous Authorized King James Version by fifty-one years, was the favored Bible of the sixteenth-century English

Protestants (used by William Shakespeare! John Bunyan!), and, fun fact, was one of the Bibles taken to America on the Mayflower. During Catholic Queen Mary I's reign ("Bloody Mary" as she came to be known), a group of anti-royalist scholars fled to Geneva, Switzerland, city of the Reformers John Calvin and Theodore Beza, under the leadership of William Whittingham to produce an English translation based on earlier translations from the Greek by Tyndale (keep reading—he acquired one of these too) and Coverdale. They even went straight to the Hebrew for the Old Testament, which was a groundbreaking move for an English translation. But what made the Geneva Bible stand out was its annotations (or "apparatus"—scriptural study aids and guides complete with verse citations that allowed cross-referencing, introductions to each book, maps, tables, woodcut illustrations, and indices), which were essentially Calvinist and Puritan in nature and thus maligned by the ruling pro-government Anglicans of the Church of England for their antipathy to the Catholic Church and monarch rule. As just one example, the 1560 Geneva Bible translates Rev 11:7 as "And when they have finished their testimonie, the beast that cometh out of the bottomles pit, shal make warre against them, and shal overcome them and kill them." The marginal note (7n) states, "That is, the Pope which hathe his power out of hel and cometh thence," and (7o) "He showeth how the Pope gaineth the victorie, not by God's word, but by cruel warre." These notes, among others, caught the attention of the Catholic Church, were eventually rejected, and are therefore absent in later editions, which became less aggressive (or perhaps passive-aggressive) and more speculative in their marginalia. Consider Rev 17:4 and its snarky marginal note to the verse in my father's 1595 edition: "And the woman was arayed in purple & skarlet, and gilded with golde, and precious stones and pearles, and had a cup of gold in her hand, full of abominations and filthines of fornication." The note reads, "A skarlet colour, that is, with a red and purple garment, and surely it was not without cause that the Romish clergie were so much delighted with this colour." Still aggressive-ish, I'd say.

The Geneva Bible (nicknamed "Breeches Bible" for its description in Gen 3:7 of Adam and Eve having made "breeches" out of the fig leaves to cover up, as opposed to "loincloths" or "aprons" which appeared in other translations), grounded in its theological undertaking of the Reformation to present God's word for God's people, became a hit with the English masses and stayed on top for over fifty years. Starting in 1575 under the reign of Protestant Queen Elizabeth (to whom it is dedicated) it was even printed there. Elizabeth's successor, King James, not a fan, and compelled by his dislike for the politics found in the margins, commissioned in 1604 the "Authorized Version," better known as the King James Bible, which was finally published in 1611, although it wouldn't be until the latter part of the seventeenth century that it would replace the Geneva Bible as the favored Bible of the English Protestants.

4

Memoir (His)

ABOUT A YEAR BEFORE he died, my father began a memoir he playfully titled *Me and My Books: Memoir of an Aging Book Rat*. He explains that he chose "book rat" (despite being "a phrase that sounds vulgar and, well, kind of ratty") over "book scout" in memory of his former colleague and good friend, Roger Nicole,[1] late professor of theology at Gordon Divinity School and Gordon-Conwell Theological Seminary in Massachusetts. "Roger once described himself in just that way," my father writes, "explaining to a society of librarians that a 'book rat' is neither mere bibliophile, librarian, or book worm but 'one who combines several of the traits of the others and who adds to it a certain scavenging instinct which leads him invariably to places where books may be obtained and which helps him to enrich his own collection or that of the institution he serves.'"[2] Here my father inserts his full disclosure, that "I'm in it not for any institution, as Roger was, but solely for myself, and maybe my heirs, depending on their tastes."[3] The memoir begins:

    1. One of my father's leisure pastimes was to make up limericks; here's one he penned about Roger:
"The eminent Dr. Nicole
Said 'Theology's good for the soul.
From predestination to propitiation
It's best if you swallow it whole.'"
    2. Nicole, *Standing Forth*, 4.
    3. Happily, *I* have ended up with most of his books.

Memoir (His)

I've had second thoughts about both the title and the subtitle. First, "Me and My Books" might be already taken. John Updike used it as a title for a piece he wrote in *The New Yorker* in 1997. But he meant books he had written, while I have in mind books I own, or have owned, books that have spent time (some only a short time) in my personal library. True, I've written a few as well, and I still take pleasure in them, but I take more pleasure in books as possessions (even as reading material!).

As for the subtitle, he explains:

At eighty-eight "aging" doesn't seem quite the right word. Everyone's aging, after all. Wouldn't "aged" be better? Or "ancient?" I decided to stick with "aging" because many of my anecdotes go back to when I was merely aging, some as far back as early childhood.

The unfinished memoir recounts his ventures and adventures[4] in acquiring some of his most treasured books, detailed descriptions of said books, his detective work in deciphering inscriptions, annotations, and marginalia, the painstaking but satisfying tracking down of provenance, his pure delight in possessing them, and—lest we forget!—negotiating deals in order to possess them for credit or trade for something more desirable. He emailed me chapters as he finished them. The evening before the day on which he did actually "croak," he emailed me (even though he was not thirty feet away in our downstairs apartment, where he'd been living for six months—he was working fervently and did not want to be interrupted) the beginning of what would be his final chapter, "Fantasy and Supernatural Horror," which covers some of the children's books in his collection. Misquoting John Updike—"The world, let us say, is full of scary things, and it's children's books that first offer to display them to us"[5]—my father concludes the chapter, "Maybe children's literature and supernatural horror [a favorite genre of ours] are not so far apart as we might think." I read this chapter on my phone in the waiting room of the ER the following morning and, later, in a curtained-off cubby as we waited for the results of various tests, we discussed it (his work in progress foremost on his mind even at such a potentially dire time), including a couple of problematic excerpts (he

---

4. An early working title of his memoir was *Encountering a Wild Enthusiast and Other Ventures and Adventures of a Book Scout*.

5. Updike, "Child Within," 35. The actual quote is "The world, let us say, is full of scary things, and it's children's-book *illustrations* that first offer to display them to us." (my italics).

notes the "dark edge" to some of the rhymes) he'd quoted from his copy of *Under the Window*, written and illustrated by Kate Greenaway, in superb condition from 1880.[6] I'd taught a course on children's literature the previous fall, and "dark edge" brought to mind "The Juniper Tree."[7] I'd rank it as the most egregious of fairy tales; the grisly descriptions of decapitation and cannibalism make it a legitimate horror story.

"Have you read it?"

He chuckled. "Well, no, but I haven't finished the chapter yet. I do own a rather old copy of *Grimms' Fairy Tales*, so I'll consider that one."

There was also *The Hole Book* by Peter Newell, published by Harper & Brothers in 1908.[8] A book of rhymes with charmingly quirky illustrations, the story centers around a gun that discharges, creating havoc in a variety of scenarios; each page has a small hole in the center. A book that would definitely get canceled today, if not for the gun violence, for at least one blatantly racist illustration of a rotund black woman gesturing toward a pierced watermelon.[9] I asked if he would include *The Slant Book*, first published in 1910, of which I'd been particularly fond, also by Peter Newell. It features a runaway buggy, which generates all kinds of mayhem as it barrels out of control.

---

6. A particularly creepy passage, accompanied by an illustration of an evil-looking man on page 63 dressed entirely in red including a cape and a tall hat, carrying off a distressed-looking little boy dressed in pajamas, was apparently dropped in later editions:

"Oh, what has the old man come for?
Oh, what has the old man come for?
To run away with Billy, I say,
And that's what the old man has come for.

Ah what will Billy's mamma say?
Ah what will Billy's papa say?
What a dreadful fright
They'll be in to-night!—
Oh, what will papa and mama say?"

7. First published by the Brothers Grimm in 1812; text by Philipp Otto Runge.

8. In a flowery script on the inside cover, "To Lewis Youngs, From, Rosemary Allen. F'eby 20th, 1909."

9. Newell, *Hole Book*, unnumbered pages.

"Who plugged dat melon? mammy cried,
As through the dor she came.
I'd spank de chile dat done dat trick,
Ef I could learn his name."

> Once Bobby's go-cart broke away
> And down this hill it kited
> The careless Nurse screamed in distress
> But Bobby was delighted[10]

Each page describes in illustration and rhyme the havoc that ensues as the cart rolls down the hill running into things. In keeping with the theme, the book itself is slanted. I tried to concentrate on our conversation but was just then feeling rather distressed myself—what were we doing here? This was a *heart* issue, not a catheter problem. I tamped down a mounting panic and, returning my attention to my father, who just then resembled a very old child, tried not to think about how vulnerable he looked in the blue printed hospital gown slipping down over one pale shoulder, a thin blanket tucked under his armpits. The pain meds had kicked in and he was now animatedly extolling his fine copy of *The Poll-Parrot Picture Book, containing Tittums and Fido. Ann and her Momma. Reynard the Fox. The Cats' Tea Party, with twenty-four Pages of illustrations, Printed in Colours by Kronheim* (London: George Routledge, n.d. [about 1870]), probably the most valuable children's book in his collection, his "best" children's book. He'd found it at an antiques barn in New Hampshire for just sixty dollars. The twenty-four illustrations are chromolithographs in spectacular color, obviously a "keeper." This is one of the very few books I've fantasized about disassembling in order to showcase the illustrations. (I would never!)

He never finished his chapter on "Fantasy and Supernatural Horror," but I want to mention one more I feel certain he would have included. When I was growing up, the subject of "the Goops" figured prominently at mealtimes for their obvious lessons in manners:

> The Goops they lick their fingers
> And the Goops they lick their knives;
> They spill their broth on the table-cloth—
> They lead disgusting lives![11]

Curious that I didn't find this book in his collection, although he might have sold it. At any rate, in a similar vein, *Der Struwwelpeter*, by Dr. Heinrich Hoffman, is a punishing yet very amusing picture book (in color) about children who misbehave; it is lauded on the back cover of the English edition as "one of the most popular and influential children's books ever

---

10. Newell, *Slant Book*, unnumbered pages.
11. Burgess, *Goops*, unnumbered pages.

written." My father's volume is an early, though not first, edition (1845); its original title was *Lustige Geschichten und drollige Bilder* (*Merry Stories and Funny Pictures*). In 1847, the book's cover incorporated an illustration of its most popular character, Der Struwwelpeter (loosely translated as "shock-headed Peter" or "slovenly Peter"), an unkempt fellow with a massive mop of yellow hair[12] and fingernails that would put Edward Scissorhands to shame. The story goes, Dr. Hoffman was searching for a book to give to his three-year-old son for Christmas, and finding nothing he liked, wrote and illustrated this one, which was immediately commercially successful. The stories describe in pictures and prose the gruesome consequences of such juvenile infractions as sucking one's thumb (it gets cut off), refusing to eat (you die), playing with matches (you are burned up), or being cruel to animals (the dog bites you and ends up slurping up your supper), among others. The English 1995 translation includes a note: "Dover Publications regrets the potentially offensive content of 'The Story of the Inky Boys' but has retained the story to avoid censorship of a work considered to be a classic." While many parents and educators predictably objected to the violence and generally drastic and sometimes fatal fates of the misbehaving children, *actual* children appreciated the over-the-top situations and the (let's face it) humorous consequences. In 1974, Joseph Wortis published *Tricky Dick and his Pals: Comical Stories by Joseph Wortis and Funny Pictures by David Arkin*, which my father also owned. Written in the vein of Dr. Hoffman's book, it is an incisive parody: "Look at this child so clean and slick / He's called obnoxious Tricky Dick! / He'd lie and cheat and hit and steal . . ."[13] You get the gist.

During the three and a half hours we spent in the ER that Saturday morning, my father shifted his body uncomfortably but was nevertheless sharp-witted. While nurses and physician's assistants came and went, doing their best to explain what was happening (a ruptured aortic aneurysm it turned out), our conversation shifted from the latest chapter in his memoir to logistics: how the next day, Sunday, would go. He was planning to go to Bible and Breakfast at Christ Church in Hamilton in the morning ("The breakfasts are free!" he crowed, adding "They have bacon!" for my vegetarian benefit, not for the first time) and hoped he wouldn't have to stay in the hospital overnight. We chatted about where to go for lunch the following

---

12. I recently learned of the condition "uncombable hair syndrome" or UHS; it is also sometimes called "Struwwelpeter syndrome."

13. Wortis, *Tricky Dick*, unnumbered pages.

Memoir (His)

Tuesday with our friend Russ with whom we had plans. Our mood was oddly buoyant. Winking, he chuckled that pain meds made him even wittier than usual. I rolled my eyes. To you maybe. He grinned. He hadn't expected to "croak" when he did, although he had been told by a cardiologist six months earlier that his aortic aneurysm could give way or "dissect" at any time. "Not a bad way to go . . .," the doctor had added. An afterthought. A silver lining.

5

Collector

My father was colorblind, had a miserable sense of direction, and in recent years, had become selectively deaf when it suited him, but set him loose in a used and/or rare and/or antiquarian bookshop or even a small town library sale, flea market, or estate sale, his navigational instincts were intact and more often than not he ferreted out something of interest, if not value, as the story of the Mormon hymnal is but one example. As he became more of a serious collector of antiquarian and rare books in middle and old age, he was drawn not to "mint" or "fine" condition books *necessarily*, but often to ones "of no particular distinction, but [having] a certain charm because of the hands through which they have passed." His collection sprang organically enough from what he called the "tools of the trade," the kinds of material he had devoted his life to research: Greek and English Bibles, especially New Testaments, a myriad of editions, languages and translations, concordances, eschatological literature, Baptist history. After a lifetime of study and research in Greek translations of the New Testament canon, the works of Josephus, the Apocryphal Books, the Nag Hammadi texts, and the Dead Sea Scrolls, among other texts of ancient manuscripts, he tended to view the historical Jesus as an eschatological, even apocalyptic prophet (which he allowed was "distasteful to many") who proclaimed a kingdom that he thought would come soon. "In short, while not agreeing in every detail with any of them, I find myself in a tradition shared with early millenarians, fundamentalists, and dispensationalists,"[1] he writes in his autobiographical essay, "Four Cords and an Anchor."

1. Michaels, "Four Cords," 181.

Collector

His interest in eschatology went way back to the influence that his Aunt Nell, a devout Seventh-day Adventist (which came out of the Millerite movement during the mid-nineteenth century), married to his mother's brother, had on him when he was a boy. "She was my introduction both to biblical piety and biblical prophecy. She talked a lot about the latter but taught me more about the former."[2] There perhaps could be found the seed of his interest in so-called "enthusiasts"[3]—the French Prophets, Millerites, Montanists, Shakers, Quakers, the Amana community, Moravians, Anabaptists, as well as such peace-loving sects as the Mennonites, the Amish, and the Brethren.[4]

He looked for first editions, preferably first printings. Presentation copies. Association copies. Dedication copies. Inscribed copies. Signed copies. Rare. Old. Obscure. Dust jackets. Annotations and marginalia. Beautiful or unusual covers and illustrations. Translations. He has 187 volumes of old and/or rare miniature books (many with type too small to read without a magnifying glass), including Bibles, hymnals, prayer books, religious instructional material, and poetry, some of them in ornate bindings, many tooled in leather, some with intricate silver clasps or locks. Before setting himself to the task of unearthing information about ownership and provenance, he examined each volume for completeness and variations between editions he looked up (in the case of English Bibles) in any number of reference books he owned, including *Herbert's Historical Catalogue of Printed Editions of the English Bible, 1525–1961*, or online sites such as ABE Books. He coveted many of these books, yes, but he was also always on the lookout for something of value that one of his book dealers or bibliophile friends might take in trade.

The price had to be right. My father did not part with his money easily. But he was open to almost anything. He was delighted with quirky notes or inscriptions. One summer afternoon, while we were sitting in his wrought iron chairs, drinking iced tea, and shooting the breeze on his porch in Portsmouth, New Hampshire, our conversation turned to handwritten notes, and he gleefully dashed into the house to retrieve the modest volume of John Bunyan's *The Pilgrim's Progress* he'd picked up for five dollars at one of the London book fairs in Russell Square years before (1994 according to a journal entry). Its only appeal at first glance was that it what was called a "provincial" imprint (not London). "Kettering: Printed and Sold by J. Toller, Market-Place, 1843." A stamped notice announced, "Kettering:

---

2. Michaels, "Four Cords," 174.

3. The word "enthusiasm" comes from a Greek word meaning "possessed or inspired by a deity."

4. See R. A. Knox's classic *Enthusiasm*, for a comprehensive survey.

Toller Chapel Sunday school." Kettering is not far from Bedford and my father inferred that J. Toller must have been both a printer and a pastor, "probably nonconformist" as dissenting churches were often called "chapels." The words "Presented to M.A. Owen, April 23, 1882, First Prize" were handwritten. Interesting that the date it was given out was so long after it was published. Perhaps a bunch of convenient remainders? On the front endpaper was a very faint signature, "Mary Ann Owen," and on the back endpaper a pointed warning in verse, letting the reader know in no uncertain terms that here "was a young lady not to be trifled with":

> Steal not this book for fear of shame, for here doth stand the owner's name. For if you do the Lord will say, Where is that book you stole away, & and if you say you cannot tell, the Lord will cast you into Hell. M.A. Owen, Kettering.[5]

---

5. Neither one of us knew this at the time, but I recently came across an article about "book cursing," a practice in the late medieval period. It seems book curses were commonly found in books owned by monks or nuns and sometimes regular folk too. They promised a variety of dire consequences to befall those who stole or damaged or hid a text: hanging, burning, drowning, excommunication. Over time, the age of the curse inscriber became younger so that by the eighteenth and nineteenth centuries the curses were more likely to have been written by children. The poet John Clare at thirteen threatened would-be thieves with "Steal not this book for fear of Shame / for here doth stand the Owner's name," seemingly the source of M.A. Owen's plagiarism (Baker, "Death to Book Thieves!," 64). Evidently, M.A. Owen was not the pioneer we thought she was.

6

Beginnings

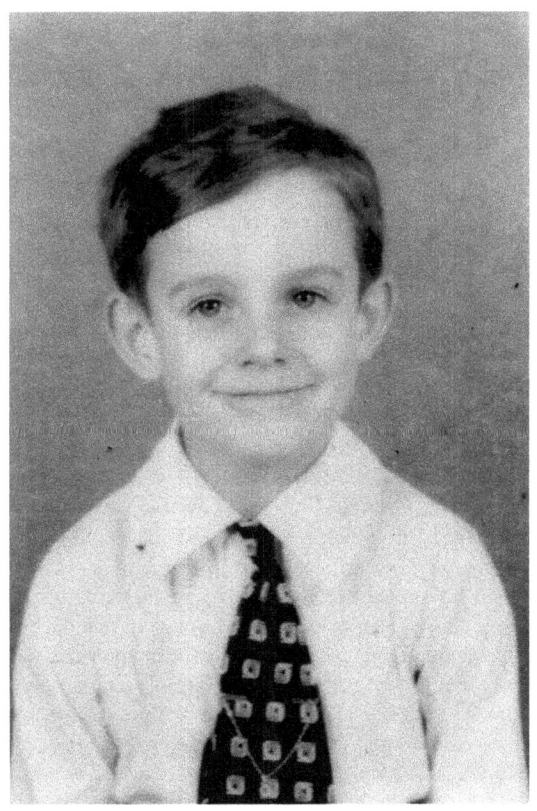

My father, circa 1938

The Book Rat's Daughter

> I spent the first five years of my life on a farm in Mattydale, on Bailey Road Route 11, between Syracuse and North Syracuse, New York.

MY FATHER WAS BORN to a sixty-four-year-old son of German immigrants, who, with a sixth-grade education, had become a successful cattle rancher, farmer, and businessman. His mother was a forty-two-year-old Methodist school teacher. Sometimes I marvel at our close brush with nonexistence: myself, my four children, and six grandchildren (so far). At this writing my father is responsible for twenty descendants.

In 1929, Peter Michaels was a sixty-two-year-old bachelor. Ethel Marie Ramsey, a forty-year-old spinster (in the parlance of the times), lived with her mother just up the hill from him on Sand Road and (according to my father) might have had "lesbian tendencies." In one audio interview[1] my father cites his mother's athleticism (basketball) as possible evidence (?!). I suspect the photographs in Ethel's scrapbook also contributed to his speculation, although the poses of girlfriends, all in a line, arms linked or draped over one another's shoulders, may have been more a matter of popular poses in the early twentieth century than signs of sexual preference. But who's to say? In any event, Peter, in his pursuit of the very shy Ethel, twenty-two years his junior, had had to do some heavy lifting to win over her widowed[2] mother, Anna, who, at sixty-nine, was only seven years older than he. Anna opposed the courtship—Peter was old (obviously), but worse, Roman Catholic. She must also have been alarmed at the prospect of losing the daughter who lived with and cared for her. When I was little, my granny told me that her mother had died of a cat scratch or maybe a

---

1. Thanks to Kenna Michaels for providing me with access to audio interviews with our father.

2. A photograph of his headstone reveals that her husband Allen (or Alling) L. Ramsey died in 1897 at age forty-two (my granny would have been eight years old), and the only story I remember my father telling me about his grandfather, whom he never met, was that at some point he had gone west in search of gold and on the way back rescued a fat woman from a burning building. I recently found the (unknown) newspaper clipping dated March 1880 that recounts the story in full: the building was called "The Insane Asylum at Osawatomie" in Kansas and the fire probably started on the third floor. Although they thought at first the inmates were all safe, they became aware that a number of the women had fled to an upper floor where the windows were barred by iron grates. Allen Ramsey scurried up a ladder, battered the grates with a sledge hammer until they gave way, and was able to rescue all of the women save one, who refused to leave the bathroom. My great grandfather ended up in a scuffle with this woman, who, at two hundred pounds, knocked him down. In the end, he was able to rescue her, earning him a glowing mention in the article of Allen Ramsey's "courage" and "true valor."

bite. I didn't much like cats after that. One of the ways he won over the old lady[3] was by putting up a clothesline for her, and as my father emphasized, Peter was *not* handy, which I have no reason to doubt as my father was also decidedly unhandy. Needless to say, Peter prevailed. A handwritten note on heavy paper verging on fabric survives, modestly stating in lavish cursive in blotchy ink that Peter Michaels and Ethel M. Ramsey "were united in marriage by me in the presence of the following named witnesses according to the laws of the State of New York." This had been signed by the city judge of Watertown and four named witnesses—so, a courthouse wedding.[4] A year and a half later, on May 1, 1931, Ethel gave birth to a son at age forty-two after two days (!) of labor. My infant father was brought home to what his father called "The Old Baum Farm." Peter had purchased the ninety-seven acres of land in Mattydale from Dr. Henry Clay Baum, younger brother of L. Frank Baum of *The Wizard of Oz* fame in 1901 (*The Wizard of Oz* was published in 1900) and in 1905 bought more of the land from Frank Matty (founder of Mattydale) who had bought it from Frank Baum's father ("So the scent of literature was in the air," my father mused). Whether or not Frank Baum ever lived in Mattydale I'm not sure, but my father thought the property should rightly have become some sort of tribute (museum? theme park?) to the *Wizard of Oz*, rather than the Kmart and its parking lot it sadly became. For years, my parents collected rent on the property until, in the early aughts, for reasons I didn't pay attention to at the time, they sold it at a loss before the lease was up.

In *The Family of the Wizard: The Baums of Syracuse*,[5] Peter Michaels is described as a "real estate and cattle dealer" who, when he died in 1945, left behind a $200,000 estate, the equivalent of over three million dollars today. Not remotely close to the fortune of a Vanderbilt or Rockefeller or Carnegie, those so-called robber barons; still, a far cry from the masses waiting in breadlines. By his own estimation, my father's father lost at least half of his wealth in the stock market crash, which, incidentally, occurred two weeks after his marriage to my granny. I wonder how the newlyweds weathered that catastrophe? Had she even known how much her new husband was worth? He was affectionately known as Diamond Pete for the rings he

---

3. I don't think I'm being remiss in calling a sixty-nine-year-old woman of 1929 an "old lady." I'd like to think, however, that in 2025, there are kinder designations. I did after all turn sixty-nine on my birthday last year.

4. Sometime after my father was born, the relatives "put up a fuss." Peter and Ethel were married a second time by a Catholic priest so that my father could be raised Catholic.

5. Ferrara, *Family of the Wizard*, 148.

bought for his wife, her sister, and her mother. I inherited several of them—four now adorn the hands of my two daughters and two daughters-in-law. Diamond Pete was either romantically generous, bought the diamonds as an investment, or maybe he just wanted to butter up the in-laws. While the rings are beautiful, they're not worth much today. Whether that's due to market forces, changing tastes, or the rise of lab-grown gems is anyone's guess. After my father moved into our downstairs apartment, I'd sometimes hear him muttering about how his father would have been a millionaire if not for the Great Depression. He often imagined conversations with his father had he lived to see his only son earn his doctorate from Harvard and publish widely: "If you're so smart, his father would scold, "why ain't you rich?"

7

Museum

The Mottville house

WHEN MY FATHER WAS five, Peter moved the family from the Baum farm to a stately brick house he'd purchased on forty-five acres where my father lived until he left for Princeton in 1948. Peter died in 1945 at age seventy-eight. The large fourteen-room Victorian was known as the Mottville Sherman Home, built by Hiram C. Sherman in 1866. According to *Skaneateles Through Time*, "[Sherman] made his fortune making yeast for area breweries. The house is built of bricks brought to Jordan on the Erie Canal and transported to Mottville by horse and wagon."[1] Between 1876 and 1914 it was the home and office of Dr. John W. Brown, thus becoming "the Dr. Brown place." The property had a "tenant house" that Peter rented out at fifteen dollars a month. The children of the tenants became my father's playmates, one of whom he kept up with well into their eighties. His mother (who never learned how to drive) had a driver and household help in the form of consecutive "girls," or maids, some of whom lived in the big house with them. During the Great Depression, Peter hired mostly itinerant workers to labor on his several farms (one of which, in nearby Cazenovia, was over three hundred acres) and tend to the cattle, wheat and corn crops, and a bounty of fruit trees planted by a previous owner: cherry, apple, pear, peach, butternut, and a row of grapevines. Ethel prepared a hot lunch for the farmhands most days. One beloved hired man named Steve Posloski (or maybe Poslovsky) lived in the big house with them, working on the farms and driving the car; he stayed on after Peter died, attending, in addition to his duties on their properties, to my granny's ironing. Steve was like an older brother to my father, who recalled playing checkers and Camelot (a board game popular in the 1930s) with him. Peter rented out some of the properties he owned, often letting folks stay even if they couldn't pay the rent. (My father noted that he was "tenderhearted.")

Establishing himself as a collector early on, my father claimed one of the unused upstairs bedrooms as his "museum," a room set aside to house his treasures:

> Stamps; coins; autographs; fossils; seashells; arrowheads and Indian artifacts; old swords; political campaign buttons and other memorabilia, including two dried up crabs and a starfish, the gift of a much older distant cousin by marriage who was a biology professor at Princeton; a brief passion for parlor magic: Gilbert magic sets, *Super Magician Comics* starring Blackstone, and books about magic, some (such as John N. Hilliard's *Greater Magic*) still collectable and pricey today if I had only hung on to them.

By his own admission, there were parts of that massive house that scared my father as a little boy. Yet he used the back stairs to get into the attic and from there scrambled into a cupula where he liked to dangle his legs and stare out at the four hills that surrounded the house. One of Peter's brothers had died in the house while visiting and another one had been laid out in a coffin in the front room when my father was a child. Sometime in the

---

1. Dibagio and Holdben, *Skaneateles*, 19.

1990s my father and mother visited the house and were welcomed in by the owner, Gene Ferguson, who had converted one of the front rooms into a gift shop. He claimed that the house was haunted by a little boy in short pants, that seven years earlier, he had seen "the apparition of a little boy" which "popped like a balloon." "It was a round face, with brown hair and flat features." When several years later a stranger visited the house, she told Gene that she'd "got a feeling. I turned around [. . .] and sensed a little boy, a very happy little boy, on the stairs," and moreover that she felt a "sincere calmness." Gene theorized that the little boy was connected to the doctor's practice; he used some of the rooms for operating and birthing: perhaps a little boy had died there? My father, however, confidently maintained that the ghost was himself as a boy, what the Scottish call a wraith, the ghost of a living person. Indeed, mediums brought in confirmed a benign presence and the story, evidently newsworthy, appeared in the local paper![2]

After he learned to read, my father would wait for the daily *Syracuse Herald-Tribune* to land with a thwack on the front porch. He told me the first thing he would do was smell the newsprint. (Doesn't everyone?) He would then go to the comics page, cut out the Buck Rogers strip, and paste it into a scrapbook so that when the Big Little Book came out a year or so later, he already had his homemade copy. He had a collection of over one hundred Big Little Books ("Always exactly 424 pages"), among them Mickey Mouse, Blondie, Flash Gordon, and Red Ryder, but Buck Rogers was his all-time favorite. Just two books remain from that collection, *Buck Rogers 25th Century A.D. in the War with the Planet Venus* (1938) and *Buck Rogers 25th Century A.D. vs. The Fiend of Space* (1940), one spineless, both shabby, and therefore worth nothing. He wasn't as into Superman, but when he was seven years old, he somehow acquired a copy of Action Comics ("At ten cents, I think"), an "item" as he called it that he "regretfully estimate[d] to have been the most valuable book I've ever owned or will own." It was either the first appearance of Superman in print (if it were in mint condition, it would fetch well over one million dollars today) or the second (which would fetch into the six figures).[3] He writes, "In that sense my subsequent ventures and adventures with books have been—at least monetarily—downhill all the way." My father once said, ruefully, "I had that sucker!"

2. *Syracuse Herald-Journal*, January 25, 1991.

3. On April 5, 2024, I read the headline on my phone, "Superman's Action Comics No. 1 Sets Record with $6 Million Sale. A rare copy, just one of around 100 in existence has topped Superman No. 1 as the most valuable comic in the world."

8

Turnbull Legacy

BESIDES THE TWO BIG Little Books, three books have survived that period, books that belonged to his Scottish Presbyterian great grandfather Thomas Turnbull (1797–1882), who arrived in America in 1820 with his widowed mother, Sarah Wood, and eight siblings. My father writes:

> Thomas found his love in America, Elisabeth Howard, nineteen years his junior, daughter of James Howard, his first employer. She was four years old when Thomas arrived in America, and Thomas watched her grow up until he married her in 1833 when she was seventeen!

Now this strikes most people (including me) as mildly creepy. But it worked out. They had nine (or ten, depending on where you look) children, the youngest of whom was born when Thomas was sixty-one, and who became my great grandmother, Anna Amelia Lyon Turnbull. Thomas's father-in-law, Anna's grandfather, and my great-great-great grandfather, James Howard,[1] was "an extensive contractor and builder of Northern New York, during the early days of progress, when it was a vast wilderness"—according to the lengthy obituary of one of his daughters who died at ninety-four.

---

1. I recently discovered that James Howard was descended from Henry Howard, Earl of Surrey (1516/7–47), first cousin to two of King Henry's wives, and remembered as one of the first English poets to write in the sonnet form. (Together with Sir Thomas Wyatt, they are considered "The Fathers of the English Sonnet.") He also holds the dubious distinction of being the last person to be executed by King Henry VIII in 1547. King Henry died the next day.

His oil portrait hung, unframed, on a landing at my grandmother's house on Lakeville Circle in Skaneateles, New York. With his combed-back white hair, white beard (but no moustache), heavy brow, pale blue eyes, and a sloping beak-like nose, he looked severe. The grim down-turned lips and the heavy black background only added to the effect. As a child, I found the painting terrifying. I would avert my eyes, take the stairs two at a time, and hold my breath, just as if I were passing a graveyard. After my granny died, my father gave it to me—my mother didn't want it in her house—and by that time I'd grown used to it. A good portion of his face had fallen off in tiny paint flecks, so I had it restored. It's been hanging in my living room, still unframed, for more than three decades and didn't seem to have the same effect on my own children.

At any rate, Thomas's books. Two of them are volumes of Scottish Calvinism from the 1750s in crude beige rawhide (goatskin maybe) bindings bound, my father suspected, by Thomas himself. One, *Human Nature in Its Fourfold State*, by Thomas Boston, "late minister of the Gospel at Etterick," twelfth edition (Glasgow: Archibald McLean, 1757), has Thomas's signature on the title page; on the back inside cover, elegantly inscribed ("Presumably after a careful reading," my father notes wryly): "Thos Turnbull. The book is most instructive. And calculated to enlighten the mind." The second, *The Marrow of Modern Divinity: The First Part*, by Edward Fisher, "touching both the covenant of works and the covenant of grace," fifteenth edition "with Notes by the late eminent and faithful servant of Jesus Christ, Mr. Thomas Boston, Minister of the Gospel at Etterick" (Edinburgh: E. and J. Robertson, 1759), has inscribed on the title page, "Thos Turnbull, from Mary Fletcher, his grandmother." The blank endpaper notes that in 1774 it belonged to his maternal grandfather, William Wood, husband of Mary Fletcher. The mention of Thomas Boston, the author of the first book, signals their connection.

The third volume, *Seven Treatises: Containing Such Direction as is Gathered out of the Holy Scriptures, leading and guiding to true happinesse, both in this life and in the life to come; and may be called the Practice of Christianity* by Richard Rogers, "Preacher of the Word of God at Wethersfield in Essex" (London: printed by the Assignes of *Thomas Man* for *Richard Thrale*, and are to be sold at the Crosse-Keys at *Pauls gate*, 1630), is almost a century older and far longer at 834 pages plus Appendix and Indices. A scrawled name (Scott?) and handwritten date of 1702 are on the title page.

On the blank endpaper is the name "John Henderson," who was among those who came to the "Scotch Settlement" in Rossi, New York, near the St. Lawrence River at about the same time the Turnbull family settled there, so Thomas may have acquired the book from him. The author, Richard Rogers, an English nonconformist (Presbyterian), frequently on the outs with various Anglican bishops, "appears to have been cut from much the same Calvinistic cloth as Thomas Boston and Edward Fisher."

My father notes, "These [books] were what heralded my future as a book collector and sometime book scout," and "without question" directed him toward theology. Mostly though, they aroused his curiosity about his ancestors, which eventually was rewarded "due to the unwillingness of my mother and her sister, Kathryne Ramsey, to throw much of anything away." Over the years, my father became increasingly interested in what he called the "Turnbull legacy," attending the occasional Turnbull reunion, researching his ancestry, and visiting grave sites. He has several folders containing pages and pages of typed genealogies, scrawled lists, and crudely rendered family trees on scraps of paper as well as letters to and from various Turnbull relatives he either met or contacted. Thomas had been a justice of the peace in Rossie, St. Lawrence County, New York, and, in addition to his beautiful desk (reverently referred to as "the Turnbull desk" in our family), my granny and Auntie Kay kept his ledger book, the blank pages of which are filled with Thomas's poetic musings about life, God, slavery, and the poetry of Robert Burns. There was more of the same scrawled on random scraps of paper. One favorite is a prayer or possibly a hymn written in Thomas's beautiful spidery handwriting on the back of a detached frontispiece of a book which my father found out was *Trials and Triumphs for three-score years and ten in the life of G. W. Henry; whilst sojourning forty years in spiritual Egypt, one year in the slough of despond, and twenty-six years in the land of Beulah: Together with the religious experience of his wife* (Frankfort, New York, 1871). The book itself is missing, but on the back of the frontispiece (an illustration of a man and his son, who sits at a small desk, pen at the ready, as if awaiting dictation. Underneath "G. W. Henry & Son"), Thomas (aged seventy-eight) wrote:

> Thomas Turnbull
> Wegatchie Aug. 1 '75
>
> Jesus my saviour ever dear
> O! bind me by loves sacred tye

> That casteth out all doubt and fear
> And hold me steadfast till I die
> O! grant to me that living faith
> That works by love and purifies
> That triumphs in the hour of death
> And anchors safe beyond the skyes
> Where Jesus my dear Savior's gone
> A mantion to prepare for me
> That I may stand before his throne
> Acquited in Eternity.
>   Amen

There were others, but this one made an impression. So much so that my father concludes his essay, "Four Cords and an Anchor," with this prayer, adding, "At eighty-three, I would like to make that my prayer as well. But if I unexpectedly deploy a Hail Mary or two on my deathbed, I know God will understand."[2] My mother put the prayer to needlework in 1980, and in 2014 my father had it printed in the bulletin for my mother's memorial service. The framed needlework still hangs where my father (actually I) hung it over the bookcase containing his oldest books in the room in my house I still call "the library."

There is a rewriting by Thomas or perhaps a sequel to Robert Burns's poem "John Anderson My Jo," written "with a robust Christian piety quite foreign to Burns himself," my father notes. Four other poems or songs in Thomas's hand—probably his own compositions—express his impassioned abolitionist convictions during the Civil War. According to my father, they belong to a genre typified in *The Anti-Slavery Harp: A Collection of Songs for Anti-Slavery Meetings* by William Wells Brown, first published in Boston in 1848. Thomas's work is noticeably similar, whether or not he was aware of such collections. One begins:

> Negros arise yourselves to release
> The lands that you labor are yours if you please
> You have earned them twice by your labor and toil
> For God gave to labor the right of the soil
> You have cleared up the fields both meadow and pasture
> Your right to command is as good as your Master.

Family lore has it that Thomas's home, located near the St. Lawrence River, was the last house in the Underground Railroad system that smuggled

---

2. Michaels, "Four Cords," 185.

enslaved blacks into Canada, although there's no way to be absolutely certain as the house is no longer there. In 1982, my father self-published, with my husband's help, *The Prayers and Poems of Thomas Turnbull, 1797–1882*, thirty-two of them in a blue paperback—pamphlet really—limited edition of 150 copies. My father concludes in his Editor's Preface:

> As a collection, they afford a poignant glimpse of a nineteenth-century man without extensive formal education, a country squire who thought about God and Christ, death and aging, life and the world around him, slavery and freedom, and his own friends and memories, a man, who, according to his granddaughters, used to pray for his "children, and his children's children, down to the last generation."

There is actually one more book from the Turnbull era that I discovered after my father died. More accurately, it is a small book that was turned into a scrapbook, the owner of which pasted newspaper clippings of hymns, poetry, news items, obituaries, some handwritten poetry, and recipes onto the pages of what appears to be some kind of reference work or study guide for the Bible. The spine announces *An Expose* by Amos Higby. Evidently not a book valued for its content! Pasted to the inside cover is a recipe in faded pencil for Ogdensburg Mountain Cake with the date 1873 or possibly '78 in the upper left hand corner. The faint name at the bottom left is that of Anna, Thomas's youngest daughter, my father's grandmother and my great grandmother. I assume she was the owner of the little volume, but there is no way to be sure. She was either fourteen or nineteen when the recipe was written.

Looking every year its age with its brittle yellowed pages coming loose from the binding and buckled with water damage, the book offers a tender snapshot of its creator: poems such as "Hope On Hope Ever," "Let Him Take All," "The Saint's Portion," "Rock Me to Sleep," "Christ Blessing the Children," "Where Is Yesterday?," "The Aged Believer at the Gate," and "Thus The Years Go By" all point to a devout and introspective (melancholic?) person. Showing an interest in opera or celebrity or both, the owner of the book has pasted in a newspaper article accompanied by a photograph of Adelina Patti, a Spanish Italian opera singer who in her prime earned $5,000 per night and once, during an American tour, sang for Abraham Lincoln and his wife, reducing them to tears. There are several loose pieces of paper tucked into some of its pages including a telegram dated October 15, 1886: "Mrs. E. C. Flack Syracuse, NY: *Mother died today funeral Sunday ten oclock will meet first train tomorrow at Gouverneur. D. S. Turnbull."* E. C. Flack (Ella) was Anna's oldest sister, an accomplished artist, twenty-five years her senior, and D. S. Turnbull would have been their brother, Dean. How the telegram came to be in Anna's possession is a mystery. Or possibly the book was Ella's. Some poems are handwritten, presumably by the owner of the book, and reveal, in addition to a guileless poet, an innocent speller:

> Yesterday there came this way,
> A parcel directed to Isabell Day,
> When opened it proved to be
> An embroidered apron for poor old me.
> I know you worked many an hour sewing and stitching with all
> your power Late and early, early and late
> you stitched on, clean and streight
> Untill it was finished, so neat and white,
> Folded and wraped and directed right.
> By Parcel Post to Gouverneur,
> I received it from Rufus safe and sure.
> Thanks to the giver, the cars, and the post
> But thanks to dear cousin Trummy, the most. Jan. 1873

The final pages of the book are given over to death in the form of obituaries clipped from newspapers ("Town Robbed of Popular Young Man," "Death of Mrs. Elenor Clarice Howard Church, in Her 94th Year," "Dead Hero Honored," "One of the Younger Pioneers, a Dakotan By Birth, Answers Final Summons") and poems with such titles as "The Mourner Comforted," "My Castles," "Thus the Years Go By," "The Saint's Portion," and "Where is Yesterday?"

9

Early Years

My father with his parents, Peter and Ethel, on the
porch of the Mottville house, circa 1935

Early Years

My father was an only child to parents who (let's face it) were old enough to be his grandparents. His mother's older sister, Kathryne Ramsey, who worked for the Department of Child Labor (Children's Bureau) in Washington, DC, until the nineteen-fifties, a spinster until she married for the first time in 1965 at age seventy-nine, was a frequent visitor. When I was a child, I thought "grannyn'anniekay" was one word. More often than not I saw them together. They were close, sometimes living together, although they didn't always get along. Auntie Kay was formidable. She was older and, if photographs can be trusted, the better-looking; she was also more independent and accomplished, a career woman at a time when few women were. Where my granny was timid, Auntie Kay was imperious and self-possessed. When he was seven years old, my father wrote this aunt (his only one) a thank-you note:

> Dear Aunty Kay
> Thank you so much
> for the shirts.
> I appreciate them
> Very much. I
> know one of them is a sport shirt.
> It is nicer than most of the shirts
> that I have and
> both are for a real he boy. You can learn
> a lot from the sport
> shirt. Thank you very
> much for them.
> your darling nephew
> Ramsey April 8, 1939

Pretty astute of my seven-year-old father to identify a "sport shirt" as such, given his lifelong (to my knowledge) apathy toward clothes. Moreover, a "real he boy." Huh. And you have to wonder what one can possibly learn from the sport shirt? Also: "*darling*?"

My Auntie Kay was a stickler for thank-you notes, as was my granny. I should know; I wrote dozens to them both at the insistence of my mother.[1] Ethel is described, in a letter addressed to my father in longhand on

---

1. I found one recently: "Dear Auntie Kay, I am glad that you were here for my birthday party. Thank you for the nice pajama's [*sic*]. I like them very much. I miss seeing you here. I Love you [*sic*] Write to me. Love, Carolyn."

Underneath, in pen, written by Auntie Kay presumably: "(Just 8 years old)." And already I knew about apostrophes even though I was using them incorrectly!

yellow-lined paper dated Saturday, August 17, 1996, as "so regal" and "so elegant" and "so strict about me standing up straight and not slumping." This from one Rosemary, an eighty-one-year-old Turnbull relative who remembered "Aunt Ethel" (who would have been in her twenties or thirties at the time), giving her piano lessons when she, Rosemary, was ten or eleven years old, in the house where Ethel lived with her mother, Anna. This would have been long before her marriage to Peter. The letter jars a forgotten memory: my granny used to call *me* Rosemary, as apparently, I reminded her of this young relative/student of hers. Not long ago, I discovered that perhaps she might have had a further reason to avoid calling me by my given name as one of her husband Peter's "old flames," also named Carolyn, despite having married someone else, was a frequent visitor to their house. Having developed a keen interest in my father, she wrote little poems to "J. R." According to my father, Ethel was "OK" with this, but perhaps not to the point of being reminded of this ex every time she saw her first grandchild. I didn't mind. I thought "Rosemary" the more beautiful name.

My mother was the second of six children, each born in a different Michigan town as the family hopscotched across the state during the Great Depression in pursuit of work. Eventually they managed to buy a farm. Had they lived close to my father's family in upstate New York, chances are they would have found themselves working for Peter. My mother grew up picking onions and slaughtering chickens[2] and wearing feed-sack dresses that her mother sewed.[3] She must have been dazzled by her new mother-in-law's "elegance" and "regality." Granny had a knack for refinement—well-made dresses and "real" (i.e., not costume) jewelry—and my mother learned a great deal from her about fine china and Oriental rugs, silverware patterns, correct place settings and proper table manners, while not always appreciating my granny's occasional and subtle interference in her efforts at child-rearing. Granny was sixty-six when I was born, so to me she was forever an old lady. She lived into her nineties, and I can't recall a single moment when she didn't seem elderly and staid. She never wore slacks, always wore stockings, and applied rouge religiously to her papery cheeks; she got her hair

---

2. This is an exaggeration. My mother told me a story of her mother ordering her to slaughter a chicken one time and my mother botched the job. This is all she said, and the look on her face told me not to ask any more questions.

3. When I looked these up, I discovered to my surprise that they are nothing like what I pictured as a child, i.e., a sack with four holes cut out for the arms and legs. In fact, during World War II, home sewing projects were encouraged, and feed-sack bags were manufactured with various designs for that purpose. The dresses looked quite smart.

"done." She seemed equally devoted to reading her Bible and watching her daily soap operas which she called "my stories." But what I remember most is her fear. Granny feared planes. Automobiles. Bicycles. Bodies of water. Fire. Robbers. Nosebleeds. For the prevention of this last calamity, she wore a length of bright red yarn around her throat, which—evidently—worked most of the time. This was hidden by a ubiquitous white scarf fitted tightly around her neck. My father, closely monitored, hovered over—he himself admitted to being "a spoiled brat"—never learned to swim or ride a bicycle, probably because his mother was afraid he'd get hurt. The outcome of one attempt at the latter as a grown man—on Mackinac (pronounced "Mackinaw" for some reason) Island as I recall—was a hernia operation.

About a year ago, a man called my husband's bicycle shop asking for me. Not your typical request at a place better known for patch kits and derailleurs. He told the employee that he had known my granny and Auntie Kay. I was a bit wary about calling him back, not recognizing his name. But after fewer than two minutes into the call, the man explained his connection to them—his mother had been my Auntie Kay's personal assistant when she worked at the Children's Bureau—and a close friend. When he mentioned that we had actually met once, a memory snapped into focus. I interrupted.

"Do you have red hair?"

He did.

Suddenly I was fourteen again, squirming through a painfully awkward seaside lunch in Gloucester, Massachusetts, with my granny, Auntie Kay, a red-haired boy named Don, and his sister, also red-haired. He was a year or two younger. I had just started to notice boys as more than muddy nuisances, and I remember feeling acutely observed. Were Granny and Auntie Kay orchestrating something? I couldn't be sure—but it felt fishy. Fast-forward fifty years. Embarrassment faded—mostly—and Don and I are now pen pals, corresponding by email like it's 1996, and we both have strong opinions about punctuation. We quickly discovered a mutual fondness for family stories, obscure connections, and a little light gossip—of the footnote variety, not the scandalous kind.

I learned that his family often visited my granny and Auntie Kay—first in Skaneateles, New York, then Woburn, Massachusetts, after Auntie Kay got married. Also, after my grandfather Peter died, Don's dad, Randy, had done handyman jobs for them and drove "the Ramsey girls" around town. Apparently neither of them ever learned to drive—true relics. Don also mentioned that Randy had taught my father how to drive. This was news to me, and I couldn't resist describing to Don my father's, shall we say, *unique* driving style. No offense to Randy, of course.

Eventually, Don, my husband Bill, and I met for a long laughter-filled lunch. Despite the decades, the connection was immediate. It made me wonder: did Auntie Kay have a sixth sense about friendships that just needed time to marinate? Could be. Also, Don brought me a gift: a cowbell once worn by one of my grandfather's steers—polished, no less. I now own a vintage livestock accessory with actual family provenance. Possibly the most obscure heirloom ever. Some folks inherit a brooch or a tea service. I have a cowbell. Honestly? I think I win.

My father was just thirteen when his own father died, and his memories of the man didn't extend much beyond his fondness for slippers and a tendency to vanish for long stretches while overseeing his various farms and properties. What he did recall was the steady stream of well-dressed men in fancy cars who showed up at the house asking to borrow money. One photograph I have of Peter shows a serious-looking man in a rumpled suit and tie, worn-looking shoes, legs crossed at the knee. On his lap, his hands are folded over my father, who, I have to say, looks remarkably serene for a three- or four-year-old. I especially like this photo for the detail of the little silk embroidered robe my father is wearing. I know it's red because I ended up with it—proof that family heirlooms come in all forms, including miniature lounge wear. Peter smoked sometimes—pipes and cigars mostly—drank rarely, and, notably, had no teeth. According to my father, he only wore his false teeth when he needed to look presentable, which apparently didn't include mealtimes. He took them out to eat—a detail that continues to confound me.

My father's childhood was quiet, lacking the necessity of work that defined the lives of so many Depression-era families. He sometimes "worked" on the farms, picking fruit, but it was for fun. Indeed, he appears to have been content to settle into the solitary and, more importantly for my granny, *safer* pastimes of reading, writing poems and stories, and collecting. In addition to stamps and coins, he was an avid autograph collector, writing dozens of letters to well- and moderately-well-known figures, mostly politicians, mostly conservative politicians, and obtained autographs (some on photographs) of Barry Goldwater, Richard Nixon, Henry Cabot Lodge, Dwight Eisenhower, Westbrook Pegler (a journalist known for his opposition to the New Deal and labor unions), Ronald Reagan, Billy Graham,

Walt Disney, Bess Truman, Harry Truman, Eleanor Roosevelt, and many whose names are indecipherable. Here's one he wrote to Republican Vice Presidential Nominee John Bricker in a shaky teenaged cursive:

> Skaneateles, New York
> August 3, 1945
>
> Dear Governor Bricker,
> I am a 14-year old autograph collector and a great admirer of yours. Needless to say, our family voted for you and Mr. Dewey in the last presidential campaign. I have already received an autographed card from Governor Dewey and I would be very pleased to have your personal signature. It would add greatly to my collection.
> Included is a self-addressed, stamped envelope for your convenience. Thank you. Most sincerely yours, J. Ramsey Michaels.

Note that "needless to say." My father was a dyed-in-the-wool Republican, becoming libertarian-leaning in his later years. He got the autograph; at the bottom of the letter, which Mr. Bricker had returned: "Sincerely, John Bricker."

When I was a teenager I too became briefly enamored with autographs and obtained just one. I loved the actress who played Agent 99 in the sitcom *Get Smart*. She was pretty, but also smart and capable, qualities I've always admired. In response to my fan letter, she (or probably her publicist) sent me a glossy 4x6 black-and-white headshot with her signature at the bottom. I remember being thrilled to receive it, but alas, I don't have it anymore. Barbara Feldon was my idea of cool when I was fourteen. I was surprised when I looked her up that at ninety-two, while she no longer performs, she is an accomplished writer.

I found two pages sandwiched in between *Ramsey's books 2004–2014* and "Ramsey's Gold Room: Some of my Most Valuable books" in his blue vinyl folder containing a typed list of thirty-nine "Autographs, not in books," and over a hundred names under "Autographs within books," including over thirty inscribed to him. Many of the latter were from my late best friend Holly Meade, who never failed to inscribe the children's books she illustrated and sometimes wrote to my parents: "For Ramsey and Betty, with love, Holly." Some are biblical commentaries written by friends and colleagues, some poetry collections, novels, and memoirs purchased at readings where you could dictate your favored inscription to the author. He has multiple William F. Buckley signatures in his books, many inscribed to his mother's sister, Katherine[4] Ramsey Wendell (Auntie Kay), who apparently generously supported *The National Review* with large checks.[5] Of the "merely" signed copies are the likes of Amy Tan, Walker Percy, Joyce Carol Oates, Anne Tyler, Joan Didion, Jimmy Carter, John Cheever, Peter De Vries, Billy Graham, Norman Mailer, Barry Moser. There are multiple John Updike novels and essay collections inscribed to my father as Updike lived in nearby Beverly Farms where, at the local bookshop, you could request a personalized inscription and every now and then Updike would stop in and oblige. This was my go-to for my father's birthday, Father's Day, and Christmas presents. In one of them, Updike included a sketch of Santa Claus (like Flannery O'Connor, he had started out as a cartoonist). After "F. Scott Fitzgerald," my father has written "(???)," and in the entry next to Kathleen Turner (a shabby paperback copy of Nathaniel West's *Miss Lonelyhearts & The Day of the Locust*): "Is it *the* Kathleen Turner? Purchased in Springfield, Missouri, where she went to college."

---

4. I've seen her name spelled several ways.

5. Every Friday night my father faithfully turned on the TV to *Firing Line*. I would fall asleep to J. S. Bach's Brandenburg Concerto No. 2 in F Major, Third Movement, *Firing Line's* theme music.

10

Devils

As soon as he began to read grown-up books, he kept and revised lists of his favorite short stories, topped by Stephen Vincent Benét's "The Devil and Daniel Webster" and Nathaniel Hawthorne's "Young Goodman Brown" about which I recently found an essay he wrote in high school. Edgar Allan Poe and H. P. Lovecraft were also favorites, as was Ambrose Bierce, who wrote "An Occurrence at Owl Creek Bridge." Upon learning that I had never read it, he located and handed me this story in one of his anthologies one afternoon, waited patiently until I had read it, and then eagerly talked about it. Another one we both liked (he retrieved it one afternoon and again directed I read it on the spot) was Stephen King's "The Road Virus Heads North." We were both delighted with this one as it takes place in Boston (briefly) and Route 1 north on into New Hampshire, a route with which we were more than familiar. This interest in devils and the supernatural never waned.[1] In 1976 he contributed an essay to *Demon Possession* (subtitle: *An unusual collection of experiences, case histories, studies, and conclusions from a wide range of professional people, including doctors, psychiatrists, scientists, historians, theologians, and college professors*) edited by John Warwick Montgomery titled "Jesus and the Unclean Spirits." In 2008, he published an article in *Flannery O'Connor Review* titled "A 'World with Devils Filled':

---

1. In 1968, he took me to see the movie *Rosemary's Baby*. I would have been thirteen. At the time, it seemed normal, and we both liked it. In retrospect, I'm surprised my mother let him, but she most likely didn't know what the movie was about. After all, "baby" was in the title! (As was Rosemary!)

The Hawkes-O'Connor Debate Revisited"[2] where he rather cleverly, I think, makes connections between Jesus's encounter with "a man with an unclean spirit," possessed by a "legion" of demons which Jesus ends up sending into a herd of pigs who hurl themselves into the sea in Mark 5:7–13 (see also Matt 8:28–34; Luke 8:26–39), and certain O'Connor stories. For example, in "The River," he argues that the (self) baptizing/drowning death of the four- or five-year-old Harry/Bevel could be interpreted as a self-exorcism: "Harry, having 'exorcised' himself, is drowning in the river like the pigs in the Gospel story, while the 'pig' [Mr. Paradise, "like a giant pig"] is on the shore desperately trying to 'save' him from his watery journey to the Kingdom of Christ!"[3] In 1988, he wrote a commentary on First Peter in which the passage, "Your enemy the devil prowls around like a roaring lion looking for someone to devour," appears (5:8), and another commentary in 1992 on the book of Revelation within which calamity and the powers of evil in the form of two beasts, a false prophet, the Whore of Babylon, and a dragon (Satan himself) lurk on nearly every page. In his memoir, he points to an early theological moment in his life while his mother was reading him the Bible. She used to tell him to say, when tempted, "Get thou behind me, Satan!," to which he thought, "Behind me? I don't want him behind me! That's the last place I want him to be!" I tend to think of his scholarly grappling with devils as his way of keeping them in front of him.

He never outgrew his penchant for making lists of his favorite reading material. On his computer is a forty-six page file titled "Anthology" where he listed (and typed out in full) his favorite poems (34), hymns (3), songs (6), limericks by J. R. Michaels (10),[4] quotations (5), palindromes by "Ye Smart Ramsey" (23), Burma-Shave for the twenty-first century ("mine too") (1), and personal reminiscences (3).[5] When I was cleaning out his desk shortly after he died, I came across a small note paper decorated with fifties-style

---

2. Flannery O'Connor famously wrote her "subject in fiction is the action of grace in territory held largely by the devil" (*Mystery and Manners*, 118). She also wrote in one letter, "I suppose the devil teaches most of the lessons that lead to self-knowledge" (*Collected Works*, 1150).

3. Michaels, "'World with Devils Filled,'" 123.

4. This doesn't include the one he came up with to honor his second great grandson, Abraham, born in Houston on September 10, 2019, whom he would never meet:
"Abraham David Sanjuan
Was thankfully born before dawn
His mother Renée was happy to say
Like his dad, he was covered with Braun."

5. See appendix for a selection of his "favorites."

birds that I recognized as one of the gifts I had given to my mother for her eightieth birthday in March 2014 (along with fancy hand cream and a copy of Elizabeth Strout's *Olive Kitteridge*, which I'm not sure she ever read), four months before she died, covered with three columns of years. Handwritten in pencil was a (clearly recent) list of the publication dates of his oldest books (thirty-two from the seventeenth century; ten from the sixteenth). On the other side of the paper were a list of seventeen dates from the eighteenth century. They were mostly Greek New Testaments.

11

High School

My father with his mother and dog Loki in front of the Mottville house

High School

The 1948 Senior Class Skaneateles High School yearbook, *The Comet*, is Indian-themed, featuring crude pen and ink sketches of Native Americans in loin cloths and headdresses sitting cross-legged in front of teepees or riding horses. The foreword invites the reader to

> travel with us now over the Indian Trail meeting the Medicine Men, renewing acquaintances with the Tribes, attending our Pow-wows and seeing our Warriors in action.

(I'm pretty sure this is not OK now either). Page twenty, titled "Prophecy," lists the names of the forty-two seniors. My father's entry reads: "Name: 'Michaels, R.,' Weakness: 'coke'; Should Be: 'professor'; Crowning Glory: 'brains'; Hang Out: 'home.'" On the next page, titled "Who's Who," my father is labeled "Most Studious." Next to his photo: "Is one of those whizzes at studies, as winner of the Wood Cup Trophy in his freshman year proves; but in being so, he has not neglected his extra-curricular activities. He was in Magic Club 2 and Student Council 4." It is not really a surprise how prescient all of this turned out to be, evidence of an early focus on books and studying over socializing that never abated. The only signed name in the yearbook appears on a back cover montage showcasing some of the highlights of the year: across a picture of a young girl, "Carolyn" is written diagonally in neat cursive ending with a jaunty flourish after the "n." Could this signature have inspired my name? Clearly, my father didn't consult his mother before he named me. He graduated in 1948. Having just turned seventeen, he was Valedictorian in a forty-two-person class and was admitted to the only university he applied to.

12

Princeton and Beyond

JOHN RAMSEY MICHAELS
Mike

May 1, 1931   Syracuse, N. Y.

Father: Peter Michaels
Mother: Ethel M. Ramsey

Skaneateles High School: Student Council.

Princeton Activities: History; Prospect Cooperative Club; Princeton Evangelical Fellowship 2, 3, 4 (Pub. Chm.); Baptist Students of Princeton 3 (Treas.), 4 (Sec.); Whig-Clio; Republican Club. Roommate senior year: Samuel L. Rochester. Plans graduate work, probably in Theology. Expects to serve in the Armed Forces following graduation; future is in Christian Work, possibly Teaching. Baptist, Republican.

Permanent Address: R. No. 2, Skaneateles, N. Y.

253

Princeton Yearbook picture

MY FATHER'S FATHER WAS nominally Roman Catholic, so my father was baptized as an infant and took catechism classes, but confessed, "My attendance was spotty, and I disliked the priest."[1] One time he hid in a chicken coop when he saw the priest coming to visit and wouldn't come out until the priest had left. Even though he never made confirmation, he "gained a certain satisfaction" from his five-dollar win of the high school Latin prize.

As a freshman at Princeton (where he started going by "Mike," a nickname that ended there as well), he registered as "Roman Catholic," but, as he writes in his autobiographical essay, during his sophomore year, he became involved in Princeton Evangelical Fellowship (PEF) through an invitation by H. Paul Pressler III. In 2018, three years after the essay was published, we spent an entire afternoon on the topic of the Paul Pressler he'd known at Princeton and the breaking news of the Paul Pressler who had become a prominent Texas judge and a leader of the Southern Baptist Convention conservative resurgence, now accused by seven men, a couple of whom had worked for him as "personal assistants," of sexual abuse. A quick Google search reveals that in 2004 Pressler paid $450,000 to one of the men to keep private the details of a fight between the two of them. In 2019, after the new allegations came to light, the Southwestern Baptist Theological Seminary removed from their chapel a couple of stained glass windows that had been made of Pressler and his wife. Honestly, the fact that he'd been depicted on a stained glass window at all (like Jesus or a saint) surprised me more than the rest of the sordid mess. He died in 2024 at ninety-four. On my father's shelves in his (now my) library, I recently came across *A Hill on Which to Die* written by Pressler in 1999. Tucked inside, I found a letter from Paul dated August 20, 1999. It is clearly a response to a letter my father wrote to him with an interest in the book, probably hoping to reconnect. Pressler's typed reply, over a page long, is warm and friendly. Channeling my father, I think: *Might it be worth something?* While many of our conversations had to do with people he had known and what became of them, this was one of the more salacious stories.

My father became a Christian at Princeton, unsure whether his mother (who read the Bible to him at least twice all the way through when he was a child) or Donald Fullerton (who was the founder and leader of PEF) was responsible. In the essay that appeared in *I (Still) Believe*, he begins:

> Yes, I still believe. We walk by faith and not by sight, and in that sense we are all agnostics until the day our faith becomes sight. Unbelief, that is, sheer atheism or nihilism, has never held any attraction for me. If pure chance or naturalistic evolution could

1. Michaels, "Four Cords," 173.

explain the origin of human consciousness and reason, I might begin to pay attention. Until it does, I remain dismissive.[2]

At Princeton, he was baptized again, making him a proud Anabaptist. He was all set to become a religion major after two religion courses introduced him to the academic study of religion. Mr. Fullerton, however, persuaded him to major in history, which turned out to be the academically superior choice. He never regretted it as it introduced him to methods of critical scholarship; his paper subjects included Origen, Augustine, and a senior thesis on Jonathan Edwards's interpretation of the Great Awakening. In *The Nassau Herald (A Record of the Class of Nineteen Hundred and Fifty-two of Princeton University)*, the activities listed under my father's photograph include History, Prospect Cooperative Club, Princeton Evangelical Fellowship, Republican Club, and Baptist Students of Princeton. "Plans graduate work, probably in Theology." As appears in the entries of many of his classmates is the phrase "Expects to serve in the Armed Forces following graduation," which surprised me. The phrase "future is in Christian Work, possibly Teaching" did not. His time at Princeton was one of his favorite topics and he spoke fondly of various professors and classmates, many of whose careers he had followed. I particularly remember his naming of Walt Litz, who graduated just a year or two before my father, ended up teaching at Princeton, and whom my father kept in touch with over the years, as the smartest person he'd ever met, which was saying something, as my father (humble as he was) was, I'm pretty sure, used to being the smartest person in the room. Another favorite topic was the eating club he'd belonged to, Prospect, a club that stood out for its acceptance of minorities (or "misfits" as my father joked): "Prospect was delighted to provide a home for those who might not be welcomed elsewhere,"[3] including African Americans, Roman Catholics, and Jews. After graduating Princeton in 1952, he went on to Grace Theological Seminary in Winona Lake, Indiana, also recommended to him by Mr. Fullerton, where he met (at the Eskimo Inn, as I recall) his future wife, an undergraduate who was waiting tables. Betty Lou Flora[4] was a shy farm girl, whose caption under her high school yearbook picture states simply, "She speaks and acts just as she should." It was undoubtedly intended as a compliment, but I'm not so sure it would be considered one

2. Michaels, "Four Cords," 173.
3. According to Woolley, *Princeton Prospect*, 65.
4. After she was married, my mother dropped the "Lou." The only person she tolerated calling her Betty Lou was my husband.

today. Upon graduating from Grace (my mother never finished her degree there), they moved to the Philadelphia area so he could attend Westminster Theological Seminary, then to Massachusetts for Harvard Divinity School, where he earned his doctorate before becoming ordained and landing a tenure-track position in the New Testament department at Gordon Divinity School (later Gordon-Conwell Theological Seminary) in 1961. This lasted until 1983, two years after he published *Servant and Son: Jesus in Parable and Gospel*, the book that, as he writes in the preface to the 2017 reprint, "facilitated my resignation and departure from Gordon-Conwell Seminary." Or as our friend Russ put it, "the book that got you canned."

13

Getting Canned

A SUCCINCT (AND GRACIOUS) account of what triggered this transition can be found in "Four Cords and an Anchor":

> All I was trying to argue in the book was that Jesus' parables were "stories his Father told him," applying a principle laid down repeatedly in John's Gospel that "The Father loves the Son and shows him all that he himself is doing" (John 5:20), so that Jesus could say "I declare what I have seen in the Father's presence" (8:38). It seemed harmless enough. I was even assuming Jesus' preexistence. Still, I made no secret of my use of literary and redaction criticism, and I discovered that the notion that Jesus ever learned anything from anyone, even the Father, was profoundly disturbing to some. This came as a surprise, because such texts as Luke 2:40 and 52 and Heb 5:8 were well known and freely discussed among us. Perhaps the difficulty was that I envisioned the Father revealing himself to the Son in metaphor no less than in propositional discourse.[1]

Recently, I came across two folders in his files; one contains dozens of letters of support from current and former students, pastors, and some colleagues. The other is comprised of the official "Decision of GCTS [Gordon-Conwell Theological Seminary] Faculty Senate concerning Ramsey Michaels' *Servant and Son*," letters to and from President Cooley, cc'd letters to President Cooley and Harold Lindsell (main Trustee) and Roger Nicole (yes, that Roger Nicole) from supporters of my father. It was not pretty. Six out of

---

1. Michaels, "Four Cords," 179.

seven senate members were "of the opinion" that the book contained some passages (twenty-eight paragraphs according to the "Decision") which they deemed inconsistent with articles 1 and 4 in GCTS's Statement of Faith. Just one person on the committee, Stephen Mott, wrote a "minority report," a five-page "Dissenting Opinion" in which he addressed, passage by passage, the "inconsistencies" and refuted them. On January 17, 1983, President Cooley wrote in a letter to my father, "The Findings of the Committee . . . were that your book *Servant and Son* was an unbalanced treatment of the lord Jesus Christ and does not represent the position of GCTS," and "the book does not represent the Statement of Faith of GCTS." Thus began a "due process" that would most certainly have ended either in his retraction of his book (that would have never happened)[2] or in his firing.

He didn't *really* get canned. Preemptively, he resigned. In an April 2, 1983, letter, my father explained to President Cooley, "When I wrote *Servant and Son*, the guidelines (that a hermeneutic of inerrancy was needed at GCTS) had not yet been made explicit," indicating that they were judging the book retroactively according to edicts only recently put in place. The bigger issue, though, for my father, was that the true humanity and historicity of Jesus Christ, the legitimacy of studying the Gospels historically, and general academic freedom was at stake. In a letter, he described the matter as the question of

> whether or not inerrancy implies a hermeneutic. The Trustees have assumed that it does, and the Faculty Senate (with only one dissenting vote) has decided not only that it does, but that my book violates that hermeneutic at certain points. . . . The reasons given by the Senate for its decision in effect prohibit any use of the historical-critical method at Gordon-Conwell in the study of the Gospels. The decision commits the faculty essentially to the hermeneutic of Harold Lindsell, the chairman of our Board of Trustees.

Ahh, there it was. Harold Lindsell, the chairman of the Board of Trustees. The fallout was swift and intense, many blaming Lindsell for the (as more than one letter writer put it) "witch hunt":

Dr. Lindsell,

---

2. There is in his files the 1969 letter of recommendation from the faculty senate and administration recommending my father be installed as professor of New Testament and early Christian literature which notes, "Although widely known for his diversity of interests, his mind is markedly uncluttered. This, in part, accounts for the fact that he is almost completely non-threatened. His security affords him the ability to listen to others."

> I have learned recently of Dr. Michaels' resignation. This saddens and angers me a great deal. I will be brief. *I hold you personally responsible.* Many others will too. . . . I cannot help but see Dr. Michaels as one of the victims of your unholy, wrong-headed and mean crusade made so (in)famous in your childish "Battle for the Bible" books. I am ashamed of Gordon-Conwell for taking this action. Even more, Dr. Lindsell, I am angry at you for inspiring it.

There are over a hundred letters from students and former students, pastors, readers of my father's books and articles, friends, and colleagues to my father directly, and copies of letters that had been sent to either President Cooley or Lindsell, or both, all beginning with variations on the letter writer "voicing [their] displeasure," being "distressed," "flabbergasted," "dismayed," "stunned," "shocked," "outraged," "extremely disappointed," and even "disgusted" and "horrified" over my father's forced resignation. Many mentioned Roger Nicole ("Just the name 'Roger Nicole' on the majority report is enough to make it of questionable value," said one) who, in one alumnus letter, included a paraphrase by Luther in his hymn "A Mighty Fortress Is Our God": "Let goods and kindred go, some professors also," (the actual phrase is "this mortal life also"), which elicited many admonitions such as this one:

> I cannot but express my sorrow and distress at your "paraphrase" of Luther's hymn. It is tasteless, insensitive to Ramsey, perhaps even cruel. It symbolizes the cavalier arrogance too often identified with the proponents of inerrancy that has caused some people to reject unnecessarily the authority of the Word of God.

Many individuals, institutions, and churches wrote to the president requesting they be removed from mailing lists, informing him of their withdrawal of financial support, and vowing to remove GCTS from their list of recommended reputable seminaries. The letters cited my father's grace, insight, and dedication in the classroom. They also noted his intelligence, caliber of scholarship, and sincerity. Nobody, even his detractors, questioned his faith ("Happily we are aware that Professor Michaels does not in fact wish to impugn or deny the deity of Christ, but this book . . ."). In May 1983, my father, in a final letter to the *Friends of Gordon-Conwell* wrote:

> The school has shifted to the right and sharply so. The trustees and faculty members who wanted to get rid of the New Testament department are not hypocrites. They are perfectly sincere; for the

present the school is securely in their hands, and the question of academic freedom is murky at best.

My father never regretted writing the book, and always maintained that aside from meeting my mother, "becoming a casualty of those tensions [at GCTS] . . . was the best thing that ever happened to me."[3] He got a year's salary from GCTS and, on his fifty-third birthday in May the following year (1984), "in a hotel in Tiberias by the Sea of Galilee," he received a phone call from Southwest Missouri State in Springfield offering him a position as professor of religious studies. "My career flourished at Missouri State, even with a heavier teaching load, for I was free of the tensions that had plagued the seminary."[4] He published a major commentary on First Peter, one on the book of Revelation, and in 1991 signed the contract with Eerdmans for the commentary on John, which took him nearly twenty years to complete. The move was hard on my mother, who was leaving behind her first two grandchildren to whom she was much attached, our son Will, who was two, and Renée, an infant at the time.

I remember the whole thing a bit differently, more rancorous for sure, but my father was (remember) "almost completely non-threatened," and also not one to hold a grudge. In 2004, my father contributed to a Festschrift dedicated to honoring Roger Nicole: a collection of essays devoted to one of Roger's favorite theological preoccupations: atonement. Toward the end of my father's contribution, "Atonement in John's Gospel and Epistles," he writes, "There are more important things than being right, and I have always found much to respect and admire in my friend, even when we did not fully agree."[5] In recent years he'd reconciled with all but the most acrimonious characters, some of whom went to my church, where my father began to go after he moved in with us. But the whole debacle was the reason for his first admonition: "When I croak, don't give them to the sem." When the publisher Wipf and Stock contacted my father in 2016 broaching the possibility of republication of *Servant and Son*, he was delighted. He noted in the new preface that "the book was a disappointment, not because of its reception at Gordon-Conwell, but because of its reception, or lack of it, in the arena of academic biblical studies," where at the time, there was apparently a glut of books and articles "on the vexed question of 'the historical Jesus.'" He considered, "I never received the feedback I coveted."

3. Michaels, "Four Cords," 179.
4. Michaels, "Four Cords," 180.
5. Michaels, "Atonement," 118.

Upon rereading, while he "found it not without its flaws (different ones, to be sure, from those that had troubled the seminary trustees!)", overall, he "was surprised at how well it had weathered the passage of time."[6]

---

[6]. Michaels, *Servant and Son*, iiv-viii.

14

(Re)catching the Virus

The collector's instinct and the scholar's instinct are at odds. Collectors want to *possess*, valuing authenticity and originality—in the book world the first edition, preferably the first printing. Scholars might want to possess in the sense of building a modest personal library, but mostly they're content with *access* to a first-class institutional library.

As MY FATHER PROGRESSED from Princeton to theological seminary and graduate work in the New Testament, his "budding collector's instinct went into eclipse." He couldn't pinpoint exactly when it started up again, but in his memoir, he cites an early purchase from a bookshop in New Hampshire in 1960 of two very old volumes entitled *Novum Testamentum Graece*, which he ("by then a budding New Testament scholar") knew to be "Greek New Testament," as a possible humble beginning. A Greek New Testament was obviously a tool of his trade, but this was not one he was familiar with. J. J. Griesbach was the editor, and the date on the first volume (consisting of the four Gospels) was 1796, and on the second (Acts through Revelation) 1806, published in London and in Halle, Germany. My father *recognized* Griesbach through surveys of New Testament textual criticism as representative of an intermediate stage

> between the early days when only a few relatively late manuscripts of the New Testament were known, the ones used by the translators of the King James Version in 1611, and the modern era when many more ancient ones had been discovered and made the basis

of the up to date [sic] "critical" editions and English translations
which I and my colleagues inflicted upon our students.

Griesbach was out of date, just not as out of date as the Greek texts used for the King James Version. Apparently, despite having noted the relevant information about manuscripts, Griesbach hadn't altered the text very much. The price was just five dollars for both, which were in "fine condition, bound in what looked like vellum over a stiff cardboard that people in the business call 'boards.'" My father was on his way home from a preaching gig at a Baptist church in Springfield, Vermont, 150 miles from his home in Essex, Massachusetts, for which he had been paid thirty-five dollars. He thus justified the purchase. Today, even though those two volumes are not for sale online, they would be worth closer to five hundred. Eventually, he "did catch the virus, as more and more collectable Greek New Testaments fell into my hands."

His friend, Roger Nicole, that old "book rat," let him have two volumes of Constantin von Tischendorf's 1869–72 edition of the Greek New Testament, which had begun to incorporate the small changes that Griesbach had collected, plus others found in his important 1844 discovery of Codex Sinaiticus at the ancient St. Catherine's monastery in the Sinai. Since the seminary already had them, Roger "graciously" let my father have them for one dollar and fifty cents! Roger also found him a first edition of Westcott and Hort's Greek New Testament of 1881, "the basis of most Greek texts and English translations ever since." For once, my father doesn't mention the price, so maybe Roger was feeling generous that day!

Much later, in his fifties, my father began to collect some noteworthy Greek New Testaments from the sixteenth and seventeenth centuries. From a dealer in Omaha, he acquired, in trade, an early Estienne, or Stephanus, edition, published in Paris in 1568–69, "two tiny museum-quality volumes in exquisite seventeenth-century bindings attributed to Charles Mearne, binder to King Charles II, signed (probably in 1637, a date that appeared within) by John Ludd, Headmaster of The King's School, Canterbury." Verse numbers were missing and the nearly unreadable cursive script looked as though it was trying to imitate the look of a handwritten manuscript before the advent of printing. He was particularly drawn to a printer's mark at the end of the second volume, a man pointing to an olive tree shedding both leaves and branches, with a banner proclaiming in Latin, "*Noli altum sapere, sed time*" ("Be not high minded, but fear"), which my father had no trouble tracing to Rom 11:20 in the Latin Vulgate Bible. The text was part of Paul's argument that "unbelieving Jews were like broken-off branches of God's olive tree so that believing Gentiles might be grafted in." He warns the Gentiles not to be "high-minded" because if God grafted them in, he could easily break them off again should they falter in their faith. Someone, perhaps John Ludd of the 1630s, had handwritten above the image the Greek text of Rom 12:3: "Don't be higher-minded than your mind should be, but make up your mind to be sober-minded." The apostle Paul here was generally repeating what he had said in Rom 11:20, as advice to anyone, not just Jews and Gentiles. My father concluded that this may well have been the printer's intention as well, "as if to say, 'So, you're proud of yourself now that you've worked your way through all four Gospels? Don't be too proud but stand in awe at what you've read.'"

My father had more recently acquired two even older Greek Testaments. One he found from an online dealer in Italy, which he promptly purchased, but which arrived much later than expected, unnerving us, warranting fraught calls to and from the bank, as he had issued a certified check for over $600. It is "a very late (possibly pirated) 'Erasmus' edition from 1543, printed in Basel with Erasmus's name on the title page whited out." He speculated that it was either not legitimately an Erasmus or possibly had been owned by an Italian Catholic who didn't want anyone to know that he was using an Erasmus text. The other is a beautiful Greek New Testament, a 1549 two-volume set published in Paris by Haltinum, one of Etienne's lesser-known competitors. These are the two oldest books in his entire collection.

In all, my father has twelve Greek Bibles and/or New Testaments and six in Latin from the sixteenth through eighteenth century, ranging in cost from about $100 to over $800. "I've come a long way from the five-dollar Griesbach!" he crowed. Five are from the seventeenth century, including three published by the Elzevir family of printers in Amsterdam (1624, 1641, 1678). He noted that all of these early Testaments kept certain "beloved passages" that were either omitted or bracketed in later "critical" editions, including the story of the adulterous woman in John 7:53—8:11, the last twelve verses (16:9–20) of Mark's Gospel, and the ending to the Lord's Prayer in Matthew ("For thine is the kingdom, and the power, and the glory, forever and ever. Amen"). The Latin preface to his 1641 edition has "*Textum ergo habes, nunc ab omnibus receptum: in quo nihil immutatum aut corruptum damus*" ("So you have a text, now received by all, in which we give nothing changed or corrupted"). First added in the 1633 edition, these words give the text the designation Textus Receptus or "Received Text." His 1624 edition has the same text without the explicit notice; however, someone had had it bound *with* the explicit notice on the spine.

His 1678 edition, "a beautifully bound little gem," has a poignant inscription by a William Whitechurch noting that he received it from the widow of a "Rev. Mr. Clarke" in 1793 at her husband's death, and added in 1805 the words, "This Book I give to my Dear James and hope nothing will ever tempt him to part with it, but always retain it in his possession as a testimony of his regard for the giver, who desires his happiness through Jesus Christ." Also in his collection is the first Greek New Testament published in the United States in 1800 by Worcester printer Isaiah Thomas and a Greek Old Testament (Septuagint) from 1665. There are also two huge, extremely heavy folios from the eighteenth century: John Mill's from 1710 in a beautiful leather binding and J. J. Wetsteins's two volumes from 1751–52. The John Mill he found in Kregel's Basement in Grand Rapids (while visiting my mother's side of the family), a "favorite haunt" of his. There he also picked up a 1699 Latin edition of the works of John Lightfoot, including a "magnificent" assortment of Hebrew and Talmudic material relevant to the New Testament. My father noted that Ken Kregel, the manager of the store ("who knew when to give a discount and when to stand firm"), had a stutter, "confirming a comment Flannery O'Connor once made that she never knew a stutterer who was not also a nice person." (John Updike also had a stutter.) My father ends with, "Alas, Ken has gone on to Glory, and Kregel's Basement is no more!"

15

The Good Book

> All those early Greek and Latin (not to mention Hebrew) Bibles were leading up to the Bible most Americans now read on the printed page, the Bible in English.

THE ENGLISH VERSIONS, FROM Tyndale in 1526 to the King James Version of 1611, generally followed the Textus Receptus, or "Received Text," retaining the old "beloved passages" noted above (the story of the adulterous woman, the longer ending in Mark, and the doxology to the Lord's Prayer). He liked to say that New Testament professors such as himself were "fond of pointing out to our students that in light of subsequent manuscript discoveries these passages were likely not part of what the New Testament authors originally wrote." Most English translations acknowledge this by printing them in brackets with marginal notes calling attention to their "secondary status." His overall point in this preamble is that these variants, whatever their origins, have been part of the Bible for fifteen centuries or more, that there is nothing "magical" about the "original" text—a text that no longer exists. When theologians claim that the Bible is "inerrant in the original autographs," what they mean is that it *was* "inerrant in the original autographs" but is no longer—"a fairly lame confession of faith," he quips. He goes on to suggest that the "unsophisticated" Christian should simply read the Bible, "almost" any Bible, as revelation; that God's word comes in many translations, in many textual traditions, even comprising different lists of books, usually just the Old and New Testament, but also sometimes including additional books outside of the canon known as the Apocrypha.

In addition to his memoir, my father had been working on a book he had tentatively titled *From Cover to Cover: Reading the New Testament Canonically*. This was a departure from the "unwritten, even unspoken, rule" *against* reading the New Testament right through "from cover to cover" in seminary classrooms, where students customarily begin not with the Gospel of Matthew, but with the Gospel of Mark, because Mark is supposed to have been written first and Matthew is believed to have used Mark as a source. Notice how Matthew revised and expanded Mark. Then read Luke to see how Luke made use of Mark. And don't forget what scholars call "Q source" or "Q" (never found) that contains material found in Matthew and Luke but not in Mark. This is only the beginning of the acrobatics required for serious biblical scholarship. While he maintained that chronological order was important and probably "substantially" correct, my father's intention was to demonstrate the value of a reader's *canonical* interpretation. Canonical order presupposes intention, not linked to the original authors or even the original readers, but to later readers after the books were collected and published. Whether or not this intention is viewed, as the fundamentalists might say, as the mind of God, or in the traditionalist fashion as the mind of, say, the fourth-century church, is not his point. The point is that the canon—the canonical books in their canonical order—presupposes some sort of plan as to how these books should be read. This is what my father was exploring—the experience of the reader in reading the Bible straight through "from cover to cover" and the value that might have in relation to the more common ways of reading biblical texts in the academy and in the church. Calling each book of the New Testament a "chapter," and reminding us that the title names are not authors naming themselves, but rather *according to* Matthew, Mark, Luke, and John (whoever they might be within the narrative, and this too was a question to be considered), placing the accent on their basic agreement as four versions of the same story, my father "equips" the reader with a King James Version, a New International Version, a basic knowledge of Greek and a Nestle-Aland Greek text, plus some familiarity with the Old Testament and "an uncommon ability to remember what he or she has read." According to his computer, he opened this file the evening of January 17, 2020, the night before he died. He had finished his commentary on Matt 26:1–13 and had typed out the text of Matt 26:14–30. He was just two and a half chapters shy of completing Matthew.

16

Oldest English Byble

My oldest complete English Bible is a Geneva Bible from 1595, my most expensive purchase ever, this in 2008, a year of severe economic recession in America.

BUT HIS OLDEST BIBLE (albeit an incomplete one), more recently acquired, is a sturdily bound volume with the words "Holy Byble" embossed on the spine. As demonstrated by his notes, my father painstakingly inspected his purchases inside and out, noting details, damages, and missing material. Consider his description of this commonly called Taverner-Tyndale Bible from 1551 he bought from David Paulus in Cornish, Maine, in 2018:

> Herbert #93 . . . like most surviving Bibles of its vintage, this one was incomplete, with some preliminary material present, but lacking the title page and the first eighteen chapters of Genesis. The rest of the Old Testament is pretty much intact except for the last chapter of Malachi (with internal pages between Deuteronomy and Joshua, and between Job and the Psalms), but it lacks the Apocrypha (which this edition is supposed to have). The New Testament title page is present, as well as the four Gospels, the book of Acts and the letters of Paul to the end of Second Thessalonians. First Timothy and most of the first chapter of Second Timothy are missing. The rest of Second Timothy, Titus, and Philemon are present (with a few gaps), and the rest of the New Testament is missing. Tyndale's Prologues are present throughout except for the beginning of the Prologue to Paul's Epistle to the Romans. The surviving title pages identify the publisher as "Day" ("John Day"

according to pictures I've seen of the missing title page), with a small image of someone waking a sleeper, and the accompanying motto, "Arise, for it is Day." Like one or two of its predecessors, it contains explanatory notes by a certain Edmonde Becke, known for his infamous note on First Peter 3:7, where husbands are urged to "dwell with a wife according to knowledge": "And yf she be not obedient and healpfull unto hym endeuoureth to beate the feare of God into her heade, that therby she maye be compelled to learne her duitie and do it."

My Taverner-Tyndale mercifully lacks this note, only because First Peter, with everything else after Philemon, has gone missing!

Underneath, he had cut and pasted the description of a similar volume he found on Greatsite.com. At the bottom of the website's lengthy and marginally intelligible description of the Bible's condition, liberally sprinkled with such qualifiers as "repaired," "mounted," "present," "lacking," "terminating," "tear":

> 1551 Taverners' Bible, Item [sic] TSF1007, Appraisal [sic] value $70,000; List price $47,000 and Your [sic] actual price on this Bible is significantly LOWER than the "List Price" shown above. For a current exact price quote on item TSF1007, please Contact Us [sic].

My father notes: "It's impossible for me to tell from this description what they are actually charging and also what's there and what's missing." A couple of months after he died, more out of curiosity than intent to sell, I went to the website and filled out the online form which asked for my information and phone number, a description of the Bible, and photographs. (Before I could do this, the website insisted that I read through several pages of "If your Bible was printed in [name the century], read this.") Because they don't do appraisals for legal reasons, they also asked me to name a price. What the heck, I thought. I took a few pictures with my phone, cut and pasted my father's detailed description and aimed high (Appraisal value 70K!), and the swiftness with which my phone rang made my head swim. It was John Jeffcoat himself, castigating me for the temerity to suggest such an exorbitant price for an incomplete "Byble." Believe me when I tell you, the "y" in Mr. Jeffcoat's pronunciation was, well, *pronounced*.

My father concludes his description with:

And even with so many pages missing, I like to think this major investment of mine may at least have saved a precious antique Bible from being torn apart by some idiotic but enterprising dealer or collector somewhere and sold off leaf by leaf (I have seen *one leaf* of the very similar 1549 edition offered for sale online at $550!).

Which is a little ironic considering that his oldest "item" is a single leaf (framed so as to be viewed from front and back) from the 1482 German translation by Anton Koberger (nearly fifty years before Martin Luther's use of Gutenberg's printing press) from the ninth edition of the Biblica Germanica, the first printed in Nuremberg. The page is from "Fourth Kings" (known to English readers as Second Kings) chapter 2 in the form of a diptych, with colored woodcut illustrations depicting, on the left side, Elijah ascending to heaven in his chariot, tossing his cloak back to his successor Elisha, and on the right side, Elisha looming over several children (according to the text, forty-two of them) and a couple of bears who appear to be devouring them. Elisha had called a curse on the children "in the name of the Lord" for calling him "Baldhead," whereupon two bears emerged from the woods and began to accost them. To be sure, *my father* didn't tear this page out of an old Bible! He found it, already framed, at D'Art Antiques, an antiques barn in Stratham, New Hampshire, for $116.[1] His (now my) only incunable.[2] Not something to hang in my grandchildren's playroom, but a keeper.

A few years ago, after I'd begun haunting rare bookstores and antique barns with my father, I bought, at my father's nudging, a probably worthless but nonetheless interesting piece at this same antiques barn: a print of the Wilton Diptych (ca. 1395–99), a late Medieval piece painted on two pieces of hinged Baltic oak, commissioned by Richard II of England depicting a kneeling King Richard II, with standing (and haloed) English saints King Edmund the Martyr, King Edward the Confessor, and patron saint John the Baptist on the left panel facing the right panel where the Virgin and Child are surrounded by eleven angels in blue, wings lifting above their heads. The two sides are related clearly, but the backgrounds are very different, the human figures on rocky ground, the heavenly figures arranged on flowers. There are plentiful details and symbols embedded in each side. The frame is painted a rather garish gold, but I considered it a bargain at thirty-five

---

1. Provenance: Ferdinand Roten Galleries, Baltimore, Brentano's and Ethel and Robert Asher, 1961.

2. From *incunabulum*, singular of *incunabula*, Latin for "swaddling clothes," referring to books published before 1501 when printing was in its infancy.

dollars. The possibly French or English artist is sometimes referred to as the "Wilton Master" but has never been identified. The much smaller original (Richard II's personal portable), painted in tempera and inlaid with gold leaf in the late fourteenth century, hangs in the National Gallery in London.

Anyway, the Taverner's Bible was my father's oldest (and, duly noted, *incomplete*) English Bible, forty-four years earlier than his Geneva Bible and sixty years earlier than the first Authorized King James Version, *and* his second-most-expensive purchase at $2,500.00 (remember, the Geneva Bible was $3,150) and nearly cost him a traffic ticket. After thinking it over for perhaps a week (I think he would have said that the only upside of my mother's death was that he no longer had to confer with her as to his book acquisitions), he left the house early one morning to purchase it from an elderly book dealer in Cornish, Maine. When I showed up at his house later that morning, he sheepishly confessed that in his zeal, he had sped through a school zone at 7 or 8 a.m. and found himself surrounded by police cars and sirens. A policeman commandeered his license and registration, leaving my father to wait in the car for ten minutes. At eighty-six years old and with no priors, he was issued a gruff warning and summarily dispatched. Sufficiently chastised, he cautiously made his way to Cornish and bought the "Byble," which he eagerly retrieved for me to admire.

17

King James Version

My father acquired a number of early King James Versions of the Bible, the oldest a New Testament published in 1662 by John Field, a printer to the University of Cambridge, the only separate New Testament that Field seems to have published. But one of his treasures was his oldest *complete* King James Bible, a tiny Oxford imprint from the press of John Baskett, "Printer to the University," dated 1722 on the title page, and with the New Testament title page dated 1723.[1] Like many early Bibles, this one is bound together with an edition of the metrical psalms (biblical psalms set to English meter) and English hymns, with a title page showing: "*The Psalms, Hymns and Spiritual Songs of the Old and New Testaments, Faithfully Translated into English Metre, For the Use, Edification, and Comfort of the Saints in Publick and Private, especially in NEW ENGLAND*." The publisher is *not* Baskett in Oxford, but John Osborn in London, and the date is 1719. It is identified as "The Thirteenth Edition." The words "especially in NEW ENGLAND" indicate that although it was published in England, it was marketed toward America.

What generally comes to mind when we think of metrical psalms in colonial America is the famous *Bay Psalm Book*, the first book ever to be printed in the colonies and published in Cambridge, Massachusetts, in 1640. One popular result of the Reformation had been the public singing of psalms and hymns. This allowed folks to participate in the church services and many families also sang together at home. Even though there was already an English book of Psalms, translated by Henry Ainsworth,

---

1. #968 in Herbert, *Historical Catalogue*.

the founders of the Bay Colony would not use it because the Plymouth Pilgrims (who were Separatists) were using it, so the Non-Separatist Bay settlers wrote their own. Its real significance now is its rarity. Of the over 1,700 copies which made up the first edition, few survive. In 2013, one of eleven known surviving copies, owned by a church in Boston, was sold at auction for over 14.2 million dollars! The *Bay Psalm Book* went through more than fifty subsequent editions, some in Boston, some in London, and some in Scotland over more than a century, the last being a twenty-seventh edition published in 1762. (More than fifty editions, but those in Boston and London—and presumably Scotland—were numbered separately. This thirteenth edition is more specifically the thirteenth London edition.)

The *Bay Psalm Book* of 1640 was turned out by a printing press that had been shipped over from England. It is said that the press operator was a locksmith who didn't quite know what he was doing: some of the pages were bound in the wrong order. Some revisions in the translation were made along the way, and hymns came to be included along with the biblical psalms. In 1651 an enlarged edition was published in Cambridge, entitled *The Psalms, Hymns, and Spiritual Songs of the Old Testament*, the same title as this copy of "The Thirteenth Edition," sandwiched in between the Old and the New Testament in a tidy 3x5x1.5-inch brick-sized volume. Having forked over fifty bucks for it at A Thousand Words, a book and art shop in Exeter, New Hampshire, my father set about his sleuthing.

The type is so small as to be almost unreadable. Tiny Bibles are generally in better condition than normal-sized ones probably because they are too small to actually read. The Bible bears in the front a signature, "Sarah Antram 1750," and on the next blank page, "Elizabeth M. Bicknell," the latter repeated on the back of the New Testament title page. Some online research revealed that Sarah Antram was the wife of Darius Sessions, deputy governor of Rhode Island, that she was born September 13, 1724, and died December 26, 1779, and that she married Sessions on May 26, 1750. This little Bible, therefore, was likely the one that Sarah Antram carried at her wedding. The setting in eighteenth-century Rhode Island indicated that the bride and groom may have been Baptists, and as a matter of fact, Sessions is known to have been a close friend of James Manning, the first president of Brown University, the earliest Baptist college in the colonies, who is said to have been instrumental in locating the university in Providence. Sarah and Darius's son, Thomas Sessions, had a daughter named Elizabeth, who married a Joshua Bicknell, explaining the two signatures of "Elizabeth M.

Bicknell" (the "M." stands for "Marchant," the maiden name of Thomas Sessions's wife, Elizabeth's mother). So, Elizabeth Bicknell (born August 5, 1792; died February 10, 1881) would have been Sarah Antram's granddaughter, who apparently inherited her grandmother's wedding Bible. My father had even downloaded a photograph of Sarah Antram's gravestone in Providence, which appeared periodically on his screen saver slideshow, which was always on. "Oh, the wonders of the Internet!" he marveled. He would have made a pretty decent private investigator.

This Bible is one of two tiny books that my father entrusted to me in the summer of 2019 to take to my house prior to his move into our downstairs apartment, as he was nervous it would get lost in the shuffle. He kept it in a "handsome clamshell box"—custom-sized—labeled simply "Holy Bible 1722" and "Psalms 1719." Placing the box carefully in my hand, he solemnly informed me that he had discovered a dealer in Maryland who was asking "$9,500 for *exactly* the same volume with the same 1722 and 1723 dates, and 1719 for the metrical psalms." He added that of course this wasn't the same as getting that much for it, but still, this gave me pause as I took the volume and placed it equally carefully on the passenger's seat of my used Volvo, worth a fraction of that.

This is not his only metrical book of Psalms. In addition to the Sternhold and Hopkins bound with the Geneva Bible, he has, from the eighteenth century, *A New Version of the Psalms of David fitted to the Tunes used in Churches*, by N. Brady and N. Tate (London: A Wilde, 1761), and *The Psalms of David translated into Heroic Verse in as Literal a Manner as Rhyme and Metre will allow*, by Stephen Wheatland and Tipping Silvester (London: S. Bert, 1754), as well as a number of Isaac Watts collections of psalms and hymns from the nineteenth century, including a split page edition published in Exeter, New Hampshire, in 1818 with musical notations at the bottom so that any psalm or hymn can be matched with any tune, calling to mind those split children's books where you can mix and match various animals' heads/torsos/feet to unusual effect.

18

The Mushroom Effect

My mother and father on vacation

The Mushroom Effect

At the end of his author's preface to his 1992 *Commentary on the Gospel of John*, my father wrote, "And of course there is my wife Betty, who has loved me and whom I have loved ever since that Spring of 1953 when I first got acquainted with the Gospel of John. To her, with my love, I dedicate this volume." In a postscript to "Four Cords and an Anchor," my father wrote: "This essay was written several months before the death of my dear wife Betty, on July 17, 2014. She was my anchor. She still is." In his *Princeton University Class of 1952 55th Reunion Yearbook*, he wrote of my mother, "The love of my life, and a wonderful companion for the long haul. She keeps my life together." And in the 2017 reprinted *Servant and Son*, he included this dedication: "In Memory of Betty Flora (1934–2014) and those precious sixty years we shared (1954–2014)." During their many years of a marriage of what looked by all accounts to be a solid and loving one, my mother kept the household and her family both functional and presentable: she kept the house and cars immaculate and maintained, prepared and cleaned up three meals a day, reminded my father to wash his hair, bought him new sweaters when his old ones got shabby (and often gave his old ones to me), made appointments for physicals, haircuts, dentists, and arranged for entertainment and travel. She *ironed*. She tidied the books in his study without undue disruption. In fact, it was she who inspired the title of his memoir:

> Betty used to tease me, saying, "You and your books," yet she incorporated them all seamlessly, the ugly ones no less than the fine bindings, into the marvelous décor she created in our successive homes.... "Me and My Books" is my grateful response.

There is a saying in my own household that originated with my father. Over a family dinner one night, he remarked on how often in the mornings their yard would be littered with mushrooms—only to vanish by afternoon. "It's strange," he said, turning his thin lips down and in, hunching his shoulders, and lifting his palms up in a gesture of wonderment. "They just disappear!" He looked genuinely mystified. My mother, ever composed, simply laughed. I—less composed—snorted into my napkin. And thus was born the mushroom effect: the coffee that gets made every morning, the laundry that folds itself, the trash that vanishes from waste baskets. All of which is to say, not only did my father lose the love of his life, but he also lost the behind-the-scenes magician whose unnoticed labor and diligence made his world function smoothly, freeing him to focus on his intellectual pursuits without ever needing to know how the dishes found their way back into the cabinets.

A week before her death, on their way home from a long weekend trip to my father's hometown of Skaneateles, New York, for a books and antiques fair, my father had driven (always a bad sign), as my mother had felt increasingly ill. After a brief stop at their home in Portsmouth, where he'd helped her down their basement stairs to turn something on which only she knew how to do (mushroom effect), my father drove her to Emergency at Portsmouth Hospital. She had never fully recovered from heart surgery nearly a year earlier and had recently been diagnosed with non-Hodgkin's lymphoma. For months, I'd been driving them to the Dana-Farber Cancer Institute in Boston for doctor's visits and treatment. The weekend before they left, at a Fourth-of-July cookout at my house, our son, Mike, had driven down our not-so-very-long driveway in order to give my mother a lift up to the house in his car because she was too weak to walk up the hill. She had remarked un-judgmentally on the chaotic state of his car's interior, gently suggesting he might benefit from a dump run. She was pale and looked exhausted but had nonetheless managed to bake two pineapple upside-down cakes for the occasion. Sitting side by side on our front steps, I asked quietly if she was sure she was feeling up to taking the trip. She sighed. "Your father has his heart set on it," she said. (*She speaks and acts just as she should.*)

Later, my father told me he'd pushed her around the fair in a wheelchair. That Sunday night he called me from the hospital—she'd been admitted—and I drove up first thing Monday morning with three of my adult children, all miraculously free. I visited again Tuesday, and then Wednesday. In the hospital, I spooned ice chips into her mouth and pointed out the swelling in her fingers to the nurse, who had a hard time removing her engagement and wedding rings. By Wednesday evening, she was visibly uncomfortable. Worried, we asked the doctor whether it might be a good idea to transfer her to the ICU, upon which he shook his head emphatically, and, patting her avuncularly on the knee, said, "We're going to turn this thing around." *Right*, I thought. When we were saying our goodbyes, I overheard my father whisper to her, "Are you ready to meet Jesus?," as if he were speaking to a child. This, more than anything else, showed me his state of mind.

Thursday morning, I was out on my bike, miles from home, when my cell phone rang. It was my father. He sounded shaken. He asked me to speak to the doctor. Between his hearing loss and his distress, the words weren't making sense. Plus, the doctor had a strong accent. Before handing over the phone, he made a choking sound and said, "I don't think she's going to make it." I pulled my bike over, sat on the ground, and listened as the doctor laid it out: at her age—eighty—things a younger person could tolerate, such as pneumonia, low blood pressure, dehydration, and kidney injury, could be devastating (i.e., deadly). I raced home and not bothering to shower hopped in the car praying I would get there before she died. I did. She was unconscious by then. But my father told me that before she slipped away, she said, "Carolyn's here. I talked to her." I hadn't yet arrived. She must have been delirious at that point, or maybe one of the nurses looked like me. But I hold on to it anyway. She never regained consciousness. I sat by her bed, trying to prepare myself for the inevitable, but mostly I worried about my father. How would he cope? Their pastor arrived. Family arrived. When everyone who could be there was there, the nurse discreetly disconnected whatever vital thing that had been keeping her alive, and my mother breathed her last. At my father's request, I wrote and delivered the eulogy (with the help of a couple of anti-anxiety pills) at her memorial service a week later.

 The days and weeks following her death were rough, filled with seemingly endless "death duties." There was a trip to the funeral home, to the gravestone store, to the church. My parents' house, once quiet and orderly, became filled with various relatives expecting to stay there with my father, either unwilling or unable to pay for a hotel. My father was not thrilled. Somehow it fell to me to diplomatically redirect (dispatch is more like it) them to alternative lodgings until the following week when the memorial service would be over, and they could go home. Then, trips to the registry, to the bank, appointments to be canceled, accounts to close, many phone calls to be made, and official documents to keep track of and send to the correct addresses. In 2008, my husband and I had gone, with my parents, to a reading given by Joyce Carol Oates in Portsmouth. She'd read an excerpt from her most recent book—a memoir called *A Widow's Story*, a powerful account of her coming to terms with her husband's unexpected death. Leave it to Oates to describe, deadpan, a hilarious scene involving her husband's death certificates and her cats' pee. Even though my parents didn't have cats, I ordered way more death certificates than we could possibly need—just in case. I still have nearly a dozen tucked away in a drawer. When does one get rid of those documents, I wonder? Once most of that was settled, I began to drive to Portsmouth once or twice a week to keep my father afloat and do my best to carry out the mushroom effect.

19

Companions

IN THE WEEKS AND months and years that followed, my father and I settled into a comfortable companionship. Growing up, I'd thought of him as a benign presence in the background of our family. My mother ran the show while he spent most of his time either holed up in his study or at school. He appeared at meals, entertained us with his wit, his sense of humor, storytelling, and aptitude for wordplay and esoteric facts, and asserted his authority only when my mother needed reinforcement, which she rarely did. He was there however for the important events. An early memory is one in which he and I are kneeling side by side at my little bed, praying. ("Down on my knees, I learned to stand," goes one song). I am in second grade; I had come home from school in tears over an injustice I'd suffered that day, something long since forgotten. But the praying stuck, thank God.

A few years later, he baptized me at Beverly Farms Baptist Church, where we were members, and many years after that, he married my husband and me in the backyard of the house we've been living in ever since. He was there for each of the baptisms of our children. I'd grown up attending church, Sunday school, Daily Vacation Bible School (a contradiction in terms as far as I was concerned), Pioneer Girls (briefly), and then Young Life. He and I became close after I learned to read and later became interested in things that mattered to him—philosophy, theology, literature, and especially Flannery O'Connor, whose brutal grace resonated with us both. While we had many theological conversations over the years, it is only since he's been gone that I've begun to grasp just how deep his scholarship really ran. As I read through his many commentaries and articles now, I wish fiercely I'd done so before he "croaked." Last October, on my birthday, Bill and I started reading his John commentary. We're over four hundred pages in, so I figure we'll finish by the end of the year. In it, my father mostly immerses himself in the text using his own literal translation—not meant for standalone reading, as he emphatically notes: "Its sole value is to give the reader without knowledge of Greek some idea of the structure and syntax of the original. It is not intended to stand on its own and it should never ever be made to do so!"[1] He engages with the big-gun commentators, ancient and modern, and draws connections across the Bible and beyond: to the Apocryphal books, to history, literature, and culture. Unlike many Biblical commentaries I've read, he has not edited out a voice that is sometimes wry, sometimes playful. He noted with amusement that "one thing that reviewers of my recent commentary on John seem not to have noticed is how very Calvinistic it is."[2]

After my mother died, our relationship took on a new dimension—more practical and also richer. I drove an hour to his home in Portsmouth once or twice a week, entire days devoted to shared meals and bookshop visits, long conversations and companionable silence. We emailed each other frequently. He was smart, engaging, easygoing. His humor was keen and infectious and often culminated in a breathless wheeze and a dab at his eyes; he could become undone by his own hilarity. We recommended books to each other, often reading them at the same time. We compared notes on teaching, read each other's work in progress, brainstormed current and future writing projects, gossiped about my students or people he had known or that we knew in common, reminisced about the past. We also seemed to talk a lot about friends or colleagues of his who were getting sick, heading to assisted living facilities, and/or dying, which they seemed to be doing in droves. In 2017, two of them, Ray Wilbur, a distant cousin of Poet Laureate Richard Wilbur, and Mildred Johnson, the 101-year-old mother-in-law of his pastor—both of whom he'd been visiting regularly—died within the same week.

I wasn't my mother—far from it. I was just the person who knew how to Google things and who had a flexible schedule. I found him a house cleaner who did a serviceable job once a month. I showed him how to run the dishwasher and operate the washing machine and dryer. Helped set up

1. Michaels, *Gospel of John*, xii.
2. Michaels, "Four Cords," 180.

online banking. Each week, I folded the laundry he had done himself, including the fitted sheet for his bed, something he for some reason obsessed about, probably because he couldn't manage it. I assured him that no one can, but he remained unconvinced. In the end I just folded it with aplomb and moved on. I went ahead and ordered a new bedspread exactly like the old ripped one, sparing us both the tedium of me trying to explain the nomenclature of mattress sizes (*why* isn't a "twin" the same as a "double?"). I cleaned out his refrigerator, throwing out bad food weekly. We bought undershirts and pajamas. And cheap frames for art he picked up at estate sales and antiques barns. Eventually, a new refrigerator. Sometimes we went food shopping together, although mostly he did this himself. I emptied the dehumidifier. Disposed of the occasional dead mouse. Tackled the ant problem two or three summers running. Tossed the butter that had turned black (which, frankly, I didn't know was a thing butter could do). I hung pictures, troubleshot Internet and phone snafus, drove him to appointments with doctors, lawyers, and his financial advisor. I picked up white wine or Fleishman's gin from the New Hampshire state liquor store on my way up. For a while after my mother died, I attempted to teach my father basic cooking skills: rice, eggs, macaroni and cheese. I would fix us a lunch that we ate at the dining room table. One morning, after his annual physical, over scrambled eggs and toast, I asked how the appointment had gone. He looked at me glumly and said, "I am disgustingly healthy."

At first he tried very hard to preserve the house the way my mother had kept it—same routines, same arrangements. (The plants didn't make it—too little watering—and neither did the grandfather clock—too much winding.) He maintained a routine—made his bed every morning, came downstairs, made coffee, looked at news, went back upstairs, had a bath, back downstairs, made himself toast, loaded the dishwasher, tried not to make any messes. Those first months were hard. I think he would have liked to find, if not another wife, a close companion, one who would manage the daily details of his life. Maybe someone who'd know how to fold a fitted sheet, for example. One friend from church, Marge P., an attractive octogenarian divorcée who had been friends with both my mother and my father, told him—preemptively—that she would never get married again. In case he was wondering. They remained good friends and went out to lunch regularly.

To my surprise, several months after my mother died, my father told me he had Googled the name of a girl he had "dated" in Kentucky while on a month-long mission trip, "evangelizing children who had memorized Scripture to get there,"[3] the summer after his junior year at Princeton. She had been fifteen years old, thus the quotes. Marietta Ball, he discovered during an Internet search, had written a book called *Horses Can See in the Dark*, which he ordered from Amazon and promptly read. Just today, I looked up the book on Amazon and was stunned to see my father's words in a review he wrote under his own name in October 2014:

> I loved it. It took me back to a world I encountered very briefly in eastern Kentucky, in the summer of 1951. There is something very personal about it. I love the way the book spans three generations, with abrupt flashbacks that catch the reader unprepared until he realizes what's going on. While I don't think the plot is in any way autobiographical, I like to think I can hear the author's own voice in the ruminations of Nora Faye as she is growing up, and to some degree in the thoughts of the grandmother as well (I forget her name; I've loaned the book to my daughter!). As the cover blurb states, it is all about loss, and survival, and moving on. On a personal level, it has helped me mightily in dealing with loss. It deserves a much, much wider circulation.[4]

My father had just turned twenty the summer of 1951. I felt as if he had reached out his hand from the grave and tapped me on the arm. The review nearly brought me to my knees for two reasons: it revealed in a way he hadn't shown me his difficulty in coming to terms with the loss of his wife, that this book helped him "mightily." And also, because he *did* lend me the book as I recall, and I read a chapter or so and "couldn't get into it" or "didn't have time," I probably said. (I'm reading it now.) I wish I could go back having read it and discuss it with him along with his memories of that summer of 1951. One other thing that bothers me is that I can't find the book, which was paperback. Did I give it back? If so, it must not have made the cut for the move. If not, shame on me. I ordered another copy. He also wrote Mrs. Ball a letter (which he asked me to read for the correct tone—he had found out that her husband had died, and my father wanted to reach out, but not in a creepy way—in a light friendly way [it was perfect]) which she never answered. And who can blame her? Sixty years is a long time. I don't really think he expected her to, but it provided him with a bit of fun anticipation for a month or two.

3. Michaels, "Four Cords," 175.
4. Michaels, review of *Horses Can See in the Dark*, Amazon, October 14, 2014.

The Book Rat's Daughter

A couple of days ago, the book arrived from Amazon. Paperback. Inside, in the upper-left-hand corner in pencil: "1.50. signed." Then on bright blue lined paper a note:

> 9–7–12.
> Hi Ron,
> I thought you might like to take a look at my novel since the first chapter won top prize as a short story in a past *Dayton Daily News* contest. When you called me with that news, I remember you mentioned your dad's background in West Virginia's mining regions. This story is set in a fictional area in the Eastern Kentucky mining area, but I thought you might find some comparisons in the chapter I have marked—and other parts.—Marietta Ball

On the title page below "*Horses Can See in the Dark*: A Novel by Marietta Ball," she had written, "All best wishes to Ron—Marietta Ball." It doesn't appear as though Ron ever read it, unless he is a *very* courtly lover of books (see chapter 25). In my experience, it's nearly impossible to read a paperback and keep it in storeroom condition. At any rate my father would have been absolutely delighted by this, a personal note from the author, and one he used to know. Just now I Googled Marietta Ball and found a site called "Conrad's Corner: July 2, 2020," where you can listen to Marietta read one of her poems, "Girl Alone," about the remains of a girl, fifteen, found frozen in the ice five thousand years ago. Grim stuff. Like the girl, his memory of fifteen-year-old Marietta Ball had remained frozen in time, and intact.

The morning after my mother died, on our way to the funeral home to deliver her clothes and a picture of her hairstyle[5] to the funeral director and to sort out burial details, my father and I stopped for breakfast at Café Espresso, one of the places he would end up going to with Marge regularly. He looked at me over his over-easy eggs and told me he had woken up with tears in his eyes. There were tears in his eyes right then. His beautiful blue eyes, the blue more noticeable after his cataract surgery because he no longer needed glasses. He said they were not tears of sadness, but of gratitude for the almost sixty years he had spent with Betty.

In the parking lot of the funeral home an hour later he backed into another car. For the duration of that summer and into the fall he hadn't been motivated to get back to any of the writing projects he'd been working on, instead spending most of his time watching Fox News and college

---

5. Even though my mother was in a closed casket, the funeral director said it was policy to make the deceased look as natural or "lifelike" as possible.

basketball. He fell a couple of times after drinking one too many gin and tonics, causing lurid purple bruises on his back and arms but no broken bones. After he started a small fire when he left some eggs boiling on the stove, we abandoned the cooking lessons, and I showed him where to find decent meals in the freezer section of Trader Joe's. These he would heat up at night. And we began to eat lunches out.

20

Lunches

Lunch at Petey's

Lunches

A ROUTINE EMERGED, AS it often does. I would arrive at his house on a day I wasn't teaching, sometimes with our dog, Blue, who showed his love for my father by annoyingly slithering back and forth under his legs. We'd fill each other in on the week—my classes, the kids, Bill, my father's appointments, meetings, lunches with friends, royalty checks, books he was considering buying, articles he was considering writing, dissertations he'd been asked to review, problems he was having with . . . anything. The fridge, the fence, the Internet, the car, the ants, the mice. We'd troubleshoot whatever and then he'd ask where I was thinking for lunch. Sometimes I had an opinion, mostly I didn't. We were similarly easygoing.

Steamed clams (sometimes oysters) for him and lobster rolls for me at Petey's in Rye. Falafel at Habibi down the street. Clam chowder and baked haddock at the Dinnerhorn. Pizza and tuna sandwiches at Galley Hatch. Chickpea garam masala at The Green Elephant. We lunched at dozens, maybe even over a hundred restaurants in the five and a half years following my mother's death. We were regulars at many of them. Next to books, food was his favorite thing. He pored over the menus as if they were ancient texts. (We both delighted in finding typos.) When the server came over to rattle off the specials, my father stared politely at the (usually female) person, looking at me periodically as if to say, *Are you getting all this?* As soon as she turned to go, my father would turn to me and ask in a loud voice, "*What did she say?*"

At Book and Bar, where we knew the owner, David L., we ate grilled cheese sandwiches and hummus and drank coffee while perusing the stacks of new and used books. David was the son of Dr. Richard L., an eccentric former colleague of my father's. After David sold the business, my father and I went back a couple of times but found the quality of the food and the selection of books much diminished. Thai Taste, across the street from Baldface Books in Dover, was also a favorite. We brought bags of our unwanted books and Clyde would take most of them for store credit. Family-owned Italian restaurant Dante's was close to the Book Barn in Lee, New Hampshire. These were recent finds, and we quickly became regulars and were both very fond of owner Vince McCaffrey, author of many books, and his wife, who had owned Avenue Victor Hugo Books on Newbury Street in Boston back in the day. I read an interview with him recently in which he says he'd just as soon "croak right in the aisles of my bookstore." No wonder we liked him.

We drove up there January 11, 2020, exactly one week before my father died. We each brought a bag of books and left with bags of different ones. We ate pasta at Dante's. He fell asleep on the way home. After he died, it took me nearly two years to go back to the Book Barn, partly because of Covid. When I entered the dusty barn alone, Vince turned and stared, registering the absence of my father. Then he shook his head, crestfallen. I thought for a minute he might cry. He said my father had seemed very frail the last time he was there. I nodded. I told him an abbreviated story of my father's rather sudden demise and then awkwardly browsed the shop for an hour or two. My father and I mostly went our own ways in the bookstores, but knowing my father wasn't there changed everything. I still haven't gone back to Dante's.

Our weekly routine was punctuated by the occasional estate sale, visits to DeWolfe's bookstore in Alfred, Maine, flea markets and antiques barns all over New Hampshire, Vermont, Massachusetts, and Maine. There were the semiannual library sales in Hamilton, Ipswich, Rowley, Georgetown, Newburyport, Manchester-by-the-Sea, and Concord, Massachusetts, Portsmouth, Dover, Concord, and Manchester, New Hampshire. The highlight of the year was the annual Antiquarian Book Fair held at the Hynes Convention Center in Boston for a weekend in November. Russ and my father, both in their eighties (neither of whom would *dream* of driving to Boston), would arrive at my house early Saturday morning, where we all gulped coffee before my antsy father shooed us out the door. Parking was usually a problem. One year I snagged a place on Boylston Street directly in front of the entrance and guiltily confessed to occasionally praying for a parking place. "But it worked," said Russ. "True," I admitted. Most of the time I found one within the labyrinthine bowels of the Prudential Center.

Once inside the sale, we'd stick together for a few rows and then go our separate ways. The space was large, but not inordinately so, or so I thought until our visit in November 2019. I searched aisle after aisle for my father for a full forty minutes (he had had an iPhone for a hot minute—his fingers couldn't manage the keys and, more importantly, it was too expensive—and he never did get the hang of the burner phone I'd bought him). The trouble was of a *Where's Waldo?* variety. Most of the people lingering at the booths, gray heads bowed reverently, gently turning pages or engaged in conversations with vendors, were disheveled white men over sixty in khaki pants, checkered shirts, and navy blue or gray cardigans wearing plaid flat caps. Thereafter, I resolved, I would insist on a red cardigan for my father and a designated place at a designated time. That never happened, as my father "croaked," and in any event, even if he hadn't, Covid happened, so in 2020 the Antiquarian Book Fair was canceled. After several hours of browsing, marveling at the price of, say, a first edition of *Absalom, Absalom!* or signed copies of Sylvia Plath, we would eat at The Cheesecake Factory in the adjacent Prudential Center and afterward get lost in the depths of the parking garage looking for my car. During what was to be our final visit together in 2019, my father had clutched my arm for support and balance on the long walk to the restaurant and then back down to the parking garage where we got lost in the basement of the Pru for the last time.

Sometimes we visited my mother's grave. The headstone was flat to the ground, simple, shared: "Ramsey 1931–." His name and birth year already engraved. On these occasions, he liked to remind me that in Syracuse, New York, he also had a stone—same name, same birth date. He got a kick out of imagining some future cemetery stroller pausing in confusion: *Well, would you look at that! This Ramsey fellow, born in 1931, still kicking in 2060! Incredible!* It never got old for him. A foot in both worlds maybe, a little ghostly mischief, like his wraith. If we thought of it ahead of time, we'd leave some random trinket we'd brought from the house—teaspoon, button, coin, once a pair of reading glasses. Our mood was always somber as we stared down at the stone and remembered my mother. But I needn't have worried about my father. I knew he missed her, but he was firmly rooted in the land of the living. Back at his place, over a glass or two of wine, we'd talk upcoming schedules and lunch plans and appointments. We'd pin down the details of my next visit. It was always a bit strange discussing such things in the same hour we'd left offerings at my mother's grave. But that was my father. Still here. Still himself. Next thing.

Taking a break at Olde Port Traders, Portsmouth

My father with Blue

21

Common Ground

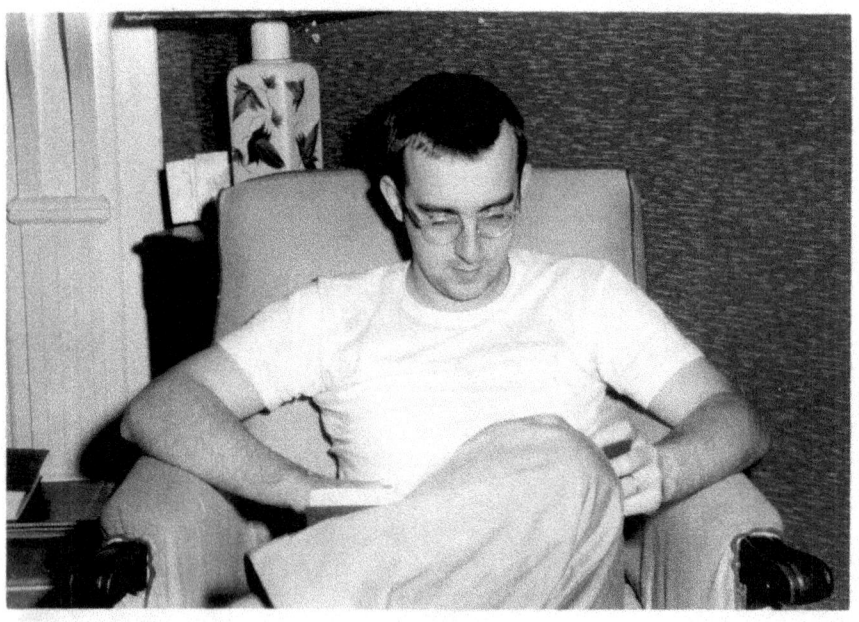

IN ADDITION TO MY father's prominent nose (so named, "The Ramsey Nose") and a disinclination to spend money, I inherited his love of books. He writes, "I can't remember a world empty of books." Nor can I. In a family photograph from August 1959, I am slouched next to him on a scratchy pink sofa, outfitted in a fancy pink dress, white ankle socks, and plastic pop pearls. My legs are crossed awkwardly, my expression one of fierce refusal to smile (I look vaguely pissed off), and I am clearly trying to hide a book under one leg. I am not yet four years old. I got my first library card at four and began hoarding books shortly thereafter. Unlike most kids, I *liked* writing book reports and research papers. My father read most everything I wrote—high school essays, college application statements, my tortured undergraduate philosophy papers on Descartes and Kierkegaard. After he died, I discovered a file with my name on it containing more than a dozen short stories and various articles or essays I'd written and sent him over the years to read and comment on. Among the things he'd saved, I found a handmade card, a thoroughly cringeworthy teenage thank-you note for letting me to go to Europe in 1973 with a friend. I'd folded a piece of brown construction paper in half, glued on some random nature scenes clipped from a magazine, and scrawled in pen, "We are the dreamers of dreams, wandering by lone sea breakers, and sitting by desolate streams." (It's Arthur O'Shaughnessy, though I'm sure I had no idea who he was.) It was a memorable trip, two months of hitchhiking around Europe (did my parents know we hitchhiked? I honestly don't remember) and visiting friends I'd made during our year in Germany two years earlier. That was during my father's sabbatical when I was in tenth grade. That year, while my father was working at the University of Göttingen on a monograph on the farewell discourses of John's Gospel and teaching himself Coptic grammar in order to read the Coptic texts from the Nag Hammadi, I was teaching myself how to smoke cigarettes, careening around our little village on a used moped, and probably giving my mother a nervous breakdown. My rebellion was relatively short-lived, the cigarette habit less so.

When I began at Boston University a couple of years later, my mother, who you may remember had grown up in a poor family on a farm during the Depression, objected to my majoring in philosophy, thereby jeopardizing my future economic security,[1] my father quietly and effectively put his foot down and told me to major in whatever I wanted. The money would follow, which it did eventually, more or less (mostly less). I was the only one of his children to follow in his footsteps as an academic (although he in

---

1. Later, I would read Flannery O'Connor's "Good Country People" and smile in recognition at Mrs. Hopewell's opinion of her daughter's degree: "The girl [Joy/Hulga] had taken the Ph.D. in philosophy, and this left Mrs. Hopewell at a complete loss. You could say, 'My daughter is a nurse,' or 'My daughter is a schoolteacher,' or even 'My daughter is a chemical engineer.' You could not say, 'My daughter is a philosopher.' That was something that had ended with the Greeks and Romans" (*Collected Works*, 268).

biblical studies and I in English and American literature and writing) and we would become cohorts when it came to Flannery O'Connor. More on this later. After I had my own family, my parents frequently accompanied us on trips, often affording my father and me quality reading time: at our yearly Canobie Lake Park outing in Salem, New Hampshire, for example, while my mother and my husband attempted to commandeer our four unruly children from ride to ride, seeing to snacks and bathroom visits, my father and I would park ourselves on a shady bench with our respective books. On overnight ski trips, I took full advantage of my mother who would tend to my kids while I read and prepared for classes.

Skiing circa 1974

22

Decisions, Decisions

WHEN I WAS GROWING up, whenever a problem presented itself, whether trivial or grave, my father would quip, "Decisions, decisions." It might have been from a TV show. I don't know. In the fall of 2018 and the early months of 2019, he had driven himself to Emergency several times in the middle of the night because of prostate/catheter-related problems. (Couldn't pee, the pee was red.) He would call me the next morning from his hospital bed, and I could picture his panic, his fumbling for keys, shoes, jacket, clumsily backing out of the garage[1] and navigating his car to the hospital in the dark. I urged him to call a taxi or an Uber (I lived an hour away) to not risk driving himself, especially if he was in pain, and even more especially if it was dark ("*Please*," I added). He was hospitalized at least twice. I took to leaving my cell phone turned on in class. I would explain the situation to my students ahead of time; several times that semester, I stepped outside of one class or another to take a call from a nurse.

He went from having a temporary catheter to a longer-term catheter to a "permanent" catheter that went directly into his bladder. The urologist, that cocky fellow we didn't much care for with a tattoo on his left forearm advertising his hard-to-pronounce last name in blocky Gothic letters, after attempting to install a larger catheter, to my father's extreme discomfort, directed him to make an appointment to "up-size the tube" in two weeks. In the end, he had to have a bladder catheter (suprapubic catheter) placed.

---

1. In the five years he lived in the house before he moved in with us, he clipped the side view mirror off his car's driver's side at least a half dozen times.

This doctor also suggested my father consult a buddy of his from urology school, a Dr. V., a specialist at Lahey Clinic in Burlington, Massachusetts, about a possible "urethrogram retrograde study" (I found this in my notes recently) to determine how bad the stricture was. Possible surgery if my father was in good health. Bottom line, he said, open surgery might enable my father to ditch the catheter. The only trouble was—this Dr. V. was booked out three months. The appointment date of June 10, 2019, is imprinted on my brain. My father looked forward to that day for three months. He would turn eighty-eight on May 1, and while he was perhaps what passed for "healthy" in vital signs and blood work, there was no arguing with the facts: he was undeniably old. I wondered at tattoo-doctor's good faith.

In April, as a result of complications with the catheter, my father landed in the same rehab facility in Rye, New Hampshire, that my mother had been in seven years earlier after her heart surgery. When I went to his house to grab the accumulated mail, I paused at the door. The place was a mess. In the four years or so since my mother's death, my father had become more relaxed about the state of the house, which I'd taken as a good sign. It was more disorderly than it had been when my mother was alive—books on the floor, mugs in the sink, sweaters draped over chairs, mail piled up—nothing terrible. But this. Granted, he had left in a hurry, having driven himself to the ER before being transferred to the rehab. But even taking all that into consideration, something had shifted, maybe some fundamental ability to take care of himself, I thought. I visited him several times during his two-week stay. On one occasion a staff member pulled me aside and asked for his trust documents, the ones that contained important end-of-life medical specifications and signatures. Back at his house, the dining room table was piled high with assorted and random papers that we had been trying and mostly failing to organize. I called his financial advisor, whose assistant—efficient, unflappable—got us what we needed immediately. I returned the next morning, dropped off the forms at the nurses' station, and went to his room. He was propped up in bed like a slightly rumpled philosopher, smiling expectantly. I sat down in the ugly chair next to his bed and said something profound like, "So!," or maybe, "Hey!"

He smiled wider. He was always happy to see me. He had struck up a friendship with his roommate John and was enjoying their theological debates. John had just shuffled out of the room. I swallowed. I'd been rehearsing this conversation in my head for days and still didn't know how to ease

Decisions, Decisions

into it. So, I just said it. "I think it might be time to think about . . . other living arrangements."

He didn't flinch. Which was good, I thought.

For years, he and my mother had had long-term care insurance, but recently—mysteriously—he'd dropped it. I suspect it was getting prohibitively expensive. Having volunteered in a few nursing homes, I had no intention of seeing him go into one. Bill and I had been talking about possibilities for months. Several years earlier, he and our sons had converted our basement into an apartment (with bathroom and kitchen) with this type of scenario in mind. (We'd both assumed my father would go first, of course. Doesn't everyone?) We had rented out the space for the past few years, and our current occupant, a college student, was fully in the loop.

I leaned in and shout-whispered: "How would you feel about moving into our downstairs apartment?" He looked at me placidly, thoughtful. I knew what he was thinking about—his books—so I quickly added, "We could turn the studio into a library space for your books." The pottery studio hadn't seen a plate or a bowl or a cookie jar in years. Arthritis and a busy teaching schedule had taken care of that. It was bare bones—cement floor, uninsulated walls. The tables and shelves and sink would all have to come out. I told him that we could hire a contractor to refinish it, including an air system for climate control.

"Not all the books," I clarified, "but . . . well, a lot of them. We could downsize. You know, curate."

I watched him as he considered this. He was quiet. The kind of quiet that means he's thinking. And then—he smiled. He looked down, then up at me, and gave a single nod. It would be a whole lot of work. We'd have to sell his house. It wasn't a perfect solution, but it was close enough.

For the next two months, I prepared lectures, graded papers, packed up my clay, tools, molds, finished porcelain work, found a buyer for my kiln and other equipment, began to pack up his house, and kept an eye on the contractors while my father held out hope that he'd eventually be able to pee "through the normal channel." In the waiting room at Lahey in Burlington the morning of June 10, my father was filling out a form and cracked an uncharacteristic joke—"What should I put after sex? 'Not anymore?' Har Har." It might have been amusing coming from anyone but my father, who had a weird/dark sense of humor but was never crass. An hour past the appointment time, a young woman in purple scrubs called "Ramsey?" and ushered us into a smaller room where we waited another fifteen minutes before a large man in a suit and tie—resembling a middle-aged Ted Kennedy[2] or maybe Alec Baldwin—made his entrance after a perfunctory knock and greeted us as if he was a celebrity (I suppose he sort of was). He announced that he could not in good conscience do that kind of operation on an eighty-eight-year-old man. Which meant that the urethrogram retrograde study was pointless. If we had any questions, Joe here would answer them. So much for the "consultation." He hadn't even examined my father. I assume he'd read the notes but can't be sure. After a three-month wait we had seen the senator for fewer than five minutes. We did have some questions for Joe, but clearly nothing we said would change the senator's mind, so we simply left. I worried that my father would be crushed, his hopes dashed, now knowing the bladder catheter would remain in perpetuity. Clutching my arm as we made our way down the hallway, we walked in silence for a while and then he made a joke about dying on the table and how that would have made the senator look bad. After a moment he chirped, "I'm starving! Cheesecake Factory sound good?"

---

2. Years ago, our family was having dinner at Anthony's Pier Four in Boston, a posh restaurant we probably couldn't afford frequently, when our father, coming out of the bathroom, announced to the table, "I peed next to Ted Kennedy!" Do with that what you will. Maybe a fascination for celebrity like his grandmother, Anna.

23

The Move

AFTER HE MADE THE decision, things progressed quickly. Our son, Mike, was working with a contractor at the time, so that part was easy. George G. gave us an estimate and got to work. My father's former pastor's wife had sold my parents the house he lived in, and she (now retired) recommended an energetic and thorough realtor to find a buyer. There was work that needed to be done on the house; my mother had taken care of all of the maintenance, and after she died, my father was loathe to spend money on things that didn't seem absolutely necessary. He had sprung six grand for a new fence, valuing as he did his privacy, but that was about it. The realtor said "not a problem" and found a young family fairly quickly who got a good deal on the house "as is." The closing was a challenge as we were missing some paperwork related to their trust. There were amended trust documents and various codicil squirreled away in several safety deposit boxes around the house. One afternoon, the realtor and I sat on the floor of my father's upstairs study for hours, methodically going through every single sheet of legal document we could find. I think it was I who found the culprit.

The move itself was more of a challenge. Eight rooms' worth of couches, beds, desks, lamps, paintings, prints, framed needlepoint my mother had done, tables, chairs, appliances, multiple sets of dishes, crystal glassware, knickknacks (Hummels, Royal Doulton figurines), sets of silverware, linens. There were more than three dozen bookcases stuffed with books in every room in the house, including the basement and the large separate building adjacent to the house they called "the studio" lined on all four sides with bookcases; here he and my mother would retreat with their glasses of wine on Halloween to avoid the trick-or-treaters. I measured the two rooms he would be moving into and drew a crude floor plan on graph paper. We set about sorting things into "Take," "Donate," "Throw Away," "Sell." We started with the big stuff: beds, dressers, chairs, tables, Turnbull desk, paintings. I led my father from room to room, putting pink sticky notes on the furniture he wanted to take to my (his) place. I took measurements to ensure it would all fit. Next, interested family members came for a weekend and put their own different-colored sticky notes on the stuff they wanted. It was a busy summer. Our first grandson had made his appearance in May, and our son Mike was getting married in August, which meant a baby shower and a bridal shower within a month of each other. I drove to Portsmouth almost daily to organize and pack. Most days, having stopped at Walmart for more boxes, I found my father in one room or another perusing one of his books, trying to decide if it was a "keeper." He must have had four or five thousand at that point, and even though I'd calculated that we could probably fit nine of his bookcases in the "library" and a few more in the apartment, he'd probably be looking at whittling his collection down to one thousand or 1,500.

It was not a clean break. As July dragged on and the apartment and the "library" at my house became more occupied with his boxed stuff, my father dragged his heels, even as his own house was being emptied. Each day, I expected to pack the last suitcase of clothes and toiletries and make the move, but he hedged. One more night. Maybe tomorrow. Finally, the man we'd hired to conduct the estate sale was coming to do whatever it was he did in preparation and the day was upon us. We started in the bedroom. I held up sweaters and pants and shirts and underwear and socks and pajamas, surprised at the number of things he didn't want. We moved on to the bathroom, down through the kitchen, grabbed a step stool on the way out and finally (*finally!*), he was buckled into the passenger's seat of my car. I started backing out of the driveway. He raised his hand. I stopped the car. We went back in for hangers. Back in the car. Then back in the house for wine glasses. And once more for a final sweep for books. We decided on The Galley Hatch in North Hampton for lunch, as it was on the way, and we ate our usual, pizza for him, tuna salad sandwich for me. They had discontinued their homemade potato chips. A minor disappointment. The following weekend, we made two more trips to the house in Portsmouth for this and that before the estate sale organizer did his sale and the new owners moved in.

24

Organization

WHILE HE ESTIMATED THAT over fifteen thousand books had passed through his hands at one time or another, my father probably never owned more than six thousand at a time in his estimation. During the summer of 2019, he culled probably close to three thousand books out of four or five thousand, housed, as I've said, in almost every room of his house in Portsmouth. Before he moved in, we got cable TV and reinstated a landline phone. The apartment had a shower only, no bathtub, which was fine as he could no longer easily get in and out of the tub, so I procured a shower chair from Hamilton's Senior Center. We got rid of the oil tank and had an electric air system installed. As for the books, "culled" is not the best word for what we did; "excised" is more like it. It was pretty painful for both of us. We spent many days going through the books. There were dozens I didn't want to let go, maybe hundreds, many of which I spirited away in grocery bags. After our sons and their friends unloaded the two U-Hauls it took to transport the essentials and placed the furniture where I directed them, sixty or seventy boxes of books lay in the middle of the floor of the "library," which was lined with empty bookshelves at the ready.

My father worked tirelessly, deriving a great deal of satisfaction from organizing and grouping his books according to his plan. Each day for about a month, after I got home from classes, I broke down the empty boxes my father had thrown onto the driveway for recycling. Most evenings I joined him for a glass of wine, and he would proudly show me what he had accomplished that day. He was very methodical and particular about his placement

Organization

and arrangement of his books. His "treasures" and "keepers" were all situated closest to where he liked to sit in a well-worn maroon upholstered swivel chair, the same one he'd occupied on his breezeway during the five years of my visits. His books on the Holy Land, oldest Bibles, concordances, and heavy Greek New Testaments were all directly in front of him, so while Fox News blared on the TV, he had only to shift his eyes to the right to see them. At least two bookcases held more Greek Bibles as well as Latin, Hebrew, and other translations. One bookcase was dedicated to Anabaptist and Baptist histories including biographies of noteworthy figures, volumes by Jonathan Edwards and Cotton Mather. One bookcase held all things Flannery O'Connor, her works in many editions, translations, some paperback, some hardcover, some with dust jackets, as well as all of the critical scholarship and anything tangentially related. This bookcase also held fictional works by Southern and/or Catholic writers as well as more contemporary fiction. J. F. Powers, Walker Percy, Muriel Spark, Eudora Welty, Richard Russo, William Faulkner, Peter Taylor, P. D. James, Graham Greene, Peter DeVries, Jean Stafford, John Gardner, Joyce Carol Oates, and Joan Didion were among those represented. One small bookcase was devoted to the works of John Updike. He kept his sectarian groups, what he called his "Enthusiasts" (see chapters 32 and 33) together; variety of books on the Apocalypse were grouped together, as were over thirty editions and/or translations of John Bunyan, most of them *The Pilgrim's Progress*. Behind his chair was a shallow bookcase filled with nearly two hundred old and/or rare miniature books, most religion-themed. Next to that was a bookcase containing the books he had either written or contributed to, some of which were translations. In this bookcase I also discovered my own few publications in literary magazines and scholarly reviews, and I was touched. Another bookcase held volumes of older poetry, obscure hymnals, old instructional religious material, family Bibles. The deep recesses in front of the basement-like windows (remember, this room began as a garage and then served as a pottery studio for thirty years) were filled with the complete works of William Shakespeare, Emily Dickinson, Richard Wilbur, T. S. Eliot, Frederick Buechner, Edgar Allan Poe, H. P. Lovecraft, C. S. Lewis, George MacDonald. There was his old paperback copy of *Moby Dick*, which had cost him at least two sleepless nights in order to finish it on time for school. He had a bookcase of material and books on states or towns or regions that meant something special to him, places he'd lived or had connections to—Skaneateles, New York, Portsmouth, New Hampshire, Grand Rapids, Michigan, Springfield, Missouri,

Sanford, Maine, Hamilton, Massachusetts. He'd also brought his complete works of Tacitus, Homer, Thucydides, Aurelius, Plutarch, St. Augustine, Tertullian, George Herbert, Dryden, Karl Barth's unfinished *Church Dogmatics*. The bookcases closest to the door held biblical commentaries on every book of the New Testament, and many on the Old, many of them written and/or inscribed by friends or colleagues. There were many books about the canon; also, Greek and Latin and German dictionaries, lexicons, books on Greek grammar, the *English Hexapla*, and histories and catalogues of English and American Bibles.

Anne Fadiman writes, "Going through a dead parent's memorabilia is a hazardous undertaking; there is a fine line between pleasure and pain."[1] She's right, of course. After my father died on January 18, 2020, it took me months to begin sorting through his books and files. Some of it was circumstantial—Covid had upended my teaching life, and I was scrambling to move my classes online—I was teaching five that semester at three different schools—while also attending to the tedious work of settling his estate, trying to work around random business hours but not being able to meet with anyone in person. But the bigger reason was harder to name. His books, his notes, his system of organization (idiosyncratic, deeply intentional) seemed to vibrate with his presence. As Fadiman recounts, a friend tasked with packing up John Clive's library described it as " like cremating a body and scattering it to the winds."[2] Which is one of the reasons I held on to most of the books. (The other reason was that I actually wanted the books.) Not long after he died, family members came to my house and collected antique paintings and photographs, my father's watch, old swords, Holly's artwork, family mementoes. One wanted the John Updike collection, which included a first edition of *Rabbit, Run* with dust jacket (under the cut-and-pasted description from Revere Books in Revere, Pennsylvania, who listed it for $1,300, my father noted, "This seems too high. I paid $18 at Aachen Books in Hamilton, MA"), another the antique Turnbull desk, another the old, framed photographs. I kept the handful of Russian icons.

---

1. Fadiman, *The Wine Lover's Daughter*, 209.
2. Fadiman, *Ex Libris*, 153.

Organization

New digs

But most of the books he brought with him to what he knew was to be his final home (that is, the one before his final, *final* home), are still where he placed them. Many are now festooned with yellow sticky notes that I affixed the summer after he died. It took me weeks to locate his Gold Room books, as a good number of them are in Greek or Latin, German or Hebrew; I have learned to not judge books by their covers as many have been rebound in later bindings masking their antiquity. While I hope to catalog everything someday (much like I "hope" to organize our family photos one day), as of now his collection of books resides in a semblance of loose clusters of thematic logic: theology here, Greek translations and lexicons there, biblical commentaries somewhere in the middle. I don't think I will ever tire of spending time in that room. His interests have increasingly become my interests. I frequently consult the reference books and biblical commentaries, and delight in arcane discoveries. The books, their smell—faint, warm, musty, *old*—is, I realize now, the smell of my father.

25

Courtly Lover

THE AFTERNOON BEFORE HE died, I went downstairs to grab his wicker laundry basket (he had emailed me, "Wash is full") and when I fetched it, I asked him if he needed anything. He was hunched over his computer, feverishly typing at his "Turnbull desk." We were blissfully unaware that it was his last day on earth. He asked me to bring him my copy of *Ex Libris: Confessions of a Common Reader* by Anne Fadiman. Sure, I told him, but where's your copy? He couldn't find it—it had probably gotten lost in the (I like to think) "gentle madness"[1] of selling his house and downsizing his book collection six months earlier. I brought it to him. (It was he who had given me this copy: "For Carolyn, bibliophile, and kindred spirit. Love *Dad*.") I'm not sure what he was looking for, but I reread this book recently and came across the charming chapter about carnal versus courtly lovers of books. In her family, Fadiman writes, "a book's *words* were holy, but the paper, cloth, cardboard, glue, thread, and ink that contained them were a mere vessel, and it was no sacrilege to treat them as wantonly as desire and pragmatism dictated. Hard use was a sign not of disrespect but of intimacy."[2] Fadiman's family's carnal treatment of books mirrors my own, and for most of my father's life, his own, whose theological books and biblical commentaries used for research and reference over the course of his career, often lay face down on the floor of his study and were filled with scribbled notes, annotations, and marginalia. Yet, paper, cloth, cardboard,

1. See Basbane, *Gentle Madness*.
2. Fadiman, *Ex Libris*, 38.

glue, thread, and ink become very important the older the book. Hence, he became the courtly lover of books of (often) carnal book lovers, enamored of the notes and scribbles and annotations found within, eager to preserve their antiquity, having older books rebound or rebacked by his aforementioned trusted book binder friend, Lynne Crocker. Sometimes he had clamshell casings made for the smaller and more delicate volumes. On those occasions he perused one of his, as he called them, "keepers," he handled gently the bindings and the pages. If they were available, he bought modern editions or facsimiles.

Two days after he died, a book arrived for him from Amazon: *Manners and Customs of the Indian Tribes* by John D. Hunter. This puzzled me: library discard, probably cost him under five bucks. He had never shown much interest in Native American material. It wasn't until I found the 1823 first edition in his library that I understood that he wanted a copy to actually read.[3] A bit of research revealed that Hunter's account of his captivity among the Osage Indians in Kansas, and of his journey across the mountains along the Columbia River, was for many years attacked as fraudulent but that Richard Drinnon in 1972 made a case for its authenticity in *White Savage: The Case of John Dunn Hunter*. This story would have been enough to interest my father.

As it happened, I *didn't* forget about Scott DeWolfe and emailed him a few weeks after my father died. This volume happened to be one of a handful of books he expressed an interest in. I ended up selling it to him for $200. Scott also bought *The Great Christian Doctrine of Original Sin Defended; Evidence of its Truth Produced, and Arguments to the Contrary Answered* (Boston: S. Kneeland, 1758) by Jonathan Edwards ($400); *Evidence from scripture and history of the Second Coming of Christ about the year 1843; exhibited in a course of lectures* (Troy: Kemble & Hooper, 1836) by William Miller ($300); *Millennial Praises, Containing A Collection of Gospel Hymns, in Four Parts; Adapted to the Day of Christ's Second Appearing* (compiled by Seth Y. Wells; Hancock: Josiah Tallcott Jr., 1813) ($325); and *An Apology for the Liberties of the Churches in New England: To which is Prefix'd A Discourse Concerning Congregational Churches* (Boston: T. Fleet for Daniel Henchman, 1738) by Samuel Mather ($300).

---

3. In one of the books my father read during that time and recommended to me, *Booked to Die* (1992) by John Dunning, a character lectures another, "Only a fool would read a first edition. Simply having such a book makes life in general and Hemingway in particular go better when you do break out the reading copies" (11).

COURTLY LOVER

Not long ago I gave my father's copy of his *Gospel of John* commentary to our friend, Russ, who has more books than anyone I know. I already had an inscribed copy ("To Carolyn and Bill with *much* love, *Dad*—aka J. Ramsey Michaels—Nov. 14, 2010"). My father's copy of *Flatland: A Romance of Many Dimensions* "with illustrations by the Author, A Square ... [pseudonym] by Abbott, Edward Abbott[4] 1884," which he picked up for twenty-five dollars, went to my brother along with an accompanying printed letter (for which he paid $600) my father believed was penned by the author himself: "Nov. 5th, 1884, City of London School, Victoria Embankment. 'My dear Moss, by all means, hold my invitation open, & come if your friend cannot take you in. As to Flatland, the Author is a friend of mine, whom I fear I love more well than wisely.'" He estimated that the book and note (if indeed it is authentic) together should be worth $5,000 or more.

In the months after he died, I located thirty-seven of the thirty-nine books listed in his Gold Room file. One of them I knew had been lost: my father had for weeks searched obsessively for *At the Back of the North Wind* in *Good Words for the Young: A Child's Devotional* by George MacDonald, which was the first appearance in print as it was serialized from 1868–70. He finally gave up and decided it must have been overlooked and left behind. The other is probably somewhere in his library, but as of yet, I haven't found it: *A Restitution of Decayed Intelligence: In antiquities: Concerning the most noble, and renowned English Nation* (London: Printed by John Norton for Joyce Norton and Richard Whitaker, 1634. Third Edition). It's got to be somewhere.

---

4. My father penned this limerick:
"Edwin Abbott Abbott
Had a habit habit habit
Of reducing three dimensions to a plane.
In his Flatland universe, what could be a greater curse
Than something round hurled through his windowpane?"

26

Carnal Lover

ACCORDING TO FAMILY LORE, when I was a toddler, I tore out and ate a page of the Greek New Testament my father was using for his dissertation. I assure you it was not venerable. My father would surely have mentioned that. Book eating in children is not necessarily uncommon, but it is telling that it was a Greek New Testament and not say *The Runaway Bunny*. In the new house in Hamilton, Massachusetts we moved into the summer after my first grade, a split-level with built-in shelving under the basement-like windows on the lower level, I carefully displayed my collection of books end to end on the ledge that ran along three sides of the sunken room. I was spectacularly hurt when my mother unceremoniously replaced them with her plants and knickknacks. In third grade, I put some no-longer-wanted books (mostly *Nancy Drew*, some Agatha Christie) into my PF Flyer and peddled them up and down the street, going from door to door. Five cents apiece!

At sixty-nine, my approach to books remains for the most part what it was at two or seven or ten: I metaphorically "devour" them, I like to own and be surrounded by them, and while I have sold and donated hundreds of books over the years, I have only thrown two books away; the titles and authors shall remain unnamed. While my father would never have allowed me to build castles with, I think it was Trollope, like Anne Fadiman's father did, I am not above using books in innovative ways, to the amusement (horror?) of the partners of my children (my children are used to me): for several years I have employed the dog-eared copy of *The Random House*

Dictionary of the English Language (1966) my husband gave me as a joke for one birthday and *Young's Analytical Concordance to the Bible* (date unknown) for propping up the two back legs of my (cheap) honey extractor so that I can (1) fit a deeper bucket under the spigot and (2) tip the extractor drum so that honey will more easily flow out. (I keep bees.) Last year the motor on the extractor died, so I extracted this year's honey by hand, sparing the books. I also have a recipe that calls for something heavy to press on a long baguette filled with cheese, tomatoes, cucumbers, olives, basil, and olive oil together overnight. Those two huge folios from the eighteenth century would be perfect, but obviously I wouldn't want to risk olive oil stains. A very used copy of volume 1 of *The Complete Works of Shakespeare (And Forty Beautiful Illustrations, with a Glossary, and a Memoir of the Author)* by the Rev. William Harness, MA—date unknown as the title pages are missing—and the 1927 *The Anatomy of Melancholy* by Robert Burton do nicely. I have also recently begun to use heavy books to lay atop blocks of tofu, which, in order to fry nicely, must be free of excess water. I sometimes buy new books entirely too readily as my husband has (finally) learned to refrain from pointing out (after pointing out to *him* that I could be buying hundreds of pairs of shoes like one person we know): anything new by Joyce Carol Oates (which I don't always read—I should have read the reviews of her latest, *Babysitter*—too dark, even for me) and new scholarship or letters having to do with Flannery O'Connor[1] are just two of my weaknesses.

Unlike my father, I don't acquire rare or collectable books if for no other reason than they are generally outside of my budget. Exceptions include a first edition of *Everything That Rises Must Converge* with dust jacket I came across at the Antiquarian Book Fair in Boston in 2015 for which I (uncharacteristically) paid eighty-five dollars (my father insisted it was a bargain). A quick Google search shows first editions going for over $300 today, so sure, let's call it an investment. I also have a copy of *My Father's Tears* published posthumously, inscribed by Updike's widow: "For Laura, who was highly esteemed by John, from Martha with admiration and affection. Aug. 2009." Seven months after John died. Who was Laura and why would she part with it? Did she die? I mean—"highly esteemed by John"! I picked it up at Manchester-by-the-Sea's annual library sale the summer of 2014. An Association copy! It was my father who nudged me into springing the

---

1. *Dear Regina: Flannery O'Connor's Letters from Iowa* (2022), edited by Monica Carol Miller, and *Better to See You With: Perspectives on Flannery O'Connor, Selected and New* (2022) by Marshall Bruce Gentry are my most recent acquisitions.

fourteen bucks for it. Besides those two, I have some signed editions bought at readings, including many by John Updike, who used to sign the copies that were sold in The Book Shop in Beverly Farms, where he lived; Richard Wilbur, one of my favorite poets, who gave a reading in Newburyport that I attended with my husband and parents; and over a dozen that Joyce Carol Oates signed for me after a handful of readings I attended. I even have a postcard Oates sent to me thanking me for a pin I sent her on a whim: "4 Dec. 2002; Dear Carolyn—Thank you for the beautiful ceramic pin! An unexpected pleasure. Warm regards, Joyce Carol Oates." The postcard is green card stock and on the front is printed:

> *Double Portrait*
> If
> opening that drawer quickly
> you hear your life rattle like hollow dice—
> we understand each other
> perfectly.
>
> *Joyce Carol Oates*

I'm not exactly sure what *that* means, but this card (ephemera if you will) is definitely one of my keepers!

27

Books He Wrote

I HAVE A COPY of all the books my father wrote, inscribed to me, including one, *Passing by the Dragon: The Biblical Tales of Flannery O'Connor*, that he *dedicated* to me: "For Carolyn." Underneath, hand printed, "With love Compliments of the Author, your Dad (That would be me!)" and a smiley face.

His title comes from O'Connor's prefatory note about the dragon that appears in *A Good Man Is Hard to Find* that in turn goes back to a letter she wrote to her good friend "A" (Betty Hester):

> Picture me with my ground teeth stalking joy—fully armed too as it's a highly dangerous quest. The other day I ran up on a wonderful quotation: "The dragon is by the side of the road watching those who pass. Take care lest he devour you! You are going to the Father of souls, but it is necessary to pass by the dragon." That is Cyril of Jerusalem instructing catechumens.[1]

Even though he writes that he took pleasure in the books he wrote but took more pleasure in books as possessions ("or even reading material"), he was proud of the fact that he had had at least one publication a year since 1960. Usually, it was several, sometimes close to a dozen. He kept track of his publications in a document on his computer titled "personal Bibliography" where he listed (again, lists!) his publications grouped by year, the major ones in bold, but also including articles, book reviews, contributions, and the like. In all there are 258, including one that had been accepted for

---

1. O'Connor, *Collected Works*, 979. See also *Mystery and Manners*, 35 for a slightly different version.

Books He Wrote

publication but was not yet finished and one that was in press. He also had a list of "possible"—three books and three articles, one of which he directed *me* to write if he croaked before he got to it: "Eraser Marks: Missing Husbands and Fathers in O'Connor's Fiction." He left behind a few notes. My next project! One of the books is his memoir, *Me and My Books*, the one I'm drawing from here, and another is the aforementioned *From Cover to Cover: Matthew and Mark*. In 2010, when he was seventy-nine years old, my father published his 1,058-page commentary, *The Gospel of John* (New International Commentary on the New Testament), over two decades in the making. (A couple of months ago, Eerdmans sent me two copies in Korean). He never failed to give me an inscribed copy. In no particular order:

I (Still) Believe: For Carolyn, who (still) believes, Love, *Dad*

Interpreting the Book of Revelation: 12/6/92. To Carolyn, Bill, William, Renée, Grace, and Michael with much love, *Dad* (Gramps).—Finished April 16, 1991. Michael Julian [our fourth child] beat me by one day.

Revelation: 10/11/97. To Carolyn, Bill, Will, Renée, Grace, Mike with love Ramsey/Dad/Grandpa . . . and yet another . . .

Word Biblical Themes 1 Peter: Christmas '89. To Carolyn and Bill with love, Dad (the Author)—I like the Chesterton quote on pp. 99–100.

World Biblical Commentary 1 Peter: 8/18/88. To Carolyn with love—Your Dad the Author—Enjoy!—For insight, information, and as a cure for insomnia. 1 Peter 5:10.

Cornerstone Biblical Commentary 1 Timothy, 2 Timothy, Titus, Hebrews [my father wrote the section on Hebrews]: To Carolyn, Something a bit different from what you've been reading . . . [smiley face]. Love, DAD. Valentine's Day 2009.

Servant and Son [remember, the book that got him canned]: To Carolyn and Bill from Dad 2/5/82.

John, A Good News Commentary: To Carolyn and Bill. Love, Dad 2/16/84.

New International Biblical Commentary: John: J. Ramsey Michaels "Dad" To Carolyn and Bill with love Christmas '89.

The News from Babylon: A Theology of First Peter: [In shaky printing] To Carolyn, Much love DAD 2/8/2018. Signed in cursive [also shaky], *J. Ramsey Michaels*.

The Spirit of Prophecy Defended: To Carolyn with love, Dad.

My copy of his first book publication, written with his friends and colleagues, Bill Lane and Glenn Barker, *The New Testament Speaks*, I thought at first was his copy as only "Ramsey Michaels Gordon-Conwell Theological Seminary 1969" appears on the inside cover. But I found a second copy downstairs on the shelf that houses his books in a dust jacket, unlike my own copy. Possibly he didn't think to inscribe it as I was fourteen at the time. There are also dozens of articles and essays that appeared in theological and literary journals, anthologies, and essay collections, all of which he has in hard copy editions.

28

More Bibles

He mostly looked for English editions other than King James, and translations other than English. His oldest English version other than the King James is a first edition of John Wesley's *Explanatory Notes upon the New Testament* (London: William Bowyer, 1755), an "indispensable key" to Wesley's interpretation of Scripture, "sturdily rebound but lacking the full-page portrait of Wesley in the front." He also has two early American Bibles, "early" as in eighteenth century, and "American" as in published in America rather than merely marketed here. These are very rare as the British did not allow the publishing of English Bibles in the colonies. Consequently, there are no American New Testaments before 1776 and no American Bibles before 1781.[1] His oldest is The Self-Interpreting Bible with extensive notes by John Brown of Haddington, first published in Edinburgh in 1778, and in America by Hodge and Campbell in 1792, the first Bible ever published in New York. It cost him $225 in credit at ABC Books in Springfield, Missouri, in the late 1980s. This volume is the largest, and at thirteen pounds, the heaviest, book in his collection, with a map of the Holy Land, twenty copper engravings of biblical scenes, and a "List of Subscribers" at the end, the first of whom is George Washington. His volume includes the Apocrypha and embossed on the heavy leather front cover are the names "Teunis T. & Margaret Johnson."

---

1. There are, however, American Bibles in German as early as 1743 (printed by Christopher Saur) and the famous Eliot Indian Bible from 1661. My father notes, "The average collector has slim hopes of ever owning the former and none at all of owning the latter."

The other eighteenth-century American Bible, much smaller and in less good shape, is an Isaac Collins publication from 1793–94, a smaller and cheaper edition of Collins's first publication of the Bible as a large folio in 1791. As a sidenote, my father at one time purchased a 1788 Collins New Testament which he found at a New Hampshire book fair from a dealer who didn't know what he had. My father didn't really either, but thirty-five dollars seemed like a good deal. His money was well spent as after keeping it for a number of years, he sold it during a trip he took with my mother for his birthday in May 2014 (just two months before she died) for $3,000 to the dealer in Cornish, Maine, from whom he would, three or four years later, buy the Taverner-Tyndale Byble. You might remember this as the one that almost cost him a parking ticket. The poor bookman later parted with it for just $2,000. My father notes, "Sad, but I hoped I cheered him up a bit with the Taverner-Tyndale purchase!"

In no particular order, he has an 1859 Welsh Bible, an 1822 German New Testament, an 1807 Scottish Gaelic Bible, a 1742 French New Testament, a 1694 Hebrew Bible, a 1583 Latin Old Testament and New Testament, an 1835 Paragraph Bible, an 1848 copy of the *English Hexapla* ("Exhibiting the Six Important English Translations of The New Testament Scriptures"), and an 1800 Diatessaron,[2] among many others. His "prize" is La Biblia Sagrada, published in New York in 1824, the first Spanish Bible printed in the New World, in New York (printing in Latin America had been going on since the sixteenth century) and not by Roman Catholics but by the mostly Protestant American Bible Society, based on a Roman Catholic translation from the Latin Vulgate, published in Madrid in 1797. When Protestants objected to the inclusion of the Old Testament Apocrypha, later American editions dropped those books, going back to the traditional Protestant canon, but this earliest edition contains the full Roman Catholic canon. He found it at the same antique mall in Rockland, Maine, on almost the same shelf on which he'd discovered the Mormon hymnal years earlier. The inscription on the front endpaper is by "someone whose first language may not have been Spanish": "La Biblia Sagrada, Presentado a Josef Lyman de su querido padre" ("The Holy Bible presented to Josef Lyman from his beloved father"). He got it for eighty-five dollars and had recently had it

---

2. An early Gospel harmony created by Assyrian apologist Titian around AD 160. Literally meaning a combining of the four Gospels into a single narrative. For a fascinating fictional story about the Diatessaron and the Shroud of Turin, I recommend *The Fifth Gospel* (2016) by Ian Coldwell. He also cowrote, with Dustin Thomason, *The Rule of Four* (2004), a novel set at Princeton that we both enjoyed.

rebacked for about a hundred more. And yes, he picked it up from Lynne Crocker *before* he croaked so I didn't have to.

As for his nineteenth-century Bibles that are not the King James Version, many come from outside traditional Christianity, particularly from the Unitarians, and many are just New Testaments. One of the "better ones," he notes, is by Gilbert Wakefield, BA, *A Translation of the New Testament* (1820), an Anglican clergyman turned Unitarian by the time he made the translation. Wakefield claimed in his preface not to have "altered in a single instance from caprice or vanity, but simply from an intention to improve."[3] His opening in the New Testament in small capitals "A History Of The Life Of Jesus The Christ, A Son Of David, A Son Of Abraham" (Matt 1:1) is arguably an improvement on the Authorized Version's "The book of the generation of Jesus Christ" but his Unitarian leanings become apparent in the opening verses of the Gospel of John. My father still considered it a "decent" translation, given his Unitarian proclivities. He also notes that Wakefield took little notice of contemporary developments in textual criticism, including in his translation the longer ending of Mark and the story of the adulterous woman in John, without comment, despite emerging doubts about their authenticity.

My father devotes some pages to "a more tendentious Unitarian edition": *The New Testament in an Improved Version, upon the basis of Archbishop Newcome's New Translation with a corrected text, and notes critical and explanatory* (Boston: Thomas B. Wait, 1809), an American edition of a version published in London by Thomas Belsham and other Unitarians, which is based in part on the "decidedly non-Unitarian" work of the Anglican Archbishop William Newcome. Quite the embarrassment to the archbishop, no surprise there. My father cites several passages as examples of the emerging Unitarian habit of editing out references to the miraculous in general and of the deity of Christ specifically. For example, his American edition acknowledges in a note after Matt 1:16, "The remainder of this chapter and the whole of the second, are printed (in the English edition) in italics, as an intimation that they are of doubtful authority."[4] A similar note appears after Luke 1:4. My father's Boston edition has no such italics, so evidently, this was taking things too far. Yet, in the Gospel of John, where Jesus' deity is most conspicuous, the editors downplay both his deity and his role in creation: for example, "The Word was in the beginning, and the

---

3. Wakefield, *Translation*, viii.
4. Belsham, *New Testament*, 2.

Word was with God, and the Word was a god" (John 1:1); "All things were done by him," not "made by him" (1:3); "He was in the world and the world was enlightened by him," again, not "made by him" (1:10). Like Wakefield, it includes the story of the adulterous woman and the last twelve verses of Mark, yet with two inconspicuous notes to the effect that some manuscripts omit them. Yet other passages are printed in italics, indicating real doubt, and the doxology at the end of the Lord's Prayer in Matthew is missing altogether!

My father mentions a "redoubtable American eccentric named Abner Kneeland" (1774–1844) who edited a Greek New Testament along with an English translation (1823) which attempted to "improve" the Newcome-Belsham version: *The New Testament in Greek and English in Two Volumes* (Philadelphia: Abner Kneeland, 1823). My father picked up volume 1 containing the four Gospels for eighteen dollars and had been looking for volume 2 ever since. Baptist-minister-turned-Universalist, Kneeland had by 1833 described himself as a "Pantheist." For his radical views he was tried and convicted of blasphemy, the last and possibly only person to be convicted of blasphemy in the United States. Yet, my father notes that his Greek text and English translation, published fifteen years earlier, is quite conventional despite his two "Universalist axes" to grind: one, that expressions of Hades or Gehenna do not refer to hell as commonly understood in traditional Christianity, and two, that the New Testament terms for "eternity" do not mean "endless" or "everlasting," but simply "agelong." My father ends the section with what appears to be either a typo or lapse in translation in Kneeland's Gospel of John. Despite printing the Greek text of John 20:8 correctly, Kneeland "inexplicably" changed the text about the anonymous "disciple whom Jesus loved," looking into the empty tomb, who "saw and believed" to "saw and believed not."

Then there is the more extreme ("notorious") Thomas Jefferson Bible, "a product of our third president's idle hours." It's basically a scrapbook made up of pages cut from two King James New Testaments printed in Philadelphia in 1804: a French New Testament published in 1802 and a 1794 Johannes Leusden Greek New Testament with a Latin translation, which my father happened to own. He discovered that Jefferson had also incorporated its two maps—one of Palestine and one of the Mediterranean world—into his scrapbook. Jefferson's original was never actually published, but the facsimile, published a century later, is, according to my father, not that hard to find: *The Life and Morals of Jesus of Nazareth. Extracted textually from the*

More Bibles

Gospels in Greek, Latin, French, and English, by Thomas Jefferson (Washington: Government Printing Office, 1904). My father notes, "The Jefferson Bible itself is no prize, a heavy-handed piece of arrogant censorship of the four Gospels" containing no virgin birth, no miracles, no resurrection, no transfiguration, no second coming. "Four Gospels with no gospel. At best a memorial to a dead Teacher."

My father offers:

> For a bracing antidote to Jefferson's depressing scrapbook, one has only to look at the work of Charles Thomson, Irish immigrant, American patriot, secretary to the Continental Congress and, ironically enough, Jefferson's close friend.

Born in 1729, Thomson came to America when he was ten and learned Latin at a young age. After a life in politics, he devoted his retirement years to learning Greek and translating the Bible—the whole thing—from the Greek. It is said that years before, he had picked up at auction volume 1 of a four-volume translation of the Hebrew Old Testament into Greek (the Septuagint) published by John Field, printer to Cambridge University, in 1665. Two years later, at the same auction house, Thomson found the other three volumes at a low price. Lucky him! My father has a compact edition of that same Septuagint from 1665—it's known as the Puritan Septuagint because it left out the Old Testament Apocrypha, also composed in Greek and usually included in the Greek translation of the Old Testament. He found it a couple of years before he even knew that it was the text Thomson had used.

Thomson's translation of the Septuagint and the New Testament into English was published in 1808. It was the first English translation of the Septuagint published in America (by Jane Aitken, the first woman to print the Bible in America) and the first English translation of the New Testament published in the New World. It met with some objection over the fact that the Septuagint itself is a translation of the original Hebrew, so he'd basically done a translation of a translation. He justified his work by pointing out that he didn't know Hebrew, but what's more, when the New Testament authors quoted the Old Testament, they followed the Greek translation more often than not, rather than translating the Hebrew for themselves. He added that his intention was not for his translation to replace the Authorized Version, only that Americans should have access to the Bible that the New Testament authors had used. His venture was unsuccessful. Most of the printed copies didn't sell, and eventually, they were destroyed. Which means that they are *rare*! The only set my father found for sale online was $8,000. With the help of Hendrickson Publishers in Beverly, Massachusetts, he was able to acquire an early twentieth-century facsimile of the two-volume Old Testament in 1904 and New Testament in 1929, almost as scarce but not nearly so expensive. As a "consolation prize," in 2011 he published an article on the New Testament volume in the *Harvard Theological Review*, "Charles Thomson and the First American New Testament,"[5] agreeing "heartily" with David Daniell's judgment that the translation was "more than just commendable" and that "to come to these books after the over-fullness developing in rival American productions by 1808 is to be refreshed."[6]

Like Thomson, Alexander Campbell was an immigrant from Ireland. He began as a Presbyterian, became a Baptist briefly, and then, in an attempt to restore the faith and practice of the earliest New Testament believers, stripped of all later ecclesiastical traditions, started his own denomination known as the Christian Church, or the Disciples of Christ. While not rejecting the Old Testament, he thought the New Testament was sufficient for his purpose, so drawing from three previous versions that had been published together in London in 1818 by George Campbell (no relation), James McKnight, and Philip Doddridge, he made his own revisions to it and self-published it in 1826. My father's copy is the "Third Edition—Revised and Enlarged. Printed and Published by Alexander Campbell. Bethany, Brooke Co. VA. 1832." Aside from the "fine colored folding map" of Caanan or Palestine in the front, another of the Mediterranean world before the book of Acts, and many prefaces as well as a long appendix, Campbell is most remembered (my father notes, "He was not bashful about supplying his own interpretation") for his "consistent rendering" of the Greek noun for "baptism" as "immersion" and the Greek verb "baptize" as "immerse." Sometimes a whole new translation would be published just to incorporate that point. My father concludes that Campbell's New Testament "deserves attention" on a wide scale as an important representation (like Thomson's) of the work of an early American scholar and theologian. The story of this acquisition is "bittersweet" as my father found it while on the last vacation he took with my mother for his eighty-third birthday in 2014. She had recently been diagnosed with non-Hodgkin's lymphoma and had been undergoing treatment but wasn't doing so well. But they did their best to celebrate, staying at a favorite inn in Freeport, Maine, and then doing some shopping in Camden. The asking price for the volume was $250, but he got

---

5. Michaels, 349–65.
6. Daniell, *Bible in English*, 645.

it for $200. He writes, "Not sure Betty was totally happy with this extravagance, my last before she died." She was there, however, when he closed the deal on the 1788 Isaac Collins New Testament and collected the $3,000 at the Antiquarian Book Fair that June. He hoped that made up for it.

One very unusual version from the 1830s is Rodolphus Dickinson's *A New and Corrected Version of the New Testament, or A Minute Revision, and Professed Translation of the Original Histories, Memoirs, Letters, Prophecies and Other Productions of the Evangelists and Apostles; to which are subjoined, a few, generally brief, critical, explanatory notes* (Boston: Lilly, Wait, Colman, & Holman, 1833). "Surely a mouthful!" my father remarks. The translation is as wordy and pretentious as the title. Consider this passage from the first chapter of Luke: "And it happened, that when Elizabeth heard the salutation of Mary, the embryo was joyfully agitated; and Elizabeth was pervaded by the Holy Spirit; and she exclaimed with a loud voice, and said, Blessed are you among women! and blessed is your incipient offspring!" (Luke 1:41–42). Or this from the parable of the prodigal son: "Bring here the fatted calf and immolate it" (Luke 15:23). Or this from the story of the suicide of Judas Iscariot: "Moreover, this man, indeed, caused a field to be purchased with the recompense of his iniquity; and falling prostrate, a violent, internal spasm ensued, and all his viscera were emitted" (Acts 1:18). *Yikes!* Or this from John's Gospel: "Indeed, I assure you, that except a man be reproduced, he cannot realize the reign of God" (John 3:3). While not all of it is quite so labored, those are the sorts of translations for which Dickinson is remembered.[7] Contemporary reviews ranged from "painfully ludicrous" to "utterly unintelligible." My father writes, "For the collector of strange and rare Bibles, therein lies its charm!"

As for Bibles since 1830 or so, he has dozens, all with stories, "some I've forgotten, some I'll never know," he confesses. One quirky example, from 1841, was printed by a Charles Lane in "Meredith Bridge, New Hampshire." He knew Meredith as a "pleasant resort" on Lake Winnipesaukee, but hadn't a clue as to where or what Meredith Bridge was. A little research revealed that Meredith Bridge, right next to Meredith Village, was the old name for what is now Meredith's "more industrial neighbor, Laconia." The little King James Bible's "only claim to fame" is that it is missing from the Hill's catalogue of American Bibles! There are Bibles published by Charles Lane in nearby Sanbornton in 1836 (#937) and 1839 (#1,041), but not this one. According to Hills, the 1839 "Sandbornton" (as it was then spelled) is

---

7. See for example Daniell, *Bible in English*, 652; Simms, *Bible in America*, 232–33.

said to have 684 pages, the same number as the Meredith Bridge edition, which appears therefore to have been a reprint.

As for more recent Bibles, my father has first editions of the Revised Standard Version (RSV) of the New Testament from 1946—signed by its editor Henry J. Cadbury—as well as the two-volume RSV Old and New Testament that followed in 1952. He has presentation copies of two translations on which he worked, the New International Version from 1973 and the New Living Translation from 1996. He also has twentieth-century facsimiles of the Tyndale New Testament (1526 and 1534 editions), the so-called Matthew Bible (1537), the Geneva New Testament of 1602, the King James from 1611, and the Aitken Bible, the first American edition of the complete English Bible (the King James Version) printed in 1782. Its compact size—small enough to fit into a soldier's pocket—gave it the nickname "Bible of the Revolution." Robert Aitken was the father of the aforementioned printer, Jane Aitken.

I have the Bible my mother's parents gave to them on their wedding day: "Presented to Betty Lou and Ramsey Michaels, Mama and Daddy July 31, 1954," as well as the one they gave my mother when she was nine: "Presented to Betty Lou Flora from Mamma and Daddy." Both of these Bibles are King James Versions and neither one seems particularly beloved (i.e., read).

My father's mother's (Scofield) Bible, though, that he himself gave her ("To Mother[8] on Mother's Day 1951. Romans 8:28") is another animal. It has a zipper, for one thing. Its pages are soft as felt and riddled (in nearly every single book!) with verses underlined in pink, penciled notes in the margins, dates in blue ballpoint pen. There are what appear to be excerpts from sermons handwritten on the inside of the front and back covers; also, on one of the blank end pages, she'd copied out "Grandfather's Prayer," the one written by Thomas Turnbull in 1875. There is a page with the heading "Meaning of Bible Numbers" from "1—no. of sovereignty, the no. of absolute unity of the Godhead" to "13—no. of rebellion," and a list of the children of Thomas and Elizabeth Turnbull—ten this time, including her mother Anna Amelia Lyon Turnbull Ramsey, my great grandmother. Scattered throughout are little pieces of paper with notes, newspaper clippings, including poems, a couple of obituaries, a feather. In the margin of Rev 13, there is a neat note, the meaning of which I had to look up:

---

8. My father never called his mother "Mom," always "Mother."

"Hebrew Letters—Nero Caesar"
N—50
R—200
W—6
N—50
Q—100
S—60
R—200
666

Most of us know that 666 is the sign of the beast but I suspect that few know why. When I research the Scofield Bible, there's that word "dispensationalism" again. Basically, dispensationalism categorizes biblical history into distinct time periods (usually seven) or "dispensations," each characterized by the way in which God deals with his human creation. Dispensationalists generally believe in a literal interpretation of the Bible—including prophecy—and therefore adhere to premillennialism, the belief that the second coming will occur before the literal 1,000-year reign of Christ on earth (the "kingdom" dispensation) as recorded in the book of Revelation. And sure enough, Scofield's notes in the book of Revelation are a source for the various end-times timetables, charts, and chronologies promoted by writers like Hal Lindsey (*The Late Great Planet Earth*), Edgar D. Whisenant (*88 Reasons Why the Rapture Will Be in 1988*) and Tim La Haye (best known for his *Left Behind* series). In 1997, fourteen years after my granny died, my father published his commentary on Revelation, which might have enlightened his mother had she read it. Regarding Rev 13 he writes,

> No passage in the entire book has captured the human imagination to quite the extent this one has. Many Americans who have little or no interest in believing or practicing anything found in the Bible suddenly become literal-minded fundamentalists when it comes to the *mark* of the beast (v.17) and the mysterious 666 (v.18).[9]

He goes on to explain gematria, an ancient numbers game "in which each letter of the alphabet was assigned a numerical value" and notes that any number of names could be found in the number representing the total number—including Adolf Hitler. In order to make sense to John's original audience, however, Nero Caesar worked. He suggests a "more cautious

9. Michaels, *Revelation*, 163.

approach" in recognizing that as seven seems to be the "magic" number in Revelation, 666 falls short three times over. He writes that "at the very least the ancient philosophical notion of evil as a lack or deficiency of the good seems to be at work in John's mysterious number of the beast." This is as far as my father will go, noting that "beyond this the interpreter is on thin ice." He concludes, "The most important thing for the modern reader to remember in connection with the celebrated 666 of verse eighteen is that its purpose is to characterize, not identify, the beast." He urges the reader to focus on verse ten: "This calls for patient endurance and faithfulness." Toward the end of the commentary, he reasonably cautions, "Once we stop looking for a blueprint of the future, we can gain insight from the picture he [John] paints into the conflict between good and evil in every generation—including our own."[10]

---

10. Michaels, *Revelation*, 163–67.

29

The Competition

MY FATHER'S INTEREST IN "the good book" naturally extended to the Holy Land—Palestine, Jordan, Syria, and Egypt—where the biblical shenanigans took place. There happens to be a literary genre of "Holy Land travel" that emerged in the early nineteenth century on both sides of the Atlantic through the Victorian era. He writes, "The title of William M. Thomson's popular *The Land and the Book* (Harper & Brothers, 1880–86) reflects a common perception that the Holy Land and the Holy Book were parallel sources of religious instruction, even revelation, mutually confirming each other."[1] This three-volume set (over 2,000 pages) "fell into my hands" in the late 1970s for a mere forty bucks.

In 1977–78, he and my mother spent five months at Tantur, the ecumenical institute outside of Jerusalem where he developed an interest in the nineteenth-century American interest in the Holy Land travel. One such volume is *Souvenir de Jerusalem: Thirty Vintage Photographs of the Holy Land* bearing the label "Maison Bonfils," for many years a prominent photography firm out of Beirut "turning out pictures of historic and sacred places, and family life in the Middle East." It includes photographs of the Mount of Olives, the Western Wall, the Holy Sepulchre, Rachel's Tomb, Bethlehem, and Jericho and the Dead Sea, among others. From Bauman Rare Books of Philadelphia, he bought a catalogue ("almost a collector's item in itself") and ordered George Williams's *The Holy City* in two leather-bound volumes from 1849, with "lithographs, a beautiful linen map and a

---

1. See Gutjahr, *American Bible*, 63–64.

tipped-in note by the author." He also has *Picturesque Palestine* by Colonel Wilson (New York: Appleton, 1881), two large volumes with gorgeous steel engravings.

His best story about a Holy Land book acquisition involves a 345-mile drive from Springfield, Missouri, where he was teaching at Southwest Missouri State, to Des Moines, Iowa, where there was a Planned Parenthood book sale. Probably needless to say (like voting Republican), Planned Parenthood was, as he said, "problematic for evangelical Christians in the wake of Roe vs. Wade." One of the fellows he was traveling with had on a previous occasion gotten into some trouble with the president of the Assemblies of God Theological Seminary, with which he was affiliated, for raving about the sale a bit too enthusiastically to the media, which was heard as an endorsement of Planned Parenthood. Although his future attendance wasn't forbidden, he was admonished to avoid the media. They drove all day to Des Moines, as the sale began at 6 p.m. This fellow, a former student of my father's, Gerry Flokstra or Flok as he was called, "was at his manic best on the road, telling anyone who would listen at gas stations or restaurants that we were headed for 'Dez Moinez' and a big book sale." In the car Flok asked my father "what would be the best of all possible finds" for him and my father "had a very specific answer": David Roberts's 1855 collection of 250 Holy Land lithographed engravings, *The Holy Land, Syria, Idumea, Arabia, Egypt, & Nubia* in six volumes, sometimes bound together as three.

My father notes, "The larger 1839 hand-colored first edition could cost well into six figures, and this smaller second edition in lithographs was even then worth $4,000 or more. My wish was more or less a pipe dream; I shared it anyway. Why not?" *Why not?* At times, my father's naïveté stunned me. Having arrived a half hour before the sale was to begin at the Iowa State Fairgrounds, they not only found themselves in a long line, but on the "wrong" side of a picket line. A pro-lifer himself, my father had some misgivings, but he confessed, "At the time my bibliophilia (make that bibliomania) banished whatever Christian scruples I may have harbored." He came away with a modest haul, including a nineteenth-century edition of John Bunyan's complete works for six bucks and a lovely little edition of George MacDonald's *Phantastes*, 1912, in a beautiful binding, signed "To Clara. Wishing her many happy returns of the day with joy and health in her life, William Ramsey/June the Ninth 1928" for a mere eighty cents. What is sort of cool about this find is that my father's uncle (his mother's brother who was married to the Seventh-day Adventist, Nell—remember her?), was named William Ramsey and my father's first-born grandson (our first son) is also named William Ramsey Kerr (the ninth, by the way), and yes, I realize this is a stretch.

Flok, on the other hand, had "struck gold." "On a raised platform featuring vintage and highly collectible books, he (not I) spotted, yes, David Roberts's *The Holy Land, Syria, Idumea, Arabia, Egypt, & Nubia*," the "item" that would have been my father's "best of all possible finds." It was in three volumes with one cover detached but present. Flok nabbed it without delay, paying $100 for it. My father didn't find out about it until they were in the car headed home. In addition to being the librarian at Central Bible College, Flok ran a bookstore on the side, where my father had purchased many "choice items" and built up a nice credit line. So, no one should have been surprised to hear that Flok was not about to pass it along to my father for what it cost him. He was asking $1,000, of which $750 had to be in cash, the rest in credit. "I was annoyed but I bought it without hesitation, and I have no regrets or hard feelings." Here my father notes that Flok, and the other fellow they were with, have "since gone home to glory." My father graciously reasoned that if he hadn't mentioned that he was looking for that book, Flok wouldn't have looked for it and odds are neither one of them would have found it. He also rationalized that he hadn't given *Planned Parenthood* ("with its track record of eugenics, racism, and abortion," my father adds) the thousand bucks but had instead supported his rapacious capitalist friend (my adjectives, not his). He considered it a bargain; the condition was "better than good." One cover needed to be reattached, and a couple of others reinforced. The "stunning" lithographs were all there. He and my mother took them to a bookman in Nashville to repair the bindings who told them that he had once shown the same set to Waylon Jennings, just back from the Holy Land, who paid cash for it on the spot.

His oldest book of Holy Land travel, *Pietro Della Valle*, with a long German subtitle, rough English translation "Description of Travel in Various Parts of the World, Namely in Turkey, Egypt, Palestine, Persia, India, and Other Far-Flung Countries," four folios in one, an enormous volume from 1694, was one of two books he bought from his friends Doran and Julie in Rye, New Hampshire, paying $350 for both. This isn't really a story about competition, as it seems Doran and Julie had no idea what they had. It was part of a collection, housed in a barn, that had belonged to a distant relative of Julie's, a German-born biblical scholar. My father helped his friends sell most of the collection to Scott DeWolfe and bought this item and a tiny Hebrew Bible printed in Frankfurt in 1694. The big volume was in poor condition externally, so he had it rebound for $350 more, a "magnificent" job done by Lynne Crocker. This volume, even counting the $500 or more my father had put into it, was selling online, he discovered, for far more. Which caused my father to question himself. "If I paid Gerry Flokstra too much for David Roberts's classic volumes on the Holy Land, did I pay Doran and Julie too little for Della Valle's travels?" These are the "qualms of conscience" that keep book rats up at night.

One more rival story that tangentially involved me is worth mentioning. In 2016 or 2017, my father picked up two volumes in plain cloth bindings in the "Religion" section of the Hamilton Library book sale. One of them, volume 3, was a facsimile of the 1582 Rheims version, the first Roman Catholic translation of the New Testament. Volume 1 was a facsimile of the 1635 Douay Old Testament, the third edition of the oldest Catholic translation of the Old Testament, Genesis through Job. Where was volume 2? He had all of the New Testament, but nothing after Job from the Old Testament. At two bucks a volume, even an incomplete facsimile of the Douay Rheims Bible was worth keeping, but what interested my father was the preface to the first volume, dated "July 27, 1987" by "Gordon Winrod, Gainesville, Missouri." He "vaguely" remembered Gerald Winrod, "a Protestant minister notorious in the 1930s (along with Gerald L. K. Smith and others) for his racism and rabid anti-Semitism, anti-Catholicism, and alleged Nazi sympathies."[2] Was Gordon Winrod a relative, "cut from the same cloth?" And if so, why on earth would he be publishing a facsimile of a Roman Catholic Bible? "Curiouser and curiouser," he notes.

He hung on to his two volumes. During the course of the sale, he ran into a Welsh bibliophile whom he knew (but did not want to name, so neither shall I), a potential rival who shared some of my father's esoteric tastes in book collecting. He showed this fellow the two volumes and asked nonchalantly if he had seen the other one floating around. The fellow said no, but said he'd keep an eye out. A couple of weeks later this fellow showed up at *my* door and offered me the missing volume, asking that I give it to my father with his good wishes, which I did. My father notes:

> I was delighted but a very naughty thought crossed my mind. Was it possible that my friend had already found the book, but was hanging on to it on the outside chance that I might give up on the two odd volumes, put them back, and they would be his? Sort of

2. See Ribuffo, *Old Christian Right*.

like a poker game ("Know when to hold, know when to fold up"). Then, when he realized this was not going to happen, he had no use for it and made sure I got it to complete the set. Would he do such a thing? Would I if I were in his shoes? I like to think not, but with bibliophiles like the two of us (book rats if you will), you never know.

Now that he had the complete set, my father set about doing research on Gordon Winrod. What he found out stood his hair on end. He was indeed Gerald Winrod's son. Born December 30, 1926, in Wichita, Kansas, he died in 2018. Everyone seems to agree that Winrod was a rabid anti-Jewish propagandist who openly attacked Jews and Judaism in his writings. Like his father, Gordon was a minister, but unlike his father, had some theological training. He was pastor to the Lutheran Church—Missouri Synod congregations in San Antonio, Texas, and Little Rock, Arkansas, but was defrocked by the Lutheran Church. In 1960 he began publishing *The Winrod Letter*, an anti-Semitic religious pamphlet. In 1965 he moved to Gainesville, Missouri, where he established *Our Savior's Independent Christian Church*. He was pastor there for many years raising his eleven children, hence his address, Gainesville, Missouri, and the 1987 date at the end of the preface to the first Old Testament volume. In 2000, Winrod, then seventy-three, was "arrested and convicted of kidnapping six of his own grandchildren from North Dakota, holding them and successfully brainwashing them on his compound in Missouri where they took turns guarding the property with rifles." He was sentenced to thirty years in prison but was released in 2012 after serving just ten years. He was also ordered to pay up to twenty-six million dollars after two of his grandchildren brought a suit against him. He was "by far the strangest, eccentric, but far more than that, and far worse" example of translator, interpreter, or publisher of "the good book."

The question of why a notorious anti-Semite and no fan of the Roman Catholics would want to reprint and distribute the very first Roman Catholic Bible in English was enough to send my father to the proverbial stacks in order to find out. The first clue appeared in volume 1's preface where Winrod's "barely coherent" argument is that the "Hebrew" (his quotation marks) manuscripts known in the sixteenth century were anti-Christian inventions, which were not faithful to the old Latin Vulgate. This is odd because the Latin Vulgate is largely a translation *from* the Hebrew original by Jerome in the fourth century. Evidently, Winrod assumed that this original was lost, that existing manuscripts were corrupt, possibly poisoned by the Jews' hatred of Christianity. The issue for him was what he considered the "systematic" removal of all references to Jesus Christ from the Old Testament.

Basically, he wanted to find Jesus in the Old Testament, not just here and there, but on almost every page. This would make the Old Testament (not the Hebrew Bible) a thoroughly Christian book, free of any references to Judaism. In the end, Winrod claimed that his reprinting of the 1582 Rheims Testament together with the 1635 reprint of the Douay Old Testament was the most faithful English version of the Bible on account of its being translated from what he considered its only authoritative source, the Latin Vulgate. My father notes that "the anti-Semitism already implicit in the sixteenth-century Douay-Rheims Bible (not least in its marginal notes) is thus highlighted and magnified in Winrod's twentieth-century preface to it." My father concludes that, while admitting that Gordon Winrod was "not a very nice man," his providing a decent facsimile of the first Roman Catholic Bible was, "in its own strange way, kind of ecumenical."

30

Concordance

IN 2017, ON ONE of our visits to Scott DeWolfe's cluttered, sprawling old-and-rare book shop, Antiquarians on the Green in Alfred, Maine, my father found *The Christian's Concordance containing the most materiall words in the New Testament* (the short title) published in London in 1622. The author, who is not identified on the title page, identifies himself in the preface as Clement Cotton. What drew him to the volume was the date, which was just eleven years after the publication of the King James Version in 1611, which might make it the first concordance for the King James Version. A modest definition of a "concordance" is that it's a dictionary or an index of all the words and proper names found in the Bible (or in this case the New Testament), arranged alphabetically, including the various pages on which they occur as well as the various meanings of the words in context. Or, as Cotton put it, "By the helpe whereof he may (onely by calling to mind some one such word in a sentence) readily attaine to any passage therein, serving his present use." He cites Acts 20:25, "Remember the words of the Lord Jesus," and Jude 17, "Remember the words—of the Apostles of our Lord Jesus Christ" as support for his enterprise. There are probably hundreds of concordances in print now, in English, in the original Greek and Hebrew, plus Latin and all the modern languages into which the Bible has been translated. When my father was in seminary, the three major concordances in English were Young, Strong, and Cruden. "In the lame seminary banter of the 1950s the word was 'Young's for the young, Strong's for the strong, and Cruden's for the crude.' Grossly unfair to Cruden's, the earliest of the three, first published by Alexander Cruden (who called himself 'Alexander the Corrector') in 1738."[1] But this concordance, found in a random pile of dusty material, was well over a century earlier than Cruden. DeWolfe was asking $200.

My father was not about to fork over that much money without ascertaining which translation Cotton was using. In Cotton's preface, "To the Christian Reader," the answer was obvious. In it, he refers to certain editions of the Geneva New Testament with annotations by Theodore Beza and also mentions "our latter translation," which would be a reference to the King James or "Authorized" Version of 1611. Thus, it appeared that this 1622 volume was in fact the first biblical concordance to take account of "our still beloved KJV." Cotton later compiled an Old Testament concordance (1627) and one based on the entire Bible including the Apocrypha (1635), but this 1622 New Testament concordance preceded them both.

My father preferred to go for this book (and all others, when possible) by accumulating trade credit. When he had enough, he emailed Scott describing the book so he could hold it for him, but alas, Scott couldn't find it. Which, if you ever do visit the shop, would not surprise you. Its loose semblance of (dis)organization is one of its many charms. A few days later, my father stopped in on the way back from a library book sale, and, with some difficulty, actually found it at the bottom of a pile on the floor near where he had first seen it. As Scott wasn't there and Scott was the only person my father did business with, his assistant told my father to take it home so as not to lose it again and bring it back later to strike a deal with Scott, which he did. As far as I know, my father never found out if it was worth only a fraction of the $200 or ten times more. It didn't matter. He considered it a keeper.

---

1. We both read and enjoyed Julia Keay's *Alexander the Corrector: The Tormented Genius Whose Cruden's Concordance Unwrote the Bible* (2005), which "argues convincingly that contrary to most historians Cruden, who was repeatedly institutionalized, was not insane but merely naïve, eccentric, and, in some ways, a saint."

31

The Christian's Dictionary

WRITTEN MORE THAN A century later than Clement Cotton's concordance is *The Christian's Dictionary: or Sure Guide to Divine Knowledge containing A Full and Familiar Explanation of all the Remarkable Words made Use of, in the Holy Scriptures, and in the Writings of the most eminent and pious Divines, whether ancient or modern* (London: J. Cooke in Pater-noster-Row, 1775). Again, "and that's the *short* title!" The author identifies himself as "the Reverend John Fleetwood, D.D. Author of *The Life of Our Blessed Lord and Saviour, Jesus Christ, &c.*" This latter work by John Fleetwood was well known, reprinted again and again throughout the nineteenth century. But *The Christian's Dictionary*, something between a concordance and a theological dictionary, is not well known at all. My father first learned of it from an early proponent of the evangelical movement and one of the founding members of Fuller Theological Seminary, Wilbur Smith, in his 1971 memoir, *Before I Forget*.[1] While Fleetwood's *Life of Christ* book, according to Smith, "had a tremendous circulation for decades" to the point that "even in the Library of Congress, not necessarily a religious collection at all—there are ten different editions of this work," no one seems to know anything about Fleetwood himself. Nothing in the *Dictionary of National Biography*. A Google search provides only information about his writings. Who ordained him Reverend? How did he become a Doctor of Divinity ("D.D.")? If "Fleetwood" was a pseudonym, no one seems to know who the

---

1. Smith, 211. An online search on WorldCat shows two known print copies, one at the British Library and one at the University of Minnesota at Morris.

actual author was. So while his *Life of Christ* was known everywhere for over a century, Fleetwood, the man, is nowhere to be found and "the same is almost true of *The Christian's Dictionary*."

My father held little hope of ever owning this work, but when it unexpectedly showed up online some years ago for a mere sixty-three dollars, he quickly scooped it up. He noted, "It's in good condition for its age, rebacked and almost complete with entries from Abaddon through Zion and twenty-nine full-page copy engravings (out of thirty called for) from 'Access' (Eph 2:18) through 'Zeal' (Gal 4:18)." Toward the end of the volume, the section titled "A Dictionary of Scriptural Proper Names" begins with "*AARON*: Heb. A mountain of praise; the first priest of the children of Israel. Exod. vi, 20,"[2] and ends with "*Zuzims*, Heb. The posts of a door; the name of a warlike people. Gen. xiv. 5."[3] This is followed by a lengthy "Appendix," addressing possible "stumbling blocks," seeming inconsistencies, or contradictory passages. The final four pages are devoted to a "List of Subscribers." What is interesting about the engravings is that most of them are not even biblical scenes, but illustrations of everyday life in eighteenth-century England (e.g., "Charity," "Envy," "Justice," "Nurse," "Learning") with accompanying Bible references and verses of poetry. The only other copy my father found online cautioned the potential buyer, "The text is incomplete in this copy," yet was still going for over eight hundred dollars. He notes with satisfaction, "My sixty-three dollars now seems well spent."

---

2. Fleetwood, *Christian's Dictionary*, unnumbered pages.
3. Fleetwood, *Christian's Dictionary*, unnumbered pages.

32

My Father's Wild Enthusiast

THE BOOK I AM most taken with in my father's library is one he found the summer of 1987 at an antiquarian bookstore in Andover, Massachusetts, while visiting us one weekend on break from a seminar he was participating in on "The Classical and Christian Roots of Anti-Semitism" at Yeshiva University in New York City. He was teaching at Southwest Missouri State by then, but my parents usually spent summers on the east coast and this particular opportunity came with a $3,500 grant from the National Endowment for the Humanities. In a bookstore a block or two from the center of town, he found a book whose title aroused his curiosity. *The General Delusion of Christians* was elegantly bound in what looked like a contemporary binding but with a detached front cover. It ran to 504 pages. The publication date was 1713, place, London, and printer, Samuel Keimer. My father found out later from Benjamin Franklin's *Autobiography* that Keimer was Franklin's first employer in Philadelphia: "He had been one of the French Prophets," Franklin wrote, "and could act their enthusiastic Agitations. At this time he did not profess any particular Religion, but something of all on occasion; was very ignorant of the world, & had, as I afterward found, a good deal of Knave in his Composition."[1] The name "Keimer" meant nothing to my father at the time, and there was no author's name on the title page. What drew him first to this volume was the extended title, *Touching the Ways of God's revealing Himself To, and By the Prophets, Evinc'd from Scripture and Primitive Antiquity. And many Principles of Scoffers, Atheists,*

---

1. See Farrand, *Benjamin Franklin's Memoirs*, 68.

Sadducees, and Wild Enthusiasts, refuted. My father was familiar with "scoffers," "atheists," and "Sadducees" as terms applied in the eighteenth century to those who did not believe that God, or the Spirit of God, was at work in the world either because there was no God or because God had "more important things to do." Or because the age of divine prophecy was now over. Sadducees were those who said, "There is no resurrection, and that there are neither angels nor spirits" (Acts 23:8). ("Therefore, they are sad you see," my Sunday school teacher told us as to a way to remember). The issue appeared to be cessationism, "the belief that the spiritual gifts in evidence when Christianity began—healing, speaking in tongues, and above all, prophetic revelation—had come to an end with the death of the last of Jesus's twelve apostles." Evidently, the book sought to "refute" these groups, according to the title. But what of "wild enthusiasts?" They sounded more suited to the other side, those who believed that spiritual gifts were still on display, "who still performed miracles, or claimed to, in the eighteenth century, who spoke in strange tongues, and who delivered prophetic oracles from heaven." What was puzzling was how the unknown author was lumping all four of them together. "Must be a truly fair and balanced individual!" my father quipped. And then he saw the marginalia, or rather, the bookseller called them to his attention. "These notes in the margin are kind of fun." I recently looked through my father's folder titled "General Delusion of Christians." The contents of this folder, along with the narrative in his memoir, tells the story of his sleuthing and research that gave birth, sixteen years later, to *The Spirit of Prophecy Defended*—"Edited and with a New Introduction by J. Ramsey Michaels." The story of how that book made it into print is a testament to my father's doggedness.

The marginalia began "modestly" with one Scripture citation on the title page ("2 Pet. 1.21") and the name of one author in the table of contents (Docter Nichols). But as my father flipped through the pages, the marginalia became increasingly frequent, with multiple asterisks and crosses in the text directing the reader to detailed comments in the margins, all executed in a careful, "almost artistic," hand in letters nearly as tiny as the type itself. They appeared to my father to be, not the notes of a reader reacting to what was written, but rather the author's own notes, perhaps in preparation for a second edition. "Who but an author would add to six observations at the end of 'Doctrine IV' the beginning of a seventh (p. 389), which then breaks off with the comment, 'See it wrote at the End of this Book?'" Sure enough, a long, cramped paragraph with the heading "Place what follows to page

389 at the end of Doctrine IV" appears in tiny cursive on one of the blank end pages of the book. The notes indicate instructions to a printer rather than annotations by a reader. The book was priced at $75 and when my father asked if the price was firm, the bookseller, who was more interested in local history than theology, said, "How does $45 sound?"

My father drove back to New York City to finish out his seminar and began work on his new project. If the author was preparing for a second edition, then had another edition ever appeared? According to the National Union Catalog, a new edition had appeared in 1832, 119 years after the first edition. This second edition was still anonymous but with a lengthy introduction by someone who identified himself as "E. I." This turned out to be Edward Irving, the Scottish Presbyterian founder to the Catholic Apostolic Church, "a self-styled prophet, and a forerunner of the modern charismatic movement." My father found a copy of this second edition at Union Theological Seminary in its rare book room. He got permission to look at it, as long as he took notes in pencil—little did they know "I had the far more precious first edition in my briefcase!" His suspicions were confirmed: Irving's 1832 edition had not included any of the marginalia. What my father had was unique. My father writes, "It was as if this anonymous eighteenth-century author had entrusted me with his secrets and was now whispering them in my ear." But who was the author? A penciled inscription on the inside flyleaf of my father's volume noted, "This work is generally ascribed to John Lacy, the patron of the French Prophets." This in fact was the most common consensus among the few sources that hazarded any guesses as to authorship, including the Harvard Library catalog and independent scholar Hillel Schwartz, author of the 1980 monograph on eighteenth-century French Prophets.[2] Others, including Edward Irving himself, were content to accept the author's anonymity.

The first thing on my father's to-do list was to either confirm or disprove Lacy's authorship. He *claimed* that that was the hard part. Transcribing the marginalia, he said, was "easy" because the notes were so neatly and legibly written. I don't know how long this took, but it must have been weeks or even months. First of all, there are 504 pages. The marginalia appear frequently, but by no means on every page, and the ink is a brownish color that, while discernible from the gray ink of the type, and somewhat

---

2. *The French Prophets: The History of a Millenarian Group in Eighteenth Century England.* My father's copy is inscribed, "For J. Ramsey Michaels/Hillel Schwartz 9-7-89/ten years after the book was completed/twenty years after I began to think about the subject."

bold, is beautiful, but terribly ornate, and must have required careful inspection. Both sides of one of the blank last pages are crammed with tiny, neat script, single-spaced. For example, "Place what follows to page 389 at the end of Doctrine IV" is the header for the top half of the first side of the page. The heading "Place what follows to page 465, 1, 38" is followed by notes covering the bottom half of that page and the entire back of the page. I'm sure he needed a magnifying glass. The marginalia ran to fifty double-spaced typewritten pages. My father was teaching full-time at Southwest Missouri State at that time and was working on several publications, so this project got off to a slow start. In 1989, he got in touch with Harvard professor Walter Grossman (who had written about a comparable group, the Community of True Inspiration in Germany, later in America known as the Amana community). I have the letter Professor Grossman wrote in response to my father's inquiry. It reads in part:

> I hope you were not too disappointed in my reaction to the marginalia. Such marginalia are very common in 17th- and 18th-century books, and they are really only of interest if they are by a major religious leader or by the author. The handwriting in a given period is very similar from person to person, and to identify it quite a task. That does not mean that you have not an important book in your hands. The very fact that it was reprinted by the Iona community, with a new introduction by McLeod (if I remember correctly what you told me)[3] shows the significance of its "Wirkungsgeschichte."[4]

At the end of the letter, he included Hillel Schwartz's address in Encinitas, California. My father had by this time read Schwartz's book, within which Schwartz explains his reasons for believing that Lacy was indeed the author of *The General Delusion*. In November 1989, the Society of Biblical Literature and American Academy of Religion was holding their annual meeting in Anaheim, California, and my father arranged to meet Hillel Schwartz at his modest trailer home near the ocean in Encinitas. After showing Schwartz his volume with its annotations, Schwartz cautiously confirmed my father's assessment that the marginalia were mostly likely done by the author himself.

---

3. He did not remember correctly: it was Irving.

4. According to the German/English dictionary I consulted, either "history of effects" or "reception history." See Tureng, "Wirkungsgeschichte."

My Father's Wild Enthusiast

My father was by no means a specialist in eighteenth-century English history, despite having written a thesis on Jonathan Edwards and the Great Awakening as an undergraduate at Princeton. From Schwartz's book, he learned that the Camisards, or "French Prophets" as the English called them, were a group of Huguenot refugees who fled persecution in the Cevennes and emigrated to England around 1706. Schwartz writes in his introduction, "My account of the French Prophets is thus an account of the survival of the millenarian impulse between mid-seventeenth-century English sectarians and mid-eighteenth-century Methodists and Shakers."[5] My father writes:

> I learned that if anyone deserved the label of "wild enthusiast" it was Lacy himself. He prophesied, spoke in tongues both Greek and Latin, performed automatic writing, wrote three volumes of prophetic *Warnings*, and on a retreat at Bushy, near St. Albans, was said to have briefly levitated, and to have cured a young prophetess named Elizabeth Gray of temporary blindness.

He and his comrades also prophesied that a member of their group, Dr. Thomas Emes, who had died on December 22, 1706, would be raised from the dead on May 25, 1707. He'd been the first of their group to die and his death challenged their belief that they would be participants in the coming kingdom:

> About 20,000 people gathered at Bunhill Fields that fateful day while Lacy and his friends conveniently spent the day in the country. No resurrection occurred.

Lacy, in a piece titled "Esquire Lacy's Reasons why Doctor Emes was not raised from the Dead" (1708), attributed the failure to the threat of mob violence. ("A wild enthusiast indeed, and a devious one at that!") Then, in the summer of 1711, Lacy received a "divine command" to leave his wife and hook up with Elizabeth Gray—yes, that one, the one he had supposedly cured of blindness, who was now sixteen years old. This action too he defended in "A Letter from John Lacy to Thomas Dutton, being Reasons why the former left his Wife, and took E. Gray a Prophetess to his Bed" (1712). In the same letter, he claimed to have been threatened with "Eternal Destruction and Hell-Fire if I disobeyed." This was taking things a bit too far even for the French Prophets, so even though many of them accepted the adultery (Lacy still considered a prominent English prophet and all),

---

5. Schwartz, *French Prophets*, 6.

he and his young paramour headed north to Lancashire, well out of the London limelight, where they proceeded to have several children.

Understandably then, the years from 1711 to 1723 were pretty silent for John Lacy; yet it was during this period, 1713, that *The General Delusion of Christians* had emerged. Given the circumstances, if he was the author, who could blame him for choosing to remain anonymous! In 1723 he came out with another book called *The Scene of Delusions*. For the title, my father was indebted to Hillel Schwartz's book, but he was unable to find a copy in America. The similarity of the title was of course compelling, and my father suspected a connection to *The General Delusion*, but he had no evidence. This did not stop him from publishing an account of his discovery in *Harvard Theological Review* titled "Marginalia to *The General Delusion of Christians*: A Preliminary Report." The title of course indicates a wish that the discovery would indeed be *preliminary* to something—publication of the marginalia at the very least, or better yet a new edition of the entire work. As a nonspecialist, he writes, "I felt like a little boy who hopes to be asked to play in the pickup baseball game, maybe even pitch, because he owns the ball. I owned the marginalia!"

A one-semester sabbatical in Cambridge the following year provided my father the opportunity to visit the British Library in London, spend some time with *The Scene of Delusions*, and have the work photocopied. What he found was that the name of its publisher (S. Noble) also appeared on the title page of *The General Delusion* as one of its distributors, and that the earlier work was featured in a full-page "Advertisement" within the latter. The similarity of the title was explained by the fact that "*The Scene of Delusions*" had first been the title of a work by a Charles Owen, from 1712, *before The General Delusion* was published, which had targeted the French Prophets and some of Lacy's earlier writings. Both it and Lacy's belated response to it are available as print-on-demand volumes. In a preface addressed to Owen in the form of an open letter, Lacy accused him of the "Sin against the Holy Ghost" described in Mark 3:21, yet signed his name, "Your Friend and Servant, John Lacy." While not explicitly claiming to have written *The General Delusion of Christians*, Lacy devoted the later book to so strenuously defending the earlier work that his authorship of both is obvious. More striking still were eight instances in certain of the marginalia my father had discovered that had been *incorporated* into the later work word for word. Pretty convincing evidence that *The General Delusion* and the later-added marginalia was the work of John Lacy, my father's "wild enthusiast."

In 1991, during a seven-month sabbatical in England, my father decided to track down the provenance of his mysterious volume. A bookplate on the inside cover ("John Fitchett"), a note in ink by an Andrew F. Reed ("Handed me Oct 25/13 [had to be 1913] by Jonathan Percy Denny, of Putney, London, Eng. who with his son was visiting me at Belmont, Mass."), the name "J. Percy Denny" in pencil at the bottom of the previous page, and an embossed stamp in the middle of the same page, "Fovant. Bramcote Road, Putney," all served as clues. My mother had abandoned him that April to help me in Massachusetts as I was about to give birth to Mike, our fourth child, so my father was on his own. The inked notice by Andrew F. Reed explained how the volume had reached Massachusetts two hundred years later. The bookplate was a dead end, but in an effort to track down the other clues, my father took a train from Cambridge to London. His April 14 entry in the travelogue he kept reads: "Found Bramcote Rd. in Putney, but no house called 'Fovant.' A pleasant affluent neighborhood." He realized, what would he do, go knocking at doors? What would he say? Does this book mean anything to you? That would be awkward. Wait. Plus, what if they said yes? The entry continues, "Had a delicious pizza at Pizza Express. Lost my London map twice, second time for good. Home about 6." "So much for provenance," he wrote later.

For the next twelve years, the project lay dormant. In 1992, my father presented a paper, "An Eighteenth Century Debate over Montanism," in Springfield, Missouri, at a meeting of the Society for Pentecostal Studies. The gist of Lacy's contention had been that the Montanists, an early Christian movement from the second and third centuries focused on prophecy and other charismatic gifts, were actually "right all along" and that the mainstream church had been mistaken in condemning them as heretics. The French Prophets saw themselves as successors to the Montanists, so in defending the Montanists, Lacy was defending himself and his cohorts in the eighteenth century. They agreed with the cessationists that prophecy and spiritual gifts had ceased for a time but contended that in their own era—the "last days"—the Spirit was back at work. In other words, the long awaited millennium of Rev 20:1–6 was upon them! The connection between early Christian movements, especially the Montanists, and modern Pentecostalism in America, which emerged around 1906 with the Azusa Street Revival in Los Angeles, intrigue scholars and the media alike.[6] The French Prophets, on the other hand, not so much, if only because they are

---

6. See for example Hoffman, *Sister, Sinner*.

less well known. His paper was well received but was published only in the proceedings of the meeting. He'd learned a lot since his lucky purchase. He'd often found Lacy "cogent and convincing," and admired the care that went into the meticulous calligraphy and detailed instructions of the marginalia. While he shared Lacy's faith broadly speaking, as well as his interest in biblical prophecy and the book of Revelation, my father pronounced himself "ambivalent," quoting the poet John Byrom who wrote in 1740:

> I no more doubt whether Heaven can or will give light &c. as in former ages, than whether the sun shines as before, but whether this writer and his friends had such communications, or whether they were not too hasty, you who have known him better can judge.[7]

Some Pentecostal and ex-Pentecostal friends of his who had started a mainstream publishing house in New England were interested in reprinting Lacy's work with Irving's preface, incorporating the marginalia, along with a new introduction my father would write (he owned the ball!). But this fell through when they began to look at cost in relation to potential sales for such an esoteric volume. Then, ten years later, a new edition was born after all. One of his ex-Pentecostal friends was by then at Brill Academic Publishers in Boston, and *The General Delusion of Christians*, incorporating Lacy's marginalia, became *The Spirit of Prophecy Defended*. The title came not from my father but from a section heading repeated four times within the original work in response to a tract entitled *The Spirit of Enthusiasm Exorcis'd* by George Hickes, one of the French Prophets' many detractors. My father wrote the introduction and Edward Irving's preface is also included. The marginalia appear in bold where Lacy had directed in his meticulous handwriting. I have two copies of this book now, my father's copy and the one he inscribed to me:

> To Carolyn with love, Dad.

On the facing page a limerick:

> *Marginalia*
> Lacy levitated—
> So they say—
> In 1707.
>
> His words still floated
> on a page—

---

7. Byrom, *Private Journal*, 2.1.302.

in a different age—
in 1987

And I retrieved them
with some hesitation:
new revelation—
no levitation.

—J. Ramsey Michaels
June 6, 2003

I don't know how many copies have been sold or even if any, but my father received a one-time payment of $500 for his labor of love. And I will venture to suggest that he may just have considered this purchase the "highlight of [his] career as a book rat."

33

More Enthusiasm

R. A. Knox, in his book *Enthusiasm* (1950, Oxford), writes of the French Prophets, "Their only lasting success was at Manchester, where they con-verted the un-happily married Quakeress Ann Lee,"[1] who in 1744 headed to America where she became known as the Mother of the Shakers, or Mother Ann. And Schwartz, in *The French Prophets*, writes, "According to the Shaker ministry in Ohio in 1808, the two witnesses chosen by God to prepare the second coming and the Second Christian Church were the Quakers and the French Prophets."[2] (The Quakers preceded the French Prophets by more than fifty years.) While my father owned a few Quaker works, including a 1902 reprint of *The Journal of George Fox* (founder of the Religious Society of Friends, known more commonly as the Quakers, or Friends), some American imprints prior to 1800, and a couple titles from the nineteenth century, as with the Mormons, he found the field too large.

Thanks in part to Scott DeWolfe and Frank Wood, he became interested in two more obscure groups, the Shakers and the Community of True Inspiration. Scott and Frank used to work for the Shaker community in Sabbathday Lake, Maine, and my father acquired several volumes from them at reasonable prices. In fact, they bought back two of the volumes after my father died. One of them (his "best Shaker item"), *Millennial Praises*, published by Josiah Talcott Jr. at the Shaker colony in Hancock, Massachusetts, in 1813, is the second edition of the first Shaker hymnal ever published (no

---

1. Knox, *Enthusiasm*, 371.
2. Schwartz, French Prophets, 211.

copies of the 1812 first edition are known to exist). I have a twinge of regret over selling this one back to Scott, which included the long hymn "Mother" in sixteen stanzas telling the story of the Shakers in England and America through the prophecies and life of Mother Ann Lee, whom they considered the female incarnation of God and the bride of Jesus Christ. As the Shakers were celibate, one of those early hymns, my father notes, "argues robustly for their chosen lifestyle":

> The cross some will not carry, but at the truth will spurn;
> The Paul says, "Let them marry, 'tis better than to burn."
> If they're in pain, and can't contain, and will not serve the Lord,
> Then sure they must live in their lust and take their just reward.
>
> Old Adam in vexation may search the scriptures through,
> And find a large relation, of Gentile and of Jew.
> But he that would be truly good, a woman will not touch
> This is the one that God will own, and Paul himself was such.

Notwithstanding his sale of the Mormon hymnal (an offer he couldn't refuse!) and his own tone-deafness, "hymnals and song books, especially of sectarian groups, have always been a conspicuous interest of mine," he confessed, revealing as it did their "enthusiasm." Among his Shaker items obtained at "quite decent prices" are two volumes of prophetic oracles, preoccupied with apocalyptic imagery, published during "the Era of Manifestations" (1837-ish to mid-1850s) reacting to the Millerite or Adventist movement[3] with their own vision of events heralding the second coming of Jesus. *A Holy, Sacred and Divine Roll and Book; From the Lord God of heaven to The Inhabitants of the Earth* (1843) by Philemon Stewart and *The Divine Book of Holy and Eternal Wisdom*, based on revelations that Paulina Bates had supposedly received, reveal a "bizarre eschatology" that didn't last much beyond the 1840s and in any event was not characteristic of the movement in the long run.

Longer lasting was their music and their simple communal lifestyle. Not to mention their simple and elegant furniture. At this writing just two Shakers survive, a man in his sixties and a woman in her eighties, both residing in the Sabbathday Lake Shaker Village. A couple of months after my father died, our daughter, Renée, who'd been living in Houston for nearly twenty years, moved back to Massachusetts with her family and bought a house in Shirley, Massachusetts, where there is a historic former Shaker community.

---

3. See Miller, *Evidence from Scripture*, the basic document of the movement.

The Community of True Inspiration was born out of Swiss and German pietism at about the same time the French Prophets were "stirring up trouble in England." Like the French Prophets they believed that prophecy was "alive and well," speaking through their own prophets whom they called *Werkzeuge*, "tools" or "instruments" of God who exhibited *Schwarmerei*, or "enthusiasm." Unlike Lacy, their founders, Eberhard Ludwig Gruber and Johann Friedrick Rock, attended to the nettlesome problem of distinguishing true prophecy from false.[4] Like the Shakers, they also came to America—though not until 1842—and settled in Buffalo, New York, where they began calling themselves the Ebenezer Community from 1 Sam 7:12, where the Hebrew *Eben-ezer* is translated "stone of help" or "Hitherto hath the Lord helped us." One of their prophets, Christian Metz, wrote in 1855:

> For hitherto the Lord has helped us and has guided
> An Ebenezer thus for us He hath provided.
> So take this vow to heart and make this pledge anew
> That you have made before: Remain faithful and true.[5]

My father found this excerpt quite by chance, reprinted in a bulletin commemorating the 150th anniversary of their journey to America, tucked into the pages of one of his purchases, *The Amana Church Hymnal. In the year of our Lord 1992*. Metz wrote it as they were about to move to Iowa, where they took the name "Amana," from a Hebrew word meaning "Remain faithful" or "true." The Amana community still thrives in Amana, Iowa, best known "not for their 'enthusiasm' which they have largely curbed," my father notes wryly, but for their Amana refrigerators and freezers.

A year after his Lacy discovery, my parents stopped in there as tourists on their way home from a trip out west. In one of their gift shops, my father found some inexpensive early Amana publications. He spent thirty or forty dollars for about four items to add to his growing collection of sectarian material. Twenty years later he would learn that his friends at Scott DeWolfe & Wood specialized in communal groups in America, specifically the Shaker and Amana communities. He brought his items in and on behalf of the Communal Societies Collection at Hamilton College in Clinton, New York, Scott offered him $150 apiece for three of the items. A year later, my father discovered a photograph of one of the items, a tiny devotional book (in English, "A

---

4. See Grossman, "Gruber," 363–87.

5. This from a bulletin, "The Journey Begins," on the occasion of the 150th anniversary of the journey to America, Sunday, November 1, 1992, Amana, Iowa. Metz, "Journey Begins."

Little Flower Garden for God-Loving Souls," Eben-Ezer, 1854) in one of their quarterlies with a note that it was the smallest and maybe even the rarest nineteenth-century inspirationist publication. The satisfaction that my father derived at having saved this little volume from the carelessness of whomever had let it get away in 1988 far exceeded his glee in the modest financial profit. (Perhaps much like his *incomplete* Tyndale Byble!)

Another volume was called *Evangelium Nicodemi*, or the Gospel of Nicodemus, an apocryphal work from the third century, bound with other early Christian apocrypha. While not something created by the Amana group, it was evidently treasured by them alongside Scripture, "perhaps as a kind of talisman," my father speculates. Although its title page was missing, it had the signature of a "Wilhelm Moershel," close friend of Christian Metz, which suggested that whatever its place of origin, it had found its place among the inspirationists in America. He subsequently learned that it was published in Germany in 1740, and in the end sold it to Hamilton College. The only known copies today are there at Hamilton College and in the British Museum.

The one volume he kept of the four was titled *J. J. J. Jahrbücher der wahren Inspirations-Gemeinden* ["J. J. J. Yearbooks of the Community of True Inspiration"] (Funfte Sammlung. Eben-Ezer bei Buffalo, 1850). In those days, the letters "J" and "I" were interchangeable both in English and German, so the "J. J. J." stood for "Jehovah, Jesus, Immanuel." What was of interest in this volume was its self-characterization as "Testimonies of the Spirit of the Lord," as given to Christian Metz, one of the community's "instruments" of the Holy Spirit in 1831, eleven years before the community came to America and nineteen years before the volume was published at Eben-Ezer in 1850. "Prophetic oracles, to them the very words of the Holy Spirit delivered to Christian Metz for the edification of the inspirationist community in Germany," had found their way into print in America.

It turned out this volume was part of a series, and while it is rare for them to come up for sale online, when they do, they are (surprise!) not in high demand, so my father acquired four more volumes, two of which he purchased and two of which the dealer threw in for free. He also acquired a metrical Psalms (1,174 pages with 110 more pages of melodies) published in Amana, Iowa, in 1871, and a modern Amana hymnal from 1992 in English. My favorite Amana "item" is a broadside he acquired in trade from Scott DeWolfe, advertising "Ebenezer Land for Sale" in English and, below, in German, "Ebenezer Land zum Verkauf," from 1855. This resides in a cheap frame we bought at Walmart as my father was loathe to spend the big bucks on framing his treasures, and like the needlework rendering of Thomas Turnbull's prayer and the incunable depicting Fourth Kings wasn't something any of the family was interested in, so still hangs in "the library."

A "rare" example from a very different group is *Divine Songs of the Muggletonians, in grateful praise to the only true God, the Lord Jesus Christ* (London: R. Brown, 1829). The folded frontispiece features a portrait of Lodowicke Muggleton, who with John Reeve founded the sect in seventeenth-century London. The first verse of the first song begins:

> In sixteen hundred, fifty and one,
> This morning GOD did freedom proclaim,
> CHRIST did declare himself GOD ALONE,
> Unto *his Ambassador, John Reeve* by name;
> *Lodowick Muggleton* was also included,
> Wisdom to the elect to make known,
> Shewing how reason is utterly excluded
> From the eternal JEHOVAH's throne:
> True saints now milk and honey
> Can purchase without money.[6]

While the poetry leaves something to be desired, the content is telling. Reeve and Muggleton were two London tailors who announced that they were the "two witnesses" described in chapter 11 of the book of Revelation. They believed that Jesus was *God alone* and not the second person of the Trinity. According to the ninth verse of the second song:

> Oh Father, Son and Holy Ghost,
> Triune in titles, never three,
> Lord JESUS CHRIST, denied by most,
> Is this hid sacred mystery.
> GOD and everlasting king,
> To whom we'll hallelujahs sing.[7]

My father notes that the Muggletonians, "enthusiasts of sorts," were around for over three hundred years, but through most of their history were "relatively harmless." The last is said to have died in 1979, leaving the entire Muggletonian archive of letters and publications to the British Library. My father has two volumes in his collection, both nineteenth-century reprints of seventeenth-century Muggletonian works. I will spare you the *very* long titles.

6. Frost, *Divine Songs*, 1.
7. Frost, *Divine Songs*, 8.

34

The Bethlehem Moravians

> Hardly enthusiasts by most definitions, the Moravians today are a small, plain vanilla mainline denomination, not unlike the Methodists.

THEY HAD THEIR BEGINNING in fifteenth-century Bohemia, now the Czech Republic, as the Unitas Fratrum ("Unity of the Brethren") under Jan Hus, and reappeared in Germany in the eighteenth century under the patronage of Nicolas Ludwig Count von Zinzendorf. R. A. Knox notes that it is "possible" that the Camisard refuges helped "to arouse the spirit of enthusiasm which gave birth to the Moravian brethren and so, indirectly, to the Methodist movement."[1] In the 1740s, a century before the Shakers, they had their own "Era of Manifestations" known as the "Sifting Time" taken from Luke 22:31 where Jesus tells Simon Peter, "Simon, Simon, Satan has asked to sift you as wheat." At a bookstore in Portsmouth, New Hampshire, my father "quite by accident some years back" came across a small, very old-looking book in German, marked down from forty dollars to twenty dollars. Lacking a proper title page, publisher and date, the Roman numeral "XII" presided over a woodcut of a lamb or sheep holding a banner at the gate of a pen filled with dozens of similar sheep. He notes, "Echoes here of the tenth chapter of John's Gospel, with Christ the Lamb in the role of Shepherd, or Door to the sheep." In the background is a very large L-shaped building. Under the woodcut the words: "Sind Wir Doch Sein Ererbtes Guth" (We are his inheritance). In the center of the front and back

---

1. Knox, *Enthusiasm*, 365.

leather cover are embossed in gold a small image of the Lamb holding the banner in a heart-shaped frame. He later learned that the emblem of the Moravian Church is, in fact, the Lamb of God with the flag of victory, illustrating the Latin motto, *Vicit agnus noster, eum sequamur* (Our Lamb has conquered, let us follow Him). My father admits, "It was slow to yield its mysteries"; years, in fact, but in 2008, he found out from an online source that it was known as *12. Anhang zum Herrnhuter Gesangbuch*. *Anhang* or "Appendix" was in fact in keeping with the absence of a title page and the odd page numbers he had noticed. Meanwhile, my father had discovered Craig Atwood's book, *Community of the Cross: Moravian Piety in Colonial Bethlehem*, about the Moravians in America, so he wrote to him about his little book. Atwood referred him to an archivist of the Moravian Archives in Bethlehem, who responded:

> Thank you for your email! It is interesting you were able to buy a copy of the Twelfth Anhang, together with the engraving. We have several copies of the Twelfth Anhang at the Moravian Archives in Bethlehem. Although they may not be rare to us, I have rarely seen copies on the market.

He learned from Atwood's book that one hundred copies of the *12. Anhang*, written by Zinzendorf in German Saxony, arrived in Bethlehem, Pennsylvania, on June 17, 1748. A notice in the Bethlehem Diary from the Moravian Archives cites, "Our brothers and sisters devoured them and enjoyed them with an especially good appetite."[2] The Sifting Time was by then well under way, having started four years before my father's *12. Anhang* arrived in Bethlehem, when a single litany known as (in English) "Litany of the Wounds of the Husband,"[3] also sent from Count Zinzendorf, was read aloud to the community. "'Everything was very bloody and heartwarming,' according to the community's diarist."[4] The *12. Anhang* simply intensified a trend, incorporating the Litany of the Wounds with a lot more about blood, wounds, and especially the spear wound in Jesus' side. The "enthusiasm" of this period embodied in this little book—not of prophecy or the second coming of Christ—is instead the community's worshipful adoration of the wounds of Jesus in his passion, most notably the wound mentioned in John 19:34, where "one of the soldiers pierced Jesus' side with a spear,

    2. Atwood, *Community of the Cross*, 143.

    3. "Husband" with reference to Christ as the Lamb of God, with the Moravian community as "the bride, the wife of the Lamb" (Rev 21:9).

    4. Atwood, *Community of the Cross*, 1.

bringing a sudden flow of blood and water." This sort of enthusiasm about blood and wounds is often associated with medieval Roman Catholicism, but it is also apparent in classic Protestant hymnody, as I well remember from my childhood Sundays in Baptist churches. William Cowper's "There Is a Fountain Filled with Blood," for example:

> There is a Fountain filled with blood, drawn from Immanuel's veins.
> And sinners plunged beneath that flood lose all their guilty stains.

Or these lines from Isaac Watts's "When I Survey the Wondrous Cross":

> See from his Head, his Hands, his Feet, Sorrow and Love flow mingled down!
> Did e'er such Love and Sorrow meet? Or Thorns compose so rich a Crown?
> His dying Crimson, like a Robe, Spreads o'er his Body on the Tree;
> Then am I dead to all the Globe, And all the Globe is dead to me.

Or these, from Charles Wesley's "Arise, My Soul, Arise":

> Five bleeding wounds he bears, received on Calvary.
> They pour effectual prayers, they strongly plead for me.
> "Forgive him, O forgive," they cry,
> "Nor let that ransomed sinner die. Nor let that ransomed sinner die."

"For the most part, such rhetoric stands squarely in the tradition of the New Testament itself, given the centrality of the cross and the passion both in the Gospels and the letters of Paul." Yet, as we will see, the Moravians in Bethlehem, Pennsylvania, in the 1740s amped it up to a whole new level.

"The Litany of the Wounds of the Husband," printed in German in his small volume (#1949, pages 1861–66) and in English translation in Atwood's book (233–37), provides a decent sampling of the blood-and-wounds theology of these colonial Moravians. The Litany begins and ends with two choirs singing responsively in Latin and Greek:

> *Ave!*   *Agnus Dei*
> *Christe,*   *Eleison!*
> *Gloria,*   *Pleurae!*[5]

---

5. In English, "Hail! Lamb of God / Christ, Have Mercy! / Glory, To the Side Wound." *Pleurae* is Latin (from the Greek) for "side."

In between is a celebration of the wounds of Christ, as if addressing the wounds themselves. Atwood features an excerpt in English translation on the opening page of the introduction to his book (my father's *12. Anhang* has the original German on pages 1864–65):

> Dearest wounds of Jesus. *Whoever does not love you, and does not give his whole heart to you, holds nothing dear.*
> Wondrous wounds of Jesus. *Holy fissures, you make sinners holy, and thieves from saints.*[6] *How amazing!*
> Powerful wounds of Jesus. *So moist, so gory, bleed on my heart that I may remain brave and like the wounds.*
> Mysterious wounds of Jesus. *I thank the pastors, who made the bruises and gashes of my Lamb known to me.*
> Cavernous wounds of Jesus. *In your treasure hoard, roomily sit many thousands kinds of sinners.*
> Purple wounds of Jesus. *You are so succulent, whatever comes near becomes like wounds and flows with blood.*
> Juicy wounds of Jesus. *Whoever sharpens the pen and with it pierces you just a little, licks it and tastes it.*[7]
> Warm wounds of Jesus. *In no pillow can a little child feel itself so secure before cold air.*
> Soft wounds of Jesus. *I like lying calm, gentle, and quiet and warm. What should I do? I crawl to you.*[8]

And as if this were not bloody enough, we find on page 1858 (#1945.2) a forty-three-word paragraph, twenty-six of which are "wunden," the German word for "wounds."

It got to be a bit much even for the Moravians, for although the *12. Anhang* was still readily available by 1753, this verse and a few others like it were by that time omitted.[9] Atwood does make a strong case that the blood-and-wounds obsession among the Moravians lasted well beyond the Sifting Time, despite the efforts of later and "more respectable" generations to sweep it under the rug. And Jesus' wounds are by no means absent from

---

6. Could this verse be looking at the Moravian community as bees or maggots, "thieves" feeding on the side wound, as if stealing precious blood like honey from the corpse of the Lamb? Such imagery is common in the community's rhetoric.

7. Such language as "juicy" (*saftige*), minimizing language ("just a little"), and the use of diminutives such as *Seitenhölgen* ("little side hole") was characteristic of Moravian rhetoric, especially useful in teaching it to children (see Atwood, *Community of the Cross*, 212).

8. Atwood, *Community of the Cross*, 1.

9. Atwood, *Community of the Cross*, 143.

respectable English hymnody. Beyond the preceding examples, consider Augustus Toplady's classic "Rock of Ages":

> Rock of Ages, cleft for me, Let me hide myself in Thee;
> Let the water and the blood, From Thy wounded side which flowed,
> Be of sin the double cure; Save from wrath and make me pure.

According to 1 Cor 10:4, Christ is the rock, so the "cleft" in the rock would be the wound in Jesus' side, where the hymnist wants to hide himself and bathe in "the water and the blood."

Adoration of the blood and wounds of Jesus is also all over the New Testament. For example:

> "The blood of Jesus, his Son, purifies us from all sin" (1 John 1:7).

> "They have washed their robes and made them white in the blood of the Lamb" (Rev 7:14).

> "For you know that it was not with perishable things such as silver or gold that you were redeemed from the empty way of life handed down to you from your forefathers, but with the precious blood of Christ, a lamb without blemish or defect" (1 Pet 1:18–19).

> "By his wounds you have been healed" (1 Pet 2:24).

> "Jesus said to them, 'I tell you the truth, unless you eat the flesh of the Son of Man and drink his blood, you have no life in you. Whoever eats my flesh and drinks my blood has eternal life, and I will raise him up at the last day. For my flesh is real food, and my blood is real drink'" (John 6:53–55).

This last example, said by Jesus himself, was even too graphic to be incorporated into the liturgy of the Eucharist, which used instead Jesus' words at the Last Supper in the other three Gospels. As for the Moravians, they seem to have drawn on this passage without (so far as we know) referring to it explicitly. Communion, according to the Bethlehem Diary from the 1740s, was a time "when we maggots shall attach ourselves individually and eternally to His gaping wounds," and twenty years later, "at last the corpse-bees approached the sacramental meal of his corpse and blood."[10] Atwood concludes that "such symbolism was not *ipso facto* pathological. It is possible that Zinzendorf's fantasy life was very healthy for him and his

---

10. Atwood, *Community of the Cross*, 210.

community. One must beware of equating the unusual or even abnormal with the pathological."[11] I'm not so sure I agree, but while the rhetoric of these "wild enthusiasts" on both sides of the Atlantic can seem extreme to the point of grotesque to us, it was not *wholly* isolated from either the New Testament or mainstream Protestant hymnody. "There is Power in the Blood!," some of us still sing. Or sing along with Randy Travis: "Have you been to Jesus for the cleansing power? / Are you washed in the blood of the Lamb?"

---

11. Atwood, *Community of the Cross*, 215. In his preface (viii) Atwood speaks of discussing these matters with a colleague over breakfast at "a small diner in Princeton, and I apologize to other patrons who found their eggs seasoned with snatches of conversation about bleeding wounds."

35

Apocalypse

> I myself have written on the Apocalypse, or book of Revelation, which seems to have fueled again and again the delusions of "wild enthusiasts" from the third-century Montanists to Lacy and his French Prophets, to the sectarian communities that followed in their wake.

HE ADDS, "NOT TO mention the Mormons, who been berry berry good to me!" Revelation, my personal favorite New Testament book, chronicles a series of visions the prophet John, otherwise unknown, received on the island of Patmos in the Mediterranean near the end of the first century AD. He regards these visions as divine revelation from the risen Christ, the Son of God, and in the first of them he is instructed to "write, therefore, what you have seen, what is now, and what will take place later" (Rev 1:19). John's visions, as well as those of Daniel and other Old Testament prophets, inspired folks like Lodowicke Muggleton of the Muggletonians, Christian Metz in the Amana community, and Mother Ann Lee and Paulina Bates among the Shakers to "replicate in some way" those visions and prophecies. My father, among those who contented themselves with reading and attempting to interpret biblical versions and prophecies *without* adding their own, counted himself as "their cousin." His first book on the Apocalypse was a kind of "how-to" book, *Interpreting the Book of Revelation*, and his second, a chapter-by-chapter commentary titled *Revelation*, was an attempt to actually "do it." His introduction to that one begins with a quote by Ambrose Bierce, author of the aforementioned "An Occurrence at Owl Creek

Bridge" from *The Devil's Dictionary*: "REVELATION: *n*. A famous book in which St. John the Divine concealed all that he knew. The revealing is done by the commentators, who know nothing."[1] To which my father responds, "Sure, we commentators should not take ourselves too seriously, but on the other hand, John was told at the end of the series, 'Do not seal up the words of the prophecy of this book, because the time is near' (Rev 22:10)."

My father has a number of commentaries on the book of Revelation, noting that through the centuries they are a "mixed bag." Some were useful to him for understanding John's Apocalypse, "tools of the trade" if you will, and others are "fascinating for what they reveal about their authors, and the times and circumstances under which they lived and wrote." Most of his older ones are focused on establishing a correlation between the successive chapters in the Apocalypse, especially chapters 4–22, and the history of the church from the first century up through the author's own time. At times, he muses, "this requires a lot of ingenuity, but in every generation plenty of interpreters are up to it."

His heaviest (and oldest) commentary on the book of Revelation is in *The Works of the Pious and Profoundly Learned Joseph Mede, B.D., sometime Fellow of Christ's College in Cambridge* (London: Printed by Roger Norton, for Richard Royston, Bookseller to His most Sacred Majesty, MDCLXXVII [1677]). He found it, five books in one, 923 pages, in the rare book room of the Archives Bookshop in Pasadena, while he was visiting professor for a semester at Fuller Seminary. Joseph Mede (1586–1639) was familiar to him from the marginalia in *The General Delusion of Christians* in which Lacy included two long quotations from Mede which Lacy must have thought would strengthen his book. After negotiating the price (of course), he bought it and counted it as one of his "treasures." Book 3 (pages 409–714) is mostly devoted to the book of Revelation and prophecies related to the second coming of Christ and the end of the world. While most of Mede's writing is in English, most, though not all, of book 3 is in Latin. At the heart of it is Mede's *Clavis Apocalyptica* or "Key to Apocalypse," all in Latin (my father writes "alas"—the five-dollar Latin prize he won in high school notwithstanding). An English translation was made in the nineteenth century, and my father has a print-on-demand copy of that. Even without the help of the English translation however, Mede provides a postscript in English addressing possible objections and/or questions. My father describes in

---

1. Bierce, *Collected Writings*, 347, as quoted in Michaels, *Revelation*, 13.

detail the "magnificent" double-page chart bound near the beginning of the *Clavis*

depicting a large circle (chapters 4–7)[2] encompassing a slightly smaller one (chapters 8–11), highlighting the "seven seals" in the Apocalypse that must be broken in order to display the contents of a mysterious sealed book or scroll (BIBLARIDION), and the "seven trumpets" introduced by breaking the seventh seal and delivering the opened book into the hands of John the prophet (Rev 10:7–8). The seventh and last trumpet yields the proclamation MYSTERIUM DEI CONSUMMATUR, "The mystery of God is completed" (10:7), and finally FACTA SUNT REGNA MUNDI DOMINI NRI ET CHRISTI EIUS, "The kingdoms of the world are made that of our Lord and of his Christ" (Rev 11:15), introducing Christ's victory over Satan, a thousand-year millennial reign on earth with his redeemed saints, and the resurrection of the dead to eternal life or eternal judgment. These inscriptions in Latin come within a third, much smaller circle introducing the remainder of the Apocalypse (chapters 12–22), the binding of Satan for a thousand years, the resurrection of the dead, and the new Jerusalem. At each of the four corners of the chart, outside the three circles, clusters of winged angels survey the whole scene. The chart itself makes no effort to correlate these elements in John's vision with the history of the world as Mede knew it, but in the course of his discussion he does make such correlations, to the point of setting dates for the coming of Christ and the beginning of his thousand-year reign on earth. Although I have not been able to verify it, Mede is said to have set dates of 1654 in one instance and 1716 in another for the end of the world as we know it. Mede actually wrote the *Clavis Apocalyptica* in 1627, and by the time my edition of his complete works was published (1677), Mede had been deceased for thirty-eight years, and any prediction of 1654 already long discredited! This despite his reputation as "the Pious and Profoundly Learned Joseph Mede, B.D.!"

Another find and purchase from the same bookshop is *Notes on Scripture (Designed for Young Inquirers)* (Edinburgh: Waugh and Innes, 1832). A WorldCat search shows just four known copies. The table of contents is a "true miscellany, a little bit of this and a little bit of that from the English Bible." However, a close reading reveals that a commentary of the book of Revelation runs to more than eighty pages. And just before the title page,

---

2. The chart ignores chapters 2–3 because they are "not generally granted to be a Prophecy" (Mede, 582).

a wonderful fold-out chart, "Chronological Map of Revelations."[3] Not as spectacular as Mede's chart, but nevertheless, impressive. Like Mede's, the chart pays little attention to the first three chapters ("Addresses to the Churches") but focuses on the seven seals in chapters 4–6 and the seven trumpets in chapters 8–9. Like Mede's chart, it identifies the content of the "Little Book" which John receives from the hand of an angel as representing the history of the Christian church from the time of Constantine to the Protestant Reformation and on to the battle of Armageddon and the end of history, which unfolds in the seven bowls or "vials" as the author calls them. The third vial brings us to 1815, seventeen years before the book was published, and the author identifies the end of the series as 1866. Whether or not this was intended as a prediction of the year of Christ's second coming is unclear, but the author is not afraid to identify events that happen in Revelation with the known history of the Christian church.[4]

Besides its rarity, another striking feature of this book is revealed in the first paragraph of the preface:

> The Author of the following pages has often smiled while reading the apologies that burden the prefatory addresses of small works and asked herself—if the writer had the humble opinion of his work which he professes, why present it to the public?[5]

The reflexive pronoun reveals that the anonymous author is a woman, somewhat unusual in 1832, especially in the field of Apocalypse interpretation. Naturally the mystery of this woman's identity piqued the interest of my father. While she seems to have gone to some pains to maintain her anonymity, the inscription on the flyleaf perhaps provides a clue: "Mrs. W.[?] Vincent, with A. M. T.'s best love and most sincere esteem Dec 4th, 1832." So just possibly, A. M. T. is the author. If so, my father, no slouch when it came to esoteric information, surmised that it might be Ann Martin Taylor, sometimes known as Ann Taylor of Ongar, wife of Isaac Taylor (1759–1829), a prominent engraver, minister, and author of books for young people. Ann Martin Taylor (1757–1830) was also an author of

---

3. Like many before and since, including some who should know better, this author repeatedly calls it "Revelations" instead of "Revelation" or "the Apocalypse," suggesting that this may be the work of a layperson, not a minister or professional scholar.

4. This is known as the historicist view of the Apocalypse, viewing it indeed as "A Chronological Map of Revelations." This was the dominant view at the time this book was written.

5. *Notes on Scripture*, i.

seven books of edification, some fiction, some nonfiction, on religion and morality, also aimed at the young. This work (*Designed for Young Inquirers*) would fit within her purview.

The catch (there's usually a catch) was that Ann Martin Taylor died in 1830, and this book was published in 1832. We don't know if there was an earlier edition, so if she was the author, it would have been a posthumous publication. Or maybe the greeting wasn't written by "A. M. T." herself. She had two daughters, Ann and Jane, and a son named Isaac after his father. Jane Taylor, known as the author of "Twinkle Twinkle, Little Star" in *Rhymes for the Nursery* (1806), died in 1824, but Ann lived until 1866 and Isaac until 1865; it is possible that one of them penned the inscription to an old friend of their mother on their deceased mother's behalf. My father notes that "if any distinction is possible between male and female handwriting, it is marginally more likely that Ann was the scribe." While there is no way of knowing for sure, my father concluded that Ann Martin Taylor was as likely as anyone to have written these *Notes on Scripture*, the culmination of a lifetime of "accumulated thoughts and musings about the Bible" aimed at those "young inquirers." One virtue of her book, my father notes, is that it does not "foster enthusiasm" in the sense in which we have been using the term. And if she is indeed Ann Martin Taylor, it is interesting to note that her son, Isaac Taylor, wrote a book, *A History of Enthusiasm* (1830), and another, *Fanaticism* (1833), calling "enthusiasm" by its "right name." Whoever she was, the author appears to have been a "proper pre-Victorian lady" far removed from the likes of such enthusiasts as John Lacy, Count Zinzendorf, or Mother Ann Lee.

William Miller, however, is another story. A clergyman, Miller became the messenger of the second coming and is credited with starting the mid-nineteenth-century American Millerite or Adventist movement. My father's copy of his *Evidence from Scripture and History of the Second Coming of Christ about the year 1843; exhibited in a Course of Lectures* (Boston: Dow, 1841)[6] was published just two years before his prediction failed to materialize and has an attached "Chronological Chart of the World" with a supplement providing an "Exposition of Miller's Chart." Taking into consideration all of Scripture, not just the Prophets and the book of Revelation, Miller presented a 6,000-year lifespan for the world as he knew it (4,157 years to the birth of Christ and 1843 years after that), followed by

---

6. You might remember that this is the work that Shakers Philemon Stewart and Paulina Bates were reacting to in their own books published during the Era of Manifestations.

the millennium, "the Great Sabbath of rest." The book of Revelation comes into view only after the end of "Pagan Rome" and the rise of "Papal Rome" in the fifth century AD. My father notes that Miller's chart is "no more bizarre" than Mede's or the anonymous author's *Notes on Scripture* and "less so" than Muggleton or the Shaker's Philemon Stewart and Paulina Bates. Yet, unlike them, it led to some "serious" enthusiasm and a movement that was firmly convinced that the end was near; a movement that, almost two hundred years later, is still alive and well despite its "initial disappointments of its hopes."[7]

> Depending on the interpreter, it seems, the Apocalypse can yield a sophisticated, though theoretical, system of eschatology (Mede), a decent and uplifting pre-Victorian concern for the education of the young (*Notes on Scripture*), or a radical religious movement (Miller).

My father's own "modest" contributions fall, he admits, somewhere between the first two, but there is more! From an antiquarian book fair in Little Rock, he acquired *Horae Apocalypticae* by E. B. Elliott, a third edition from 1847 in four beautifully bound volumes connecting the dragon and beasts in the latter chapters of Revelation with the perceived growing apostasy of the Roman Catholic Church through 1,500 years or so. This with the expected charts, amazing but practically "incomprehensible." My father goes on to list a number of other respectable scholarly works on the Apocalypse in his library as well as several others that would find no such respectable place, but "yet are not without their charm."

I end this chapter with an Atlas-sized (eleven inches square) Apocalyptic book ("bound in cloth, making it more convenient to handle and carry about," the author informs us helpfully) I found in his library that he doesn't mention in his memoir but which I find fascinating, titled *Dispensational Truth or God's Purpose in the Ages* "By Clarence Larkin, Author of a Work on The book of Revelation, and a Pamphlet on The Second Coming of Christ, Twentieth Printing," published in Philadelphia in 1920. It is dedicated "to the Lord Jesus Christ who, through the Holy Spirit, has imparted to me the knowledge and mechanical skill to construct these Charts." There are thirty-four chapters, ninety charts, and fifteen "Cuts," small woodcut illustrations. In his foreword, the author explains that the book was created

---

7. My father's note reads, "That is, in the worldwide Seventh-day Adventist movement brought to birth later in the century by the prophecies of Ellen G. White, and the more mainstream Advent Christian denomination."

and published as a result of "Divine leading." A mechanical engineer and architect by profession, Larkin entered the "Gospel Ministry" at age thirty-four and, thinking he'd have no more need for those skills, sold all his books and "appliances" except for his "drawing instruments." While he wasn't a premillennialist at the time of his ordination, he soon became one thanks to his study of the Bible and various books that "fell into his hands." He began creating large colored wall charts on "Prophetic Truth" to accompany his sermons and this led him to design and illustrate the charts and write the copy for this book, which he claims took three years, although the charts and illustrations are so detailed and so meticulously rendered that I wouldn't have been surprised had he said thirty years. The copy I have is a third edition, evidently greatly expanded and enlarged by many more charts and descriptions. As just one example (out of the ninety!), the chart titled "The Tribulation Period or Daniel's Seventieth Week, The Reign of Antichrist" (between pages 133 and 134) folds out to twenty-two inches, and if you think of it as a graph beginning at the bottom left, illustrations of "The Grave," "The Church," "The Rapture," and "The Glorified Church" snake their way up the Y axis, while along the top of the X axis moving from left to right we encounter the "Seals" (including the four horses), the six "Trumpets," the "Interval" ("The Little Book and The Two Witnesses"), the seventh "Trumpet" with its third woe, the "War in Heaven," the "Beast out of the Sea," the "Beast out of the Earth," the seven "Vials" ("Boils, Blood on Sea, Blood on Rivers, Great Heat, Darkness, Euphrates dried up, Hail") and so on, ending with the "Battle of Armageddon." Beneath this, "The Great Tribulation," with illustrations of the "Rise of Antichrist," "The Little Book," "The Two Witnesses," "Moses and Elijah," "The Dragon," "The Beast," "The False Prophet," "The Scarlet Woman," "Babylon," and "Armageddon." And at the bottom of the page is evidently what is happening under the earth, "The Bottomless Pit and Lake of Fire." Everything is neatly categorized and labeled according to the corresponding chapters of Revelation and connected when appropriate by little arrows. The "Week" of the title is "explained" (ha ha) at the bottom of the page: "First Half of the Week=3 ½ years," "The Middle of the Week" is "Daniel's Seventieth Week," and the "Second Half of the Week=Times Time and A Half Time=42 months=1260 days=3 ½ years." There is much, much more: the illustrations throughout are painstakingly detailed and connect events recounted in the book of Revelation to events that the author believes will unfold according to a very specific timeline. Each illustration is explained in short paragraphs on the next few pages. Whatever your beliefs about the Apocalypse, this book is sure to impress.

My father ends his chapter on this note: "Whether or not the Apocalypse fuels 'enthusiasm' depends less on the text than on the interpreter, and sometimes the interpreter's own story is more interesting, perhaps more authentic, than the interpretation." Amen to that.

36

Bunyan

No personal library is complete without a sampling of John Bunyan's works. "A tinker out of Bedford," Rudyard Kipling called him, "a vagrant oft in quod, a private under Fairfax, a minister of God. Two hundred years and thirty ere Armageddon came, his single hand portrayed it, and Bunyan was his name."

MY FATHER IS QUOTING from *The Holy War* (1917), where Kipling is referring to Bunyan's 1682 novel, *The Holy War made by King Shaddai upon Diabolus*, Bunyan's version of Armageddon, and to Kipling, a fitting prediction of World War I. My father "shamefully" confessed he'd never read it. "It's on my bucket list." He never got to it.

John Bunyan's *The Pilgrim's Progress*, first published in 1678 with part 2 added in 1684 is his more well-known book. Huck Finn called it a story "about a man that left his family, it didn't say why, I read considerable in it now and then. The statements was interesting but tough."[1] The book was a "late discovery" for my father; he didn't recall it among the books his mother read to him. And in any case, it's not really a children's book. I read it in high school but promptly forgot all about it until I married my husband, whose father, it turned out, was an avid collector of John Bunyan's work, particularly *The Pilgrim's Progress*. In fact, my father credited my father-in-law, William Nigel Kerr, professor of church history, as well as dean of Gordon-Conwell for a time, with sparking his interest in both. Nigel had in his collection over three hundred editions in many languages,

---

1. Twain, *Adventures of Huckleberry Finn*, 134.

many bindings, old and new, common and rare with all manner of illustrations and annotations. My father kept an eye out for Bunyan "items" to pass on to him or to trade for something he had that my father wanted, and in so doing acquired a modest collection of his own. My father deemed Nigel's "a magnificent collection." When Nigel died in 1998, he left it to Gordon-Conwell to be housed in a special collection.

On the morning of July 17, 1998, I was making the beds when I heard from an open bedroom window a high voice exclaiming wordlessly—softly at first, building into a staccato scream. I finally identified it as that of my mother-in-law. It was high-pitched and panicked. I threw on a bathrobe, told my two youngest, Grace and Mike, who were on the couch, probably watching a movie, to stay put (they were nine and seven), and raced down our driveway which ran into my in-laws' to find my father-in-law sprawled on his back on the ground, half in the carport, half in his driveway. My mother-in-law was fluttering uselessly beside him. I knelt down. His head was bleeding. I told her to get me a blanket which she wandered off to do, during which time I called 911. Apparently, I'd come a long way since my father's lawn mower accident. (I'm jumping ahead. See chapter 40.) The ambulance took forever, but it may have just seemed that way as I was right there, watching my father-in-law expire and my mother-in-law lose it. Before he died, he turned his head and growled at me, a phenomenon that I looked up later on Google and have chosen to believe wasn't directed at me per se. It is called, more or less officially, a death rattle. My own father, unbeknownst to me, had plans to go to a book sale with my father-in-law that afternoon. When I arrived home from the hospital hours later, after my father-in-law had been pronounced dead (heart attack), I found my father and my favorite cousin Chuck sitting in lawn chairs in my front yard. I had to break the news to them.

Gordon-Conwell recently contacted the family informing us that they are "downsizing" and looking to deaccession the collection, inquiring if any of us would be interested. I told my husband I was, book rat that I have become. Turned out, his sisters were glad we were willing to take it. My father must be swooning in glory right now. Except: I underestimated my father-in-law's Bunyan collection. Twenty-one good-sized boxes now sit in the middle of my father's library. I've contacted the British Museum in London as well as the John Bunyan Museum and Library in Bedford, neither of which have gotten back to me. Therefore, I am now in the process of combining (!) our collections of Flannery O'Connor material and duplicate volumes of modern and contemporary novelists and poets in order to make room for Nigel's "magnificent" collection. A formidable undertaking.

My father's oldest copy of *The Pilgrim's Progress* is from 1755, the twenty-ninth edition, published in London "by A. W. for W. Johnston, at the Golden-Ball, in St. Paul's Church-Yard." The frontispiece is nearly the same as the one from the earliest editions from the 1680s with the pilgrim Christian dreaming, surrounded by small vignettes from his journey. It's bound with the twenty-second edition of part 2, by the same publisher in 1758, with a note on the title page: "The THIRD PART, suggested to be J. Bunyan's, is an Imposter." My father concurs, "And indeed it is." Evidently, after Bunyan published *The Pilgrim's Progress* in two parts, an "anonymous someone capitalized on its popularity, imitating Bunyan's style with yet a third part, and a pilgrim named Tender Conscience." Despite its imposter status, part 3 came to be included in some editions with parts 1 and 2 for a century or more. This volume happens to be one of those. And its blunt warning about the "imposter" notwithstanding, the second part is followed by "the third part," eighteenth edition, 1760, on yet a third title page facing a frontispiece portrait of Bunyan, with the note, "*To which is added,* The *Life and Death of John Bunyan*, Author of the *First* and *Second* Parts, [Compleating the Whole Progress]." My father writes, "While part 3 stops just short of explicitly claiming Bunyan as its author, it tries its best to give that impression." Very strange indeed. Having paid a mere five dollars for it, he replaced the fragile paper cover and had it bound in hardcover. "Big mistake," he confesses. While the binding was fine, the bookbinder had put a protective film of some kind over the title page, "making it blurred and hard to read, and reducing the value considerably." But "never mind, it's a keeper, not an investment, my oldest Bunyan," he groused. He has a "splendid" 1804 edition published in Exeter, New Hampshire, with all three parts, no mention of an "imposter," and "a shameless attribution" to "'John Bunyan' on the title page to part 3." And his earliest American edition (in German no less) was published in Germantown, Pennsylvania, in 1796 (parts 1 and 2 only).

Most of his collectable editions of *The Pilgrim's Progress* are from the nineteenth century. Some are what he calls "novelty items" such as the one in which M. A. Owen issued her dire warning. He has a translation into Greek by American missionaries to Greece with a handwritten inscription on the front endpaper. There are classics, such as the 1830 edition with a *Life of Bunyan* by Robert Southey, and George Virtue's "elegant edition" from 1850 with many steel engravings and a colored chart (much like the charts of the book of Revelation) where the reader can follow in concentric circles the "Plan of the Road from the City of Destruction to the Celestial City." He has a smaller volume from Samuel Bagster and Sons from 1845 that features tiny black-and-white drawings by Samuel Bagster's eldest daughter Eunice. Of these illustrations, Robert Louis Stevenson once wrote (not knowing they were the work of a woman), "Whoever he was, the author of these wonderful little pictures may lay claim to be the best illustrator of Bunyan." Her "unpretentious cartoon-like drawings, not even announced on the title page" can also be found in one other edition in his Bunyan collection: *The Illustrated Polyglot Pilgrim's Progress*, in English and French (part 1 only) from D. Appleton & Co. in New York, 1876.

And from the end of the nineteenth century, he has a "very collectable" Essex House edition (1899), fat like the Big Little Books but bound in a medieval-looking vellum. In 1991 he saw it in bookshops in Cambridge and London but couldn't afford it. While not a facsimile, it was modeled after the first edition of 1678 and was limited to part 1. Unexpectedly, he happened upon one in a small bookshop south of Conway, New Hampshire, for a "modest" fifty bucks, number 651 in a limited edition of 750. "Naturally I took advantage."

My father considered *The Pilgrim's Progress* to be "a fictionalized equivalent of either 'the good book' with its story of human salvation, or 'the Apocalypse' in particular with its vision of what is still to come." The full title of its first edition was *The Pilgrim's Progress from This World, to That which is to come: Delivered under the Similitude of a Dream wherein is Discovered, The manner of his letting out, His Dangerous Journey; and safe Arrival at the Desired Country*. Not quite an enthusiast, Bunyan was foremost a storyteller and *The Pilgrim's Progress* is his own story. My father thought it best read in tandem with his previous book, *Grace Abounding to the Chief of Sinners*, published twelve years earlier in 1666 while Bunyan was in prison for preaching without a license. That book is told in a straightforward manner as an autobiographical spiritual struggle against a worrying sense that he was irredeemable. *The Pilgrim's Progress* tells the same story in "the similitude of a dream" rather than as a straightforward narrative. In it, Bunyan (in his dream) encounters Christian, his alter ego and "pilgrim" who leaves his wife and children to embark on his "progress" and introduces himself wherever he goes with "I am come from the City of Destruction and am going to Mount Zion." This because he had been "for certain informed that this our City will be burned with fire from Heaven," perhaps like the recent great fire in London in 1666, and "Mount Zion," with *Grace Abounding* and Heb 12 in mind. My father concludes that the books (*Grace Abounding* and *The Pilgrim's Progress*) are a "matched pair." In 1994, he was "finally able to inflict this insight of mine on to a group of American students in London," a program that included students from several universities. One of the courses my father taught was "Religious Dissent in England" and he led a field trip to (among other sites) Bunyan's Bedford, a visit which was "uneventful" and "not an overwhelming success."

Three years earlier, however, on a sabbatical at Tyndale House in Cambridge in 1991, my father's visit *had* been, shall we say, "eventful." He had parted with my mother and her sister Lucy, who was visiting, venturing into Bunyan territory on his own, his first and only time driving on the "wrong" side of the road. Having checked out some of the usual sites, he wanted to see the Houghton house, which is said to be the inspiration for the House Beautiful (or Palace Beautiful) in *The Pilgrim's Progress*. In his memoir he details his encounter with first one dog, who merely sniffed him, and then the "lineup" of five more dogs bounding his way. Not one to take chances, he hightailed it back to his car and said goodbye to the world of Bunyan. Since then, he "delights" in telling folks how he was "chased off by dogs at the House Beautiful!"

37

The Baptists

SOMETIME DURING THE PROCESS of going through his books, discerning which ones would make the cut to Hamilton, Massachusetts, my father rediscovered a book titled *Select Works of the Rev. Robert Robinson, of Cambridge. Edited, with Memoir by the Rev. William Robinson* (London: J. Heaton & Son, 1861). There on the front endpaper, in his own hand, the note, "Purchased Bedford, Bedfordshire, June 26, 1991." He writes, "There you have it, the very day twenty-eight years ago when I was chased off by dogs at the House Beautiful!" It was published by "The Bunyan Library: for the publication and republication of standard works by eminent Baptist authors. Vol II. Select Works of the Rev. Robert Robinson." Not surprising, since Bunyan was a Baptist. My father notes, "Evidently I had been up to my usual tricks that day in June 1991." Robert Robinson is mainly known today as the author of "Come Thou Fount of Every Blessing" (1758), a hymn popularized in recent culture by Sufjan Stevens. During his sabbatical in 1991, my mother and father lived for seven months in Cambridge and attended the St. Andrews Street Baptist Church, "named in typical Baptist fashion not for a saint but for its street location." My father remembered Stephen Hawking and his wife occasionally attending, he in a technologically advanced wheelchair that allowed him to communicate with parishioners after the service. The church was founded in 1721 as the Stone-Yard Baptist Church and appointed Robert Robinson as its pastor in 1761, where he remained for almost thirty years until, in later years, through his friendship with Unitarian Joseph Priestly, he drifted toward Unitarianism. A year or two after his first visit to Bedford, my father found Robinson's "key book on the subject," *A Plea for the Divinity of Our Lord Jesus Christ, in a Pastoral Letter Addressed to a Congregation of Protestant Dissenters at Cambridge* (fourth edition; Cambridge: Francis Hodson, 1780) dedicated "to the Congregation of Protestant Dissenters assembling at the Meeting House in St. Andrews, Cambridge." While older and rarer than the *Select Works*, not to mention pricier, the fact that it was "beautifully rebacked and eminently readable" made it impossible to resist.

In fact, Robinson was never a Unitarian like Priestly, but what theologians call a Modalist (similar to the Muggletonians who believe that Jesus Christ was "God alone"). Modalism was an ancient heresy going back to the third-century Bishop Sabellius, an early prominent proponent. Sabellianism held that one God was revealed in three distinct ways or "modes" as Father, as Son, and as Holy Spirit rather than existing as three distinct persons within one divine entity. By contrast, Unitarians believe in one God; Jesus was merely a human being (albeit an important one!) and wise teacher. But Robinson, looking for a common cause with Priestly and the Unitarians, was "asking for trouble" by repeatedly calling himself a Unitarian:

> We are, say they, *Unitarians*. We reply, So are we. Our dispute is not, Whether there be one God, or three Gods, but whether the divinity of Jesus Christ be incompatible with the unity of God, which unity both sides believe.[1]

While technically a heresy, Robinson's theology is still represented today among the so-called Oneness Pentecostals, or Apostolic Church, that are widely recognized as broadly "evangelical" in character. My father's point was that Robinson's "defection from orthodoxy (if it is that) simply underscores the fact that Baptists can be, and often are, all over the map theologically." Calvinistic Baptists believe in divine election and predestination, while Free Will Baptists insist on (drum roll) free will. Children of the Protestant Reformation, fundamentalists or biblical literalists, as well as social gospel or social justice warriors, may all identify as Baptists. My father writes, "The American Baptist historian Edwin Gaustad has said, 'I'm not a member of any organized religious group. I'm a Baptist.'[2] As for Robinson," my father notes, "he suffered from depression at about the same time that he fancied himself a Unitarian. It's tempting to assume that the two things

---

1. Robinson, *Plea for the Divinity*, 11.
2. Gaustad, *Baptist History Celebration*, 200.

are related, but this is by no means clear." In the second-to-last verse of "Come Thou Fount," he pleads with God to

> Bind my wandering heart to Thee.
> Prone to wander, Lord I feel it, Prone to leave the God I love;
> Here's my heart, O take and seal it, Seal it for Thy courts above.

My father recounts an anecdote, unverified, that Robinson, in his later years, was riding in a stagecoach with a lady who asked if he knew the hymn she was humming. He supposedly answered, "Madam, I am the poor unhappy man who wrote that hymn many years ago, and I would give a thousand worlds, if I had them, to enjoy the feelings I had then."[3]

When I was growing up, our family mostly attended Baptist churches. Occasionally, my father took an interim pastor position, and we would travel to a new church for a few months. When I was twelve or so my father baptized me (by dunking of course) in the tank at the front of Beverly Farms Baptist Church in Beverly Farms, Massachusetts.[4] My parents attended many Baptist churches over the years, many of which they didn't actually join. One of these was the one they found in Springfield, Missouri, Sovereign Grace Baptist Church, southeast of town. My father found it off-putting at first: they used the King James Version only and served Communion to members only—and on a weekday evening, not Sunday morning (probably so as not to make the nonmembers feel left out). They defined themselves as "Particular Baptists," a "technically separatist" group that emerged from the Puritan movement within the Church of England. They combined the practice of baptism with the belief that Christ died for believers in particular, not the world in general. Yet, my father notes, they knew their Bibles better than any other congregations my parents had attended and had an appreciation for Baptist history "in all its diversity." One of the church's ministries was the publishing of books on Baptist history, reprints of classic works, and biographical essays on prominent Baptist leaders of earlier generations, both British and American, focusing on "Particular Baptists," their imprint bearing the name Particular Baptist Press or PBP. Later, after my father retired from teaching and moved to New Hampshire,

---

3. See Banks, *Immortal Hymns*, 253–54.

4. Interestingly, my husband's father, William Nigel Kerr, had been the pastor of that church several years earlier. Early in my courtship with Bill, it had been fun to compare notes: my future husband (PK or pastor's kid) turned out to be the bad boy shooting pellets down on the emerging congregants from the roof of the church. My own rebellion had taken a more legitimate form of skipping the service by volunteering in the nursery.

they recruited him to write abbreviated biographies of early American Baptist preachers and teachers from New England, some whom my father had never heard of, for a series called *A Noble Company: Biographical Essays on Notable Particular-Regular Baptists in America*.

> I wrote on John Clarke, Henry Dunster, John Comer, Samuel Shepard, Job Seamans, John Peak, Baron Stow, and Roger Nicole. John Clarke and Henry I knew, Clarke the father of Baptists in America and Dunster remembered as the first president of Harvard who shocked his Puritan colleagues by refusing to have his infant son baptized. Of course, Roger Nicole was an old friend and fellow "book rat" and I got acquainted with Baron Stow because back in 1826 he became the first real pastor of the church Betty and I joined in 2002, Middle Street Baptist Church in Portsmouth, New Hampshire.

He actually owned *The Riches of Bunyan, Selected from His Works, for the American Tract Society* by Jeremiah Chaplin, published in 1850 by the American Tract Society and inscribed by Baron Stow to his brother-in-law who was a deacon in his Boston church, dated March 7, 1851. This volume was one of his "treasures." While my father was unfamiliar with the other four men, Terry Wolever, a layman at Sovereign Grace Church, supplied him with photocopies of obscure documents from the past available through the Baptist Historical Society at Colgate-Rochester Divinity School and later Mercer University, making my father's task "ridiculously easy." He notes that Wolever's "ecumenical gesture" helped him to become a "contributor to books that within a generation would themselves be rare and collectable."

One of the "Four Cords" my father writes about in his essay is Anabaptism. "Baptist" is actually short for "Anabaptist," the belief that baptized infants need to be rebaptized when they are old enough to know what baptism means. While English and American Baptists disliked the term because they didn't believe infant baptism even counted (therefore they were not "rebaptizing" anyone), most of their European branches (which came to America mostly from Germany and Switzerland by way of Russia or the Netherlands), the Mennonites, Amish, and certain Brethren groups, have no problem calling themselves Anabaptist. My father notes that while some, like the English Baptists, were "enthusiasts" in their early history, most today are what we would call "plain people," committed to peaceful ways. Something I learned recently is that the reason Amish men do not have moustaches is because moustaches were associated with the military. While the Amish do not have extensive surviving literature like the Shakers or the Amana community, my father was lucky to have found a fourth American edition of an ancient hymnal known as the *Ausbund*; the long German title can be roughly translated as "Paragon [or model or epitome], that is, some beautiful Christian songs, as composed in the prison at Passau in the Castle, by the Swiss brethren and other genuine Christians here and there" (Germantaun: Liebert and Billmeyer, 1785). It's a collection of hymns and testimonies first published in 1564, when their forebears were imprisoned at Passau in Bavaria. A sturdy volume that "looks its age, every year of it" (much like my father himself), its 140 songs in German take up 812 pages, followed by an index, fifty-six pages of "Confession" including testimonies of those imprisoned at Passau, and ending with an *Anhang* or "appendix" of six more songs, taking up another forty-six pages. "Truly long, long songs, with many, many stanzas!" Apparently, the most famous song in the *Ausbund* is number 131, known as the *Lobelied*, or "Song of Praise," always the second hymn in every Amish service; the English translation is my father's own "modest effort":

> Oh Father God, we bless thy name,
> And all thy goodness praise,
> That thou, O Lord, so graciously,
> Hast been to us always
> And brought us all together, Lord,
> To be admonished through thy word
> For this grant us thy grace

This is only the first stanza of four in one of the shortest hymns in the whole collection, but in the Amish services it can take anywhere from eleven to twenty minutes to sing.[5] My father notes that their "fast tunes," designed for the young people at Sunday evening gatherings, were not taken from the *Ausbund* but from the *Unpartheyisches Gesang-buch* (or "Non-Denominational Songbook"), published by the Mennonites for a variety of congregations, including Anabaptist.[6] And—wait for it—my father has this in his collection as well, two volumes bound together, published in Lancaster, Pennsylvania, in 1808.

My father's acquaintance with the Amish was "limited, tourist-level at best." I remember one such tourist visit yielded a present from my mother

---

5. Hostetler, *Amish Society*, 125.
6. Hostetler, *Amish Society*, 128.

The Baptists

to my two young daughters of dolls from Amish country. These were clearly handmade—soft bodies with muslin bonnets, long dresses, and aprons. The problem, I soon discerned from my daughters' puzzled faces, was that these dolls *didn't* have faces.[7] Unbleached beige canvas. My daughters were *not* OK with this. I had to agree the blank faces *were* a bit unsettling. My modest effort at sewing crude eyes, nose, and mouths onto the fabric ended up meeting with their satisfaction and the dolls were thereafter allowed to join the ranks of their ragtag collection. My father considered himself to be an "Anabaptist cousin" of the Amish through his marriage to my mother, who grew up attending the Church of the Brethren in Grand Rapids, Michigan, a similar group with similar simple customs. That church eventually moved over to the Grace Brethren, a more "progressive" group in manner of dress and customs. But her father, my grandfather, Chester Flora, and his siblings grew up in the most conservative branch, the Old German Baptist Brethren, or Dunkards, "Dunkards" because they believed in baptism by immersion. Unlike the Amish (or the Mennonites or the Hutterites), who are descended from sixteenth-century Anabaptists, the Brethren began in the German village of Schhwarzenau as a small group of separatist Pietists in 1708. Their customs include the holy kiss (a kiss on the mouth when Brethren meet), foot washing, and "dunking" three times during baptism—one each for the Father, the Son, and the Holy Spirit.

Photographs of my grandfather's family show folks who could easily be mistaken for Amish: men with untrimmed beards (no moustaches), broad-brimmed hats, suspenders holding up baggy khaki pants, white shirts, sometimes with vests, and women in bonnets fitted closely to their heads, long dresses, and short cape-type things around their shoulders. Sensible shoes of course. These folks my parents called "Old Orders" and, despite a promise to his mother to stay with the Old Orders, my grandfather had not done so and "carried with him a burden of guilt." Two of my grandfather's sisters (who had remained in the group) had married two brothers and raised their families within the Church. One of these brothers, Uncle Ralph, "had a charm that we all loved," writes my father. After many years with the Old Orders, this brother, Ralph, left as something of a free thinker. He wrote a tract called "Seventy-Two Hours" wherein he argues that Christ was crucified on the Wednesday of Passion Week (rather

---

7. Depending on where you look, this is either because faces on dolls make them appear more worldly (duh), facelessness indicates that all are equal in the eyes of the Lord, or the makers are following the second commandment which forbids the creation and worship of graven images.

than Friday) using Matt 12:40 as evidence: "three days and three nights in the heart of the earth," from Wednesday to Sunday. More problematically, he argued for universal salvation, which got him booted from the group. Nevertheless, he continued to dress in the manner of the Old Orders and had a "rich sense of humor," according to my father, who cites a couple of his one-liners: "I'd rather stay up with you all night than to see you go to bed hungry," and "I'd rather owe it to you all my life than cheat you out of it." My father's memories of family reunions on that side of the family include "abundant comfort food" like biscuits and gravy and heavy cream pies, and the "inevitable" horseshoes.

My father's "best" Old Order item is a first edition of their hymnal, published in 1882, the year the Church of the Brethren split into three groups: the "progressive" Brethren Church, the "moderate" or mainstream Church of the Brethren, and the Old German Baptist Brethren. Unlike the Amish *Ausbund*, this smaller hymnal (397 pages) is in English because by 1882 the Church of the Brethren had transitioned to English: *Hymns and Songs, suited to both private and public devotions, and especially adapted to the wants and uses of the Brethren of the Old German Baptist Church* (Kinsey's Station, Ohio [near Dayton]: Office of the Vindicator, 1882). When my father found it online, he bought it for his brother-in law, my mother's older brother, Chuck Flora, who had kept in close touch with the Old Order relatives in Indiana. When Chuck died, his son, my favorite cousin, Chuck, thoughtfully returned it to my father. Thanks to them both, my father also has the twelfth edition from 1927 and the thirty-first from 1999, both of which remained unchanged. The hymnal's use of the detail in John 19:16, that Jesus "bowed his head" when he died on the cross, and the same image that appears with Jesus' baptism, becomes the model for baptism by immersion:

> 'Tis done, the precious ransom's paid,
> Receive my soul, he cried:
> See where he bows his sacred head!
> He bows his head and dies! (#149)
>
> Down to the sacred wave
> The Lord of Life was led,
> And he who came our souls to save
> In Jordan bowed his head. (#271)

Among the Old German Baptists, this took place by kneeling and bowing face down into the water. This, my father heartily concurred, was an "eminently practical kind of immersion," confessing that "I have had at least one near accident in attempting to immerse a rather large person in the more common Baptist way, backwards."

> O Thou who in Jordan did'st bow thy meek head,
> O'erwhelmed in our sorrow, did'st sink to the dead.
> Then rose from the darkness to glory above,
> And claimed for thy chosen the kingdom of love.
>
> Thy footsteps we follow to bow in the tide,
> And are buried with thee in the death thou hast died.
> Then wake in thy likeness to walk in the way
> That brightens and brightens to shadowless day. (#273)

My father ends with, "What better way to conclude a chapter on the Baptists: 'We were therefore buried with him through baptism into death in order that, just as Christ was raised from the dead through the glory of the Father, we too may live a new life' (Rom 6:4)?"

38

Mary Abigail Dodge, aka Gail Hamilton

> Mary Abigail Dodge (1833–96) grew up and lived most of her life in Hamilton, Massachusetts, an hour northeast of Boston, where I lived for seven years in the 1960s (plus fifteen more in neighboring Wenham), and where I find myself again in late retirement with my daughter and son-in-law.

I CAN BEAT THAT: I've lived in Hamilton for far longer: the seven in Hamilton in the sixties with my parents, plus just four in Wenham before I moved to Boston for college; then, having married someone from Hamilton, have been back here for another forty-six years. The other day I looked for Gail Hamilton's (her pen name) house, which was located somewhere in the vicinity of 500 Bay Road. I even have a picture of it, but I suspect the house has either been altered or replaced. I couldn't find it. My father discovered her *not* in Hamilton, Massachusetts, but in Kregel's basement in Grand Rapids (probably on a visit to my mother's parents) where he found several of her books, including *Woman's Wrongs: A Counter-Irritant* (Boston: Ticknor and Fields, 1868) with "two inscriptions in pencil on the flyleaves dedicating the book to two different individuals." One is:

> To Rev. Henry M. Harman, D.D., Professor of Ancient Languages in Dickinson College, this work is humbly dedicated, as a token for the many helps derived from *Egypt and the Holy Land* and also to the late work of this renowned scholar, *The Introduction to the Holy Scriptures*. I met him in Palestine & enjoyed the eloquence with which he defended an apple woman whose cart had been

overthrown by little Arabs. I have many other pleasant reflections of this highly esteemed and honest man. Gail Hamilton.

My father happened to have in his collection a signed copy of *Egypt and the Holy Land* (Philadelphia: Lippincott, 1873), and he calls this dedication "strange indeed." For starters, *Women's Wrongs* was published in 1868, five years *earlier* than Harmon's book, which means she must have written the dedication at least five years *after* her book was published. Since my father's copy of her book is ex-library with a bookplate of the Union Philosophical Society of Dickinson College, would it have been *before* she donated the book to Dickinson College or *after* the Union Philosophical Society discarded it from their collection? Stranger yet, my father had not the "slightest evidence" that Hamilton ever visited Palestine. Her only biography (*Gail Hamilton's Life in Letters*, 1901) includes travels in 1887 to England, Scotland, France, and Italy, but no mention of the Middle East. My father questioned whether her creative imagination was at work, perhaps prompted by Harmon's work? According to my father, there is nothing in that book even "remotely" resembling her description of the apple woman. "We have a mystery!" he declares. On the facing flyleaf page is the second dedication, this one sardonic, in keeping with the actual content of *Woman's Wrongs*:

> To the Rev. John Todd, D.D. as a token of the appreciation manifested for his manly labors in the spread of the gospel, and the clear manner in which he has indicated to woman her "true sphere," this work is respectfully dedicated by the Author. Gail Hamilton.

In fact, her entire book was a response to this Rev. John Todd's book, *Woman's Rights*, and on pages 3 to 4 she is far more direct than her handwritten dedication: "The Rev. John Todd, D.D. has lately been moved to announce and expound the laws of human life, especially in their bearing upon the relations between man and woman. He has done so with a wisdom accurately described by James in the fifteenth verse of the third chapter of his Epistle."[1] In the language of the King James Version, "This wisdom descendeth not from above, but is earthly, sensual, devilish." My father notes:

> It's all downhill from there: "He touched a sacrament and it shriveled into profanity. Marriage became in his hands a base commercial transaction. Woman was reduced to the level of the beasts that

---

1. Hamilton, *Women's Wrongs*, 3–4.

perish." And so on. Like young Mary Ann Owen of Toller Chapel, Kettering, this was a lady not to be trifled with!

His favorite Gail Hamilton publication, one he wrote about, was published much later, *A Washington Bible Class* (New York: Appleton, 1891). In it she recounts her time as a Bible teacher in Washington, DC, in 1890, during the presidency of Benjamin Harrison. The Bible class was initially for the wives of congressmen, cabinet members, and diplomats, but over time "men crept in singly and in pairs." Of herself, she writes "with a modesty bordering on mockery":

> The woman who had first suggested the mode of study, and who by parliamentary courtesy was placed in the chair as leader, speedily abused the position. The novelty of being able to speak her mind bore down every instinct of justice, till she completely monopolized the talk, and, instead of seeking the views of others, spent the whole time in expounding her own.[2]

Which endeared to her my father, who loved a snarky feminist. Prompted by the participants begging her to provide them with manuscript notes, she did one better and wrote *A Washington Bible Class*, "a small biblical theology of sorts, from the standpoint of nineteenth-century liberalism in the tradition of Ralph Waldo Emerson." My father's article "*A Washington Bible Class*: The Bloodless Piety of Gail Hamilton" which appeared in *Strangely Familiar: Protofeminist Interpretations of Patriarchal Biblical Texts*, examined her theology in detail, which was indeed bloodless, deriding as it did the Mosaic sacrificial system: "Not like God. It is not gentle, gracious, seemly, harmonious. It is violent, brutal, bloody, barbarous. It is not spiritualizing, it is brutalizing."[3] She sides with Cain and "his harmless fruit-offering" over Abel with his "violent beast-offering," warning, "We have not yet heard Cain's side."[4] If her view of Judaism bordered on antisemitic, her opinion of orthodox Christianity was even lower:

> This is not an improvement on the Jewish ritual, it is a retrogression to the pagan ritual. If there must be a sacrifice, it is better to sacrifice an animal than a man. If that man is the prince of life, the Son of God, then to sacrifice him is a crime without a name.[5]

2. Hamilton, *Washington Bible Class*, 4–5.
3. Hamilton, *Washington Bible Class*, 83.
4. Hamilton, *Washington Bible Class*, 97.
5. Hamiton, *Washington Bible Class*, 130–31

My father observes that she "misreads" Hebrews which she claimed abolished the whole Jewish sacrificial system, substituting it with the worship of God "in spirit and in truth." In fact, Paul (or whoever wrote Hebrews) "abolished 'altar, sacrifice, priesthood' in order to establish a *new* altar, sacrifice and priesthood built around redemption through the blood of Jesus Christ."[6]

My father concludes that her theology was "not so much feminist as feminine—the theology of a proper Victorian lady, feisty and formidable in debate, but ladylike nonetheless, and easily shocked."[7] His admiration for her "trumps but does not overcome my considerable misgivings about her theology." She certainly was no enthusiast and quite the opposite of the bloody Moravians, and "sadly of the Bible as well." When an unnamed former student, by then a well-established New Testament professor, responding to a paper about Hamilton my father presented at the 2008 SBL meeting in Boston, pointed out that he should have chosen Phoebe Palmer as his subject, as she had a more "enduring impact" than Gail Hamilton, my father was annoyed. "Why should I write on Phoebe Palmer just because I mostly agree with her? Why not deal with a worthy antagonist instead?"[8] My father concluded that while Hamilton and Palmer each advanced the feminist movement in different ways, in a culture whose secular forces were likely more determinative, probably neither woman had had all that much impact.

A year before her death, Gail Hamilton wrote, "I died on the 10th of May 1895." After seven weeks' "divorce of body and soul, a partial reunion was effected" and she discovered the newspapers "festooned with obituary biographical sketches wholly friendly and equally inaccurate"[9] and thus began to put together her "reminiscences" in order to set the record straight. What happened was, she'd had a stroke. What remains of these reminiscences can be found at the beginning of volume 1 of *Gail Hamilton's Life in Letters*. Her last book, *X-Rays* (copyright May 4, 1896), was a self-published paperback with an inserted note promising that "to all who address me at Post Office Building, Hamilton, Massachusetts, enclosing $.50 I shall be

---

6. Michaels, "*Washington Bible Class*," 194.

7. Michaels, "*Washington Bible Class*," 196.

8. As it happened, this "unnamed" fellow's article on Phoebe Palmer's "lasting impact" appears in the article following my father's in *Strangely Familiar*: "Women in High Places, or Women of Lasting Impact?" Let's go ahead and name him then: Ben Witherington III.

9. Hamilton, *Gail Hamilton's Life in Letters*, 3.

glad to forward the book as they direct."[10] The small book contains her reminiscences about the towns of Hamilton, Essex, and Ipswich, along with some essays about death and the afterlife with such titles as "The Valley of the Shadow of Death," "Failure," "Hints of Heaven," and "Holy War." More than a year after her stroke, on August 16, 1896, she died, "for real this time," my father notes helpfully.

10. Hamilton, *X-Rays*, page insert.

39

Flannery[1]

IN STARK CONTRAST TO Gail Hamilton's "bloodless piety," the work of Flannery O'Connor (1925–64) contains its fair share of bloody piety, although the blood is mostly offstage. Unlike Hamilton, who sought to worship God "in spirit," O'Connor was a sacramentalist. The Word became flesh, not spirit. She wrote famously in a letter to a friend about a dinner party during which the hostess, Mary McCarthy ("a Big Intellectual"), remarked that she thought of the Eucharist as a symbol ("and implied that it was a pretty good one") to which Flannery replied ("in a very shaky voice"), "Well if it's a symbol then to hell with it."

> That was all the defense I was capable of but I realize now that this is all I will ever be able to say about it, outside of a story, except that it is the center of existence for me; all the rest is expendable.[2]

Flannery O'Connor's Catholic sacramentalism fully informed her fiction as did the region of the American South, where she lived for most of her life. Even though she was Catholic, most of her characters are Southern Protestant fundamentalists (many of them "enthusiasts"). In a letter to Sister Mariella (May 4, 1963) she begins, "About the fanatics." She observed that many Protestants she knew considered monks and nuns fanatics while

---

1. For reasons that remain obscure—to me anyway—Flannery O'Connor, unlike most writers, is more often than not referred to by scholars by her first name, much like some performing artists and celebrities. Beyoncé, Cher, Madonna, Oprah come to mind. Brad Gooch's excellent 2009 biography is titled, aptly, *Flannery*.

2. O'Connor, *Collected Works*, 976–77.

to the monks and nuns, "my Protestant prophets are fanatics." She observed that if you're a Catholic fanatic, you can go ahead and join a convent, but if you're a Protestant fanatic, "you go about in the world, getting into all sorts of trouble and drawing the wrath of people who don't believe anything much at all down on your head." She adds, "The prophet is a man apart. He is not typical of a group."[3] She is referring here to old Mason Tarwater, self-proclaimed prophet who dies within the first few pages of *The Violent Bear It Away*. Like many of her characters, Mason's great nephew, Francis Marion Tarwater, on whom old Mason has bestowed his legacy, is resistant to his prophetic calling, but eventually, like another character, Hazel Motes, is "unable to resist the action of grace in territory held largely by the devil."[4] In Francis's case, by accidentally baptizing the hapless "dim witted" Bishop as he is drowning him: "The words just come out of themselves, but they don't mean nothing. You can't be born again."[5] In "The River," four- or five-year-old Harry/Bevel drowns on his way to the kingdom of heaven while trying to escape the evil Mr. Paradise ("like some ancient water monster"[6]) shouting on the shore. In "A Good Man Is Hard to Find," the grandmother dies when "The Misfit sprang back as if a snake had bitten him and shot her three times in the chest."[7] In "Good Country People" Joy/Hulga's wooden leg is stolen by Manley Pointer, a Bible salesman, who "been believing in nothing ever since I was born!"[8] Hazel Motes, a character in *Wise Blood*, blinds himself in order "to pay," explaining, "If there's no bottom in your eyes, they hold more."[9] And in her perhaps darkest story, a grandfather has a heart attack while smashing his granddaughter's head on a rock. Grim stuff.[10] My father observes, "Sometimes the dragon is offstage, but you can bet he's lurking."

Passing By the Dragon: The Biblical Tales of Flannery O'Connor, published in 2010, was another labor of love, uniting my father's biblical scholarship with what he called his "O'Connor habit." Much has been written

---

3. O'Connor, *Collected Works*, 1183.
4. O'Connor, *Mystery and Manners*, 118.
5. O'Connor, *Collected Works*, 458.
6. O'Connor, *Collected Works*, 171.
7. O'Connor, *Collected Works*, 143.
8. O'Connor, *Collected Works*, 283.
9. O'Connor, *Collected Works*, 126.
10. See O'Connor's short story "A View of the Woods" in *Collected Works*, 525–46, esp. 545.

about the religious and theological dimensions of Flannery's work, but not very much about her use of biblical stories and biblical references in her fiction. After some introductory chapters on O'Connor's own Catholic Douay Bible, her book reviews, and "her wayward readers," he closely examines her two novels and seventeen of her stories in the context of her many references to biblical texts and the bigger picture of what emerges: the aforementioned "action of grace in territory held largely by the devil."

The next year in a lecture ("The Fiction Writer and His Country"), she added, "No matter what form the dragon may take, it is of this mysterious passage past him, or into his jaws, that stories of any depth will be concerned to tell, and this being the case, it requires considerable courage at any time, in any country, not to turn away from the storyteller."[11] I recall that my father was somewhat puzzled at the cover art chosen for the book: a red-and-gold Asian-themed etching of a dragon which seems to be slithering off the cover made us wonder whether the person who had chosen the design had actually read the book. Still, it *was* a dragon. At any rate, he was delighted to get it into print, and I was more than delighted that he dedicated it to me. In the last paragraph of his preface, which begins, "So, I have people to thank," he writes, "Above all, my daughter Carolyn, who has both joined and inspired my journey in retirement, and who now has major publications of her own on O'Connor, in *Christianity and Literature* and *The Flannery O'Connor Review*. In one sense, this book is for her." Does it get any better than this?

As he and I both aged, my father out of teaching and me out of keeping four children alive (and educated—they were heading toward college by then), we became a cohort of sorts. His interest in Flannery O'Connor (whom he didn't discover until 1975 when he picked up a paperback copy of *Three* by Flannery O'Connor [Signet Books, 1964] for ten cents), was fueled less by his collector's instinct than by her strange and compelling fiction. That she elucidated that fiction and her no-nonsense Catholic sensibility in her letters and published essays and lectures made it even more appealing and accessible. Her letters reveal a prickly and immensely likable young woman with a dry of sense humor. He taught her work at Gordon-Conwell and Bangor Theological Seminaries as well as at Southwest Missouri State University. I'd read "A Good Man Is Hard to Find" in high school but much later my father encouraged my interest in Flannery, and I began to study her stories in earnest and then to include her work in my own

---

11. O'Connor, *Mystery and Manners*, 35.

teaching. Her fiction became a mainstay in my introductory writing and literature courses. On occasion, I participated in the O'Connor seminar he sometimes taught at Bangor Theological Seminary after he was officially "retired." In 2006, he and I presented papers at a Flannery O'Connor conference in Grand Rapids: "Flannery O'Connor in the Age of Terrorism." My mother came with us, and we stayed with her younger sister, Lucy. My father expanded his paper into an essay, "Eating the Bread of Life: Muted Violence in *The Violent Bear It Away*," which was included in *Flannery O'Connor in the Age of Terrorism: Essays on Violence and Grace*, edited by Robert Donahoo and Avis Hewitt (who had hosted the conference at Grand Valley College in Grand Rapids and who came to be a dear friend to both of us). My copy is inscribed "Remembering Grand Rapids 2006, with love, *Dad* (aka J. Ramsey Michaels, pp. 59–69) Mother's Day 2010."

In 2007 we each received a $3,000 grant from the National Endowment for the Humanities (NEH) to participate in a month-long Summer Institute at Georgia State College, Flannery's alma mater, which houses the O'Connor Library in Milledgeville, Georgia. Thrilled at our acceptance, we were two of twenty-four and got to work with some of the big guns in O'Connor scholarship: Marshall Bruce Gentry (editor of *Flannery O'Connor Review*, who hosted the seminar), Sarah Gordon, Virginia Wray, Patricia Yaeger, Robert Donahoo, Avis Hewitt. We spotted Louise Florencourt,[12] an elderly cousin of Flannery's, at Sacred Heart Church, the only Catholic Church in Milledgeville. We met William Sessions, who had been a friend of Flannery's and who was working on a biography, *Stalking Joy: The Life and Times of Flannery O'Connor*. He died in 2016, and I'm not sure where or if the book is in publication. Although no other spouses attended, my mother accompanied my father, much to my relief (see above: mushroom effect). Most of the twenty-four participants were put up in dorm rooms; mine was adjacent to my parents', divided by a shared bathroom. The four weeks included lectures, panels, movies, seminars, one-on-one conversations with the scholars in order to develop and discuss research topics, and *one whole week* in Special Collections where we were able to access unpublished material and take notes. There were also plenty of informal discussions and chats over wine and the occasional cigarette with the rest of the participants. We were given volumes of all of O'Connor's work, including

---

12. Wilhelmina "Louise" Florencourt died on July 31, 2023, at the age of ninety-seven. I sat next to her during one lecture given by an O'Connor scholar and distinctly heard Louise mutter under her breath, "We can read that on our own."

her letters, essays, and the complete set of the *Flannery O'Connor Bulletin* and *Reviews*. There were field trips: to Andalusia, the farm where O'Connor had lived with her mother, and where most of her stories were written, and where we met Flossie—a thirty-five year old mule—and a couple of peacocks. We visited Sacred Heart Church, where O'Connor worshiped daily; the house in Lafayette Square in Savannah, where O'Connor spent her early years; Eatonton, to visit the Alice Walker sites and the Uncle Remus Museum; and the massive Central State Hospital (founded as the Georgia State Lunatic, Idiot, and Epileptic Asylum), which in the 1960s was among the largest mental hospitals in the world. Early on there was no distinction between lunacy, retardation, and epilepsy. In 2007, its population was down to 850.

We frequented Blackbird Coffee; The Brick, a pizza place; The Velvet Elvis Grill and Tap, where we had our first fried green tomato (pretty good!); and my favorite destination, a neatly maintained secondhand shop where I picked up, among other bargains, a heavy ornate cross for six dollars, all on Hancock Street in downtown Milledgeville. Every day I went for a run in the Memory Hill Cemetery where Flannery is buried and fell in love with the whole town—including its aggressive kudzu and insects (cicadas?) that sounded like machinery. I was introduced to the work of the printmaker Barry Moser and bought a print of Flannery O'Connor. (My father bought one too—slightly different.) I emailed Barry several months later and obtained one of Joyce Carol Oates as well, and later, one of John Updike. Our last couple of days in Milledgeville were devoted to presentations by each participant on their research interests, many of which became published articles, including my father's and my own. In addition to that month being one of the most memorable of my life ("Flannery O'Connor Camp" as my kids called it), it resulted in more teaching opportunities (in addition to including her stories in my literature classes, I was invited to focus a handful of seminars on her literature, essays, and letters) and more published articles for both of us. My interests ran to Joyce Carol Oates and Jean Paul Sartre, while my father predictably veered into biblical and theological arenas. We each kept notes during that month in moleskin notebooks, both of which I still have, and are fun to look at eighteen years later, tracing as they do our scrawled observations and impressions and hurried notes, and the sometimes unlikely ways in which they evolved. My father and I have similar styles when it comes to note-taking and using space on a page: pretty chaotic I admit, but even after so many years, it makes (almost) perfect sense to me.

We presented papers at more literary conferences over the years, in Savannah, Milledgeville, and Boston. These were always fun trips, begun collaboratively as paper proposals, tentative emailed suggestions and tweaks, then the actual solitary writing of the papers, the sending of drafts back and forth, the booking of the plane tickets and hotels, the excitement of presenting, the reuniting with old friends from the NEH Institute, the hunt for good restaurants and used bookstores, the conversations over wine back in our hotel rooms.

When it came to Flannery, my father's collecting instinct was limited by the high prices of first or signed editions. He mostly contented himself with early editions (preferably with dust jackets), first paperback editions, editions with interesting (often weird, even lurid) cover art,[13] first English editions and first French editions of *Wise Blood* (one signed by the translator), and first German editions of *The Violent Bear It Away*. He also accumulated most of the important critical studies of Flannery's fiction, more for the scholarship than collectability. This is where our libraries overlap the most. I now have doubles of just about everything—all of her fiction, two biographies, her essays, collection of letters, and dozens of volumes of critical scholarship, which continue to be published, including all the issues of the *Flannery O'Connor Bulletin* and *Flannery O'Connor Review*, which span fifty years.

One of his collector's stories is from 1987 when he attended a colloquium at Conception Abbey in Northwest Missouri, a few hours north of Springfield where he was teaching. There he met two people who had known Flannery personally. One was Paul Engle, her mentor at the University of Iowa where she studied creative writing and began writing what would become her first novel, *Wise Blood*. As it happens, *Dear Regina: Flannery's Letters from Iowa*, a collection of her letters to her mother during her time there, has recently been published, edited by Monica Carol Miller. My copy came a few weeks ago and is proving to be a fascinating window into twenty-year-old Flannery's time there. What has struck me so far is how often she writes about food (potential article there?). The other person my father met was Sally Fitzgerald, Flannery's lifelong friend, who, with her husband Robert, provided Flannery a room above their garage

---

13. The cover art on two early paperbacks of *Wise Blood* (1953, 1955) suggests a bodice ripper!

next to their Connecticut home in which to write in exchange for babysitting. This would have been after Iowa and before the onset of lupus necessitated her return to Milledgeville and her mother. By 1987, Sally, along with Flannery's mother, Regina, was a sort of guardian of the O'Connor literary legacy. Sally's lecture that day was on *Wise Blood*. She was talking about Haze's encounter late in the book with a patrolman, who stops him and "in an apparent act of police brutality" releases the brake on Haze's car and pushes it into a gully with the comment, "Them that don't have a car don't need a license." The car was important to Haze: "No one with a good car needs to be justified," he once said, and while his second- (or third- or fourth-, who knows!) hand Essex was anything but a "good car," it had served as Haze's pulpit from which he preached his "Church without Christ," his second home, and his preferred method of transportation. It also became a deadly weapon when he ran over and killed Solace Layfield, the hired prophet with consumption whose sin, according to Haze, was that he "ain't true" and "mocks what is." The patrolman asks Haze if he can give him a ride and then asks if he was going anywhere. Haze says no, walks three hours back to the city, buys some lime, and blinds himself. "The patrolman had relieved him of the last thing standing between him and where he was actually going—the kingdom of God"—or so my father thought. So, in the question period my father asked Sally Fitzgerald if the patrolman who had "a red pleasant face and eyes the color of clear fresh ice" and spoke "in a kindly voice" might be an angel.[14] Sally Fitzgerald did not say very much, notes my father, but he thought she looked pleased. The attendees had been given free paperback copies of the 1983 second edition of *Three*, and when my father asked her to sign his copy, she wrote at the top of the title page, "For Ramsey Michaels, who knows an angel when he sees one—Sally Fitzgerald." For my father, it was the "next best thing to a note from Flannery herself!"

Which segues nicely into the next story. In 2013, while browsing the Internet, amazed at the prices that first editions of Flannery O'Connor were fetching (some into the five figures), my father came across what he came to call "the Flannery O'Connor item" going for $3,100. Not just a signature, but an entire paragraph written on a Christmas card in Flannery's own hand with a photograph of her on a porch smiling and facing right, framed together side by side. The note reads:

I appreciated those kind

14. O'Connor, *Collected Works*, 117–19.

words in the Commonweal—an
excellent selection of adjectives,
said I to myself. Did you
see the *editorial* in America
about *Rabbit, Run*? Nausesous [sic].
I hope your various projects
are going well and I wish
you a Merry Christmas.
      Flannery OC

My father writes, "Who but Flannery O'Connor would ever use the word 'Nausesous' (misspelled at that! She was a notorious speller) on *a Christmas card*?" He was intrigued, but it was "way out of [his] price range." The reference to John Updike's *Rabbit, Run* published in November 1960 dated it to Christmas of that year, but more sleuthing was needed. The card is "about as modest and generic as a Christmas card can be," he notes, with two small ornaments on either side of a larger one. The design is retro, very 1950s. The inscription is written on both sides so that the beginning of the note actually appears on the back side of the frame while just the last ten words appear on the front (underneath the ornaments). Letters to two of her friends place her in Piedmont Hospital in Atlanta between December 13 and 22, 1960, and it was probable that she wrote the card from there—perhaps on one provided by the hospital? Providentially the "item" showed up at the 2013 annual Boston Antiquarian Book Fair at the Hynes Auditorium. We usually parted ways soon after we arrived, but he hurriedly found me and dragged me over to the dealer's booth. While we were leaning over to examine "the item" more closely, the dealer must have seen how serious we were and said he'd take $2,500. My father was sorely tempted but resisted, wanting to find out more about its provenance.

The main thing he wanted to know was who the card had been addressing—*who* had written "those kind words in the *Commonweal*?" Later that year, after he had done his research and made sure it hadn't been sold, my father contacted the dealer and requested he bring it back to the Boston Fair in 2014 for further examination. I was cheering him on when he closed the deal for $2,000 (his third-most-expensive purchase after the Geneva Bible and the 1551 Taverner-Tyndale Byble). By then, he had learned who the recipient was, and some of the background story. About a month after Christmas of 1960, Flannery wrote to her publisher of *The Violent Bear It Away*, Robert Giroux: "I like the idea of the brochure on my book because all the good reviews are stuck off where nobody will ever see them. If you do get it up, I wish you would include Richard Gilman's remarks on it in the Christmas book issue of *Commonweal*."[15] A recent survey of the earliest reviews of Flannery's work includes a short unsigned piece in the *Commonweal* (December 9, 1960) on *The Violent Bear It Away*:

> For nothing I read this year satisfied me more than this story of a prophet *malgre lui*, written with the surest hand—antic, stern, deft, strong and revelatory. I might add that Miss O'Connor seems to me to be the only novelist writing today out of a religious sensibility who has stayed obedient to the laws and purposes of fiction; next to her I think Graham Greene, for instance, is a con-man.[16]

The Christmas card seems clearly to be Flannery's response to "those kind words." Her phrase "an excellent selection of adjectives, said I to myself" is a dead giveaway: "antic, stern, deft, strong and revelatory." An educated guess would be that Flannery knew the author of these words was Richard Gilman because Richard Gilman had most likely sent the review to her. Hence her note to Robert Giroux, who appears not to have heeded her suggestion. Gilman's reference to young Tarwater as "a prophet *malgre lui* [in spite of himself]" might even have prompted her to characterize Hazel Motes in such a way as "a Christian *malgre lui*" a year or so later in her author's note to the second edition of *Wise Blood*. Who knows?

"Who was Richard Gilman?" Turns out he was a freelance writer, a Jewish convert to Roman Catholicism, who converted in 1954 but left the church in 1959. In 1960 he was still a drama critic for the *Commonweal* (a major Catholic news journal). Twice in print he recalls his acquaintance with Flannery, including a visit to her home in Milledgeville, Georgia, in September of 1960, three months before she sent him the card.[17] Clearly, she knew him well enough to be candid about her literary opinions: "Did you see the *editorial* in America about *Rabbit, Run*? Nauseous." *America* was another Catholic news journal, a rival to the *Commonweal*. *Rabbit, Run* had appeared just a month earlier with a blurb on the front flap of the dust jacket by—you guessed it—Richard Gilman. The plot thickens. Gilman called it "a minor epic of the spirit, thirsting for room to discover and *be* itself, ducking, dodging, staying out of reach of anything that will pin it down and impale it on fixed, immutable laws that are not of its own making

---

15. O'Connor, *Habit of Being*, 429.
16. Scott and Streight, *Flannery O'Connor*, 158.
17. See Magee, *Conversations with Flannery O'Connor*, 44–57.

and do not consider its integrity."[18] *America* had run not just a book review, but an editorial, attacking John Updike and *Rabbit, Run* for its treatment of sex as "revoltingly gratuitous, obsessively all-pervading and restless until it can sink to descriptions of perversion."[19] Flannery agreed that sex in the novel was "laid on too heavy," to the point of "sheer boredom," yet she attributed to Updike "a real religious consciousness. It is the best book illustrating damnation that has come along in a great while."[20] Thus, her pronouncement of the editorial in *America* as overdone or "nauseous." That she brought up the matter to Gilman at all indicates that she may have read his words on the dust jacket, words that in some ways echoed her own: "The modern hero is the outsider. His experience is rootless. He can go anywhere. He belongs nowhere."[21] Something like Tom T. Shiftlet in "The Life You Save May Be Your Own." My father's account of his acquisition of this framed Christmas card was published in the 2015 issue of *Flannery O'Connor Review*,[22] including photographs of the "item."

Sometime in 2015, one of our conversations turned to J. F. Powers, another Catholic writer from the same time period. I sometimes assigned his story, "Death of a Favorite," in one of my literature classes and I was telling my father how positively my students responded to it—despite it being told from the point of view of a rectory cat, or maybe because of it. This conversation led to a lengthy back-and-forth about "A Good Man Is Hard to Find" in which a cat named Pitty Sing prominently figures. When Powers's collection of letters, *Suitable Accommodations*, came out in 2013, my father wrote a review for the 2014 *Flannery O'Connor Review*, the first paragraph of which contains a parenthetical aside: "Try to imagine 'A Good Man Is Hard to Find' as told by the cat!"[23] This was my inspiration. In the introduction to the essay I wrote, "Survival of a Favorite," I began, "I imagined it, and then wrote it, complete with a cat who can remember six lines of lyrics from *The Mikado* by Gilbert and Sullivan."[24] It was a fun project,

---

18. On the dust jacket of first edition of *Rabbit, Run* by John Updike.

19. "Run from Rabbit," 257. Although O'Connor suspected that the author of the review was Harold C. Gardiner, the editor of *America*, the review was one of several unsigned editorials on the page, so there is no way to be certain.

20. O'Connor, *The Habit of Being*, 420.

21. O'Connor, *Collected Works*, 856.

22. Michaels, "Flannery O'Connor Christmas Card," 16–66.

23. Michaels, review of *Suitable Accommodations*, 139.

24. Kerr, "Survival of a Favorite," 71.

a retelling of O'Connor's story from the cat's perspective. My father wrote his piece, "The Same Kind of Horns: Flannery O'Connor and J. F. Powers," at the same time and we submitted both articles to the *Flannery O'Connor Review*. The editor, Bruce Gentry, emailed me one Saturday in November, letting me know that our articles had been accepted for publication for the fall 2018 edition. I was beside myself with excitement and couldn't wait to share the news with my father. Trouble was, he wasn't here. He was giving a paper at an SBL (Society of Biblical Literature) meeting in Boston.

Rather than registering early and getting a discount, he had waited until almost the last minute, not wanting to pay ahead of time in case he "croaked" before the meeting, thereby wasting his money. That was my father. We had gone shopping the previous week to buy a couple of new dress shirts for the occasion. I'd hand him a pile of shirts, and he'd periodically open the dressing room curtain in just the shirt and his underwear. He had to ask me what color each one was. I felt a pang to see how wrinkly he was, how shrunken, how skinny his legs. I have no idea why he took his pants off; we weren't there for pants. The next weekend, I dutifully drove him to the Weston Hotel in Boston, parked the car, rode the escalator with him to the conference area and found his hotel room. The plan was for me to pick him up Sunday afternoon. I had been nervous, as he'd been having some trouble with sciatica and had a temporary (or so we thought at the time) catheter. He had brought a cane at my suggestion, but I doubt he used it. And, he had no phone. I could only pray that he would be at the designated meeting place two days later. He was, and on the way home I excitedly told him the publication news from Bruce, and he told me all about the conference. The following summer we were giddy as schoolgirls upon receiving the 2018 issue of *Flannery O'Connor Review* containing our articles side by side. Two years later, when I received the 2020 issue of *Flannery O'Connor Review* seven months after he died, I was touched by Bruce's inclusion of an "In Memoriam" that concluded his "From the Editor" note: "To J. Ramsey Michaels (1931–2020)." He was in the very good company of Harold Bloom (1930–2019), Josephine Keese King (1941–2019), and Elaine E. Whitaker (1942–2020).

40

Something Bad

There is an hour, a minute—you will remember it forever—when you know instinctively on the basis of the most inconsequential evidence, that *something is wrong*.[1]

Life changes fast. Life changes in the instant.[2]

January 18, 2020. Sometime before eight a.m.

I awoke to a commotion outside our bedroom. The dog barking, the door from the downstairs creaking open, my father's voice in the hall. Was *this* the minute I knew *something was wrong*? Not exactly. Or . . . maybe. My father had been living with us for six months, yet each morning Blue barked—seemingly surprised to find that someone was living downstairs. So, I can't blame the dog. Even so, something was off: my father was upstairs unusually early. And, as I would soon see, still in his pajamas. He usually didn't come upstairs until later—and never before he was fully dressed. Bill was already up. Hauling myself out of bed, I heard my father say, "Something bad happened." I caught up with him as he shuffled into the living room and sank heavily into the red chair by the window. He smiled when he saw me.

"Hey, good morning!" I said. "What's going on?"

He repeated, "Something bad happened."

1. Oates, *Widow's Story*, 10.
2. Didion, *Year of Magical Thinking*, 3.

He looked disheveled, but that was nothing new—and like I said, he was smiling. How bad could it be? I smiled back. Asked him what had happened. He'd woken early, he said, and was watching a YouTube video—Obama, he explained—as if that detail might prove important later on. Then he'd felt a sharp pain. He patted his chest. Managed to lie down on the rug next to his desk, he said, and then, with much difficulty, to get up again.

"I feel a little bit better now." He patted his catheter bag.

"That's good," I said.

I offered him coffee, but Bill—visible in the kitchen to me but out of my father's sight—dragged a finger across his neck.

Confused, I tried again: "How about some tea?"

"Sure," he said.

Bill was on the phone, enunciating our address. Abruptly, he announced, "An ambulance is on the way."

Bill alone recognized the situation for what it was. Unfailing optimist that I am, I'd been ready to forget about the whole thing, blame it on indigestion, and go back to bed. My father, who clearly knew better, had been expecting us to drive him to the hospital. Meekly, he hoisted himself out of the chair. I hovered behind him as he made his way down the stairs to his apartment. From the doorway I watched him slowly and carefully get himself ready: off came his pajamas and on went the khaki pants (accommodating the catheter), a green plaid short-sleeved shirt, and a navy cardigan. I offered to help. He waved me off. He asked for help when he needed it. He looped his belt through the belt loops; despite our lunches out and Bill's cooking, he'd lost weight since my mother died, and his trousers no longer stayed up without one. He didn't bother with socks or shoes, wore his slippers. He didn't take his billfold (as he called it) or put on his watch, which I didn't register until later.

Then three men from the ambulance company appeared, all big men who seemed to dwarf the apartment, commandeering the situation. "What were you doing when you felt the pain? Shingling the roof?" one of them asked, too loudly. Another gave him a handful of aspirin. Which must have been protocol, but which was probably not ideal in his case. They helped him onto a gurney, which had somehow materialized without me noticing. They expertly maneuvered it out of the bathroom door, out of the apartment, past the foot of the stairs, into the library, and out the front door, all of which had been made wider than standard for this eventuality. Within minutes they were gone. Bill and I dressed quickly and followed in our car.

There was a long wait in the waiting room of the ER, during which time I read the chapter of his memoir he had sent me the night before.

The clock above his hospital bed reads 9:30 a.m.—three hours before they will load my father into the back of another ambulance, bound for the only cardiac surgeon in Boston willing to operate on an eighty-eight-year-old man.

Three hours before I will next notice the time: 12:23.

Three hours before I will jog beside the stretcher, while he struggles to breathe. Before I'll tell him they won't let me ride in the back; before I will say *I'll be sitting up front with the driver*; before I'll say *I love you*. Before he'll say *Love you too*.

Three hours before I will hear:

"Ramsey! Ramsey! Stay with me!"

"Joe! Turn the ambulance around—and don't put on the siren."

Right now, though, my father. Life hasn't changed just yet, but I'm wary. I'm staring at the mangled toenail on his left big toe, an injury from a lawn mowing accident more than fifty years ago.

Where is his slipper? I look around.

We'd been at what my family called "the farm," a weathered farmhouse and barn on sixty acres in Shapleigh, Maine, a summer getaway my parents owned for a few years. It was the summer the Manson girls killed those people. I was fourteen—just about the same age as some of those girls—lying on a towel, working on my tan, listening to the news on my little transistor radio. My friend Martha P. was up for the week. My father was mowing the grass in his loafers. The grass was wet. He slipped. His foot slid under the mower and chewed up his leather loafer and practically took his big toe off. I remember loads of blood. I remember being immobilized by panic. My mother wasn't home. Lucky for him, Martha clicked right in. She ran into the house, came back with a bucket of soapy water, a washcloth, some towels. She gently washed his foot and wrapped it in a towel. We were too young to drive so he drove himself to the hospital—with his left foot wrapped in a towel.

I lost track of Martha soon after, but about four months ago, I ran into her and her mother—Bill recognized Mrs. P. first—at a local diner. Martha had been a teenager last time I saw her and bore little resemblance to the sixty-something-year-old woman sitting in the booth. After a polite round of "Still in the area?" and "Any kids?" she asked, "Do you remember that time when your father slipped under the lawn mower and almost cut his toe off?" And after my initial surprise, of course it made sense that that memory had stuck with her. It had certainly stuck with me, in part because my father used to occasionally like to gross me out by taking his sock off and showing off the disgusting toenail. I asked her if she'd become a nurse. She frowned. "God, no. Grant writer. But now I work at Home Goods." Pity. Missed her calling.

In the ER I force myself to not look at the toe (since the accident, he's had to visit a podiatrist periodically to cut the toenail, which is grossly misshapen) which right here, right now, heralds my father's mortality. I turn my body away from the foot and I look at his face instead, which is pretty wrinkly. (The other day, he'd been flipping through photos from Mike's wedding the previous August and, with good humor, had declared his face "a mess.") Our conversation now brims with the certainty (hope?) that this whole morning is but a blip in an otherwise long(er) life. We talk about the possibility that he may have to spend the night in the hospital.

"But then I'll miss Bible and Breakfast," he says, smirking. (They've given him a strong pain medication.) For lunch the coming Tuesday with Russ, after a bit of back and forth, we settle on Adea, an Israeli restaurant in Salem, tucked between a dentist's office and a hardware store, the one that serves killer Falafel. In passing, he mentions to Bill he is out of wine (another smirk). Don't spend more than twelve bucks for two, he says. He likes to reimburse us for wine. I tell him I'm not worried about the cost of the wine, but I *am* going to buy him a nightcap (not that kind) so our electric bill won't be so high next month. I picture him in the seriously red wool stocking cap I saw on the L. L. Bean website. After an hour or two, a doctor's assistant strides through the curtain and announces—mostly to me—that (1) what is going on is *extremely* serious and (2) while no one at this hospital can perform the kind of cardiac surgery my father requires, she's found a surgeon at Massachusetts General Hospital in Boston who's willing to operate.

Before she leaves to confirm with the cardiac surgeon, I ask if this is serious enough for me to call the family. She emphatically nods "yes." My father looks at me with a "What-did-she-say?" look.

My father is presented with a choice: Take an ambulance to Mass. General where the surgeon will be waiting, or go upstairs where he'll be "made comfortable"—a phrase so absurd and blatant we all register it for what it is.

Bill asks, "Are you ready to go?"

At first my father deliberately misinterprets. "Yes! Ready for the table!" Then he snorts. "I kind of want to stick around and see who will win the election."

A beat. Then gleeful: "On the other hand, if I croak, I won't have to do my taxes!"

And finally: "Why not? It wouldn't be so bad dying on the table—for me anyway, heh, heh. Can't vouch for the doctor."

I turn to the assistant, shrug. "Let's do it."

To my father, I say, "I'll be right back." I touch his hand, try to smile, and step out of the room; I have to walk down the hall a ways before I can get a signal on my phone. When I return, Bill asks me to look up G. K. Chesterton's "A Second Childhood"[3] on my phone. This is my father's idea. I find it, bend close to his ear, read.

> When all my days are ending
> And I have no song to sing,
> I think that I shall not be too old
> To stare at everything;
> As I stared once at a nursery door
> Or a tall tree and a swing.
>
> Wherein God's ponderous mercy hangs
> On all my sins and me,
> Because He does not take away
> The terror from the tree
> And stones still shine along the road
> That are and cannot be.
>
> Men grow too old for love, my love,
> Men grow too old for wine,
> But I shall not grow too old to see
> Unearthly daylight shine,
> Changing my chamber's dust to snow
> Till I doubt if it be mine.

---

3. Chesterton, "Second Childhood," 40-41.

Something Bad

Behold, the crowning mercies melt,
The first surprises stay;
And in my dross is dropped a gift
For which I dare not pray:
That a man grow used to grief and joy
But not to night and day.

Men grow too old for love, my love,
Men grow too old for lies;
But I shall not grow too old to see
Enormous night arise,
A cloud that is larger than the world
And a monster made of eyes.

Nor am I worthy to unloose
The latchet of my shoe;
Or shake the dust from off my feet
Or the staff that bears me through
On ground that is too good to last,
Too solid to be true.

Men grow too old to woo, my love,
Men grow too old to wed;
But I shall not grow too old to see
Hung crazily overhead
Incredible rafters when I wake
And I find that I am not dead.

A thrill of thunder in my hair:
Though blackening clouds be plain,
Still I am stung and startled
By the first drop of the rain:
Romance and pride and passion pass
And these are what remain.

Strange crawling carpets of the grass,
Wide windows of the sky:
So in this perilous grace of God
With all my sins go I:
And things grow new though I grow old,
Though I grow old and die.

He chuckles weakly—more of a snort really—in appreciation and tries to lick his lips. I take the hint, and spoon ice chips into his mouth, as his diet is now restricted. Eventually, two large ambulance drivers (I briefly wonder if all ambulance drivers need to meet a weight requirement) clatter into the cubicle in all their bluster and heavy gear and, talking loudly, rather too brusquely I think, hoist my father from the hospital bed onto a gurney. He is short of breath. He catches my eye and points to his chest; says he feels as though he has run a race, although I am fairly certain he has never run a race in his life. I do remember him jogging around the dead-end circle at their house in Wenham. Some doctor's idea. Sometimes I would accompany him. He would have been in his late forties then and I'm sure we never jogged more than two miles. The ambulance guys set him up with oxygen in his nose, adjust his catheter. Bill leaves to follow the ambulance in his car. Things speed up. Meet you there, he calls over his shoulder. I trot alongside the gurney, past closed curtains where other families' tragedies are unfolding, and out the emergency room door. The men open the double doors of the waiting ambulance and slide my father in, feet first. He is still out of breath. I put my hand on his shoulder, and he reiterates the feeling of having run a race.

On the way out of the hospital, I glance at the wall clock to my left: big, round, rimmed in black, a white face and large black numbers. I have stared at hundreds of clocks just like it—through elementary school, junior high, high school, college, graduate schools. Later, as a professor, it was often behind me. They must be standard-issue for official spaces.

12:23.

Outside, I put one foot on the bumper (fender?) of the ambulance, about to hoist myself up onto the bench beside his stretcher and am surprised when Joe tells me "no."

"You can't ride in the back," he says. "You sit up front with Bob."

Rule-follower me—why don't I ask *why not?*

"What did he say?" my father manages.

Over the noise of the engine, I shout, "They won't let me ride in the back." Then, more quietly into his ear, I say, "But I'm right here, Dad. I'll be sitting up front with the driver."

I take his hand. Bony. Warm. For as long as I can remember, the way I and my parents have ended any type of parting (letter, phone call, email, departure) is with "I love you." "I love you," I say. "Love you too," he says weakly. Unless he said something to Joe in the back of the ambulance, those were his last words. Love you too.

41

Ramsey! Ramsey! Stay with Me!

I'M CHATTING WITH THE driver, telling him this is the first time I've ever ridden in an ambulance (I get chatty when I'm nervous). He tells me I'm lucky. I look around the cab, noting all the gadgets, and we're not even three minutes out when I hear the voice from the guy in the back—Bob? Joe? I can't remember—loudly and briskly instructing the driver: *Turn the ambulance around and don't put on the siren.* At the time, I thought it was a bad sign—*Is he dead?* Since then, I've learned that they don't use the siren for heart patients, which makes sense given its shrillness. In response, the driver, protesting that he has a red light, nonetheless executes a not-quite-seamless U-turn at the intersection and retraces our route. At the ER entrance, the ambulance doors open, the hospital doors burst open, and my father is wheeled swiftly back to the cubby he vacated not five minutes earlier. I speed walk behind. Stop just short of the curtain. I watch a swarm of hospital personnel converge, fraught in a frenzy of activity, swirling around my father like bees. This seems to go on for a long time, but it's probably only a matter of minutes. Abruptly, as if signaled by some unseen force, some cosmic movie director, they all stop. Cut! File out of the cubby, silent, eyes downcast. Scene over. No one looks at me. I tentatively enter the room. My father lies alone and small and motionless in the bed and I make my way around to his left side, where I have so recently stood, reading a poem from my phone. To my father, who was listening. I put my hand on his age-spotted forehead. Look up at the clock: 12:34. Three hours, start to finish.

Four if you count when the "something bad" happened. Fewer hours than most births. *Not a bad way to go.*

It isn't the first time I have been present when the person dies, and maybe that's a good thing. I'm "a pretty cool customer."[1] I was there with my mother in Portsmouth hospital when they pulled the plug. I'd been there to put a blanket under my father-in-law's head after he'd collapsed in his driveway next door to my house. As a volunteer, I had been at the bedside of a number of hospice patients when their ends came. The last time I saw Holly, I was pulling out of her driveway in Sedgwick, Maine, on my way home after a weekend Holly had almost perfectly orchestrated. She was on hospice. We hit her favorite Mexican restaurant, the best pizza in Maine, the Russian Orthodox church she'd been going to on and off, some bougie tourist shops on Mount Desert Island, her favorite seaside walks. Almost perfectly because after the Mexican restaurant she started bleeding, and when we got back to her place she disappeared into the house to call the doctor. It was either on this visit or a previous one that I had smoked pot with her daughter Jenny who had acquired some weed from an elderly couple she knew specifically to alleviate her mom's discomfort. When Holly flatly refused, I felt sorry for Jenny and we shared a clumsily rolled joint, tried to focus on the movie Holly had chosen (*Gosford Park*), and failed (to focus). And on my final day, Holly had canceled the breakfast place she'd planned to take me to. She'd eaten an entire pizza the night before, at a place that had taken forty-five minutes to drive to. It was the best pizza I had ever tasted, but she'd overdone it. That morning, before I left, she'd been watering her many potted flowers and hanging laundry on a clothesline in the yard and said to me in passing:

"I hope I'll know when to lie down."

When I left that afternoon, I looked in my rearview mirror. We'd been best friends for over forty years. She was standing in front of her studio/gallery in stained overalls, one arm around Jenny, the other waving. I remember thinking that it would be the last time I'd see her. I braked in order to postpone the moment. As soon as she was out of sight, I lit a cigarette. I'd quit smoking twenty-five years earlier, with her help in fact, but when she got cancer I started up again. Those five-hour car rides to her house in Maine. I needed something to do. A few days later, Jenny called me—Holly was in the hospital. I offered to come up, but she said no need.

---

1. See Didion, *Year of Magical Thinking*, 15.

Years earlier, on our way to my father-in-law's memorial service, Mike had lamented from the back seat, "Who will play checkers with me now?" He was in first grade. I looked at him in the rearview mirror.

"Aww Buddy," I said. "I'm sorry."

Who will go to bookstores and library sales with me now? Who will discuss with me the finer points of the Gospels? Who will want to talk endlessly about Flannery O'Connor's characters and stories and get excited about article topics? Who will read the same books and articles and eagerly look forward to discussing them? Who will ooh and ahh over my library sale finds? Who will ever be so pleased to see me? Who will need me now? These last questions are frivolous and self-pitying as there are quite a few people who are not only pleased to see me but who actually need me, including Bill, our kids, and six grandkids who call me "Gram."

Yet my relationship with my father was unique and nontransferable. I am bereft. What did I expect? Did I think he would live forever? Of course not, but I had never really anticipated his death. Or rather, I had, too many times, arriving at his home in Portsmouth, ringing the doorbell, finally letting myself in with my key, calling his name, going from room to room to room, becoming ever more frantic, imagining him dead in bed, sprawled on the floor of the bathroom, lying in a disorganized heap at the bottom of the basement stairs. *Not a bad way to go*, the cardiologist had said. But I always found him alive; he hadn't heard the doorbell, hadn't heard me calling for him. I usually found in him in one of his many studies, nose in a book. He was like a piece of gristle. For as long as I can remember, even before he went (selectively) deaf, he'd had the uncanny ability (superpower as I thought of it) to be fully absorbed in whatever thought or book that happened to engage him to the exclusion of all else.

"Honey," my mother used to chide him, "where *are* you?"

I lift my hand from his cooling forehead, rest it on his shoulder, thin and bony under the cotton johnny. I whisper: Where *are* you? *Don't go.*

Bill hasn't yet returned. I'm feeling unmoored, unsure of the next step. Is there a protocol? Should I stay? Leave? Is there a form I need to fill out? I'm alone, but I don't exactly feel alone. I stare at my father and wait. I can't yet think of him as "a body."

Eventually, someone in scrubs appears, takes my arm, and guides me down the hallway to an empty room. Somber gray walls. A lot of Kleenex. A room designed, apparently, for grief. The door closes with a soft click. I slump into an ugly chair, cover my face with my hands. And weep.

42

Postscript

LATER, I TRIED TO convince myself that it was all for the best. The timing anyway. He had sold his house and dispersed many of his possessions to children and grandchildren, saving me quite a bit of work. Had his aortic aneurysm held fast for two months longer, I likely would not have been allowed into the ER or the ambulance with him. Maybe he would have gotten Covid. But I doubt that. I'd never seen my father with so much as a sniffle. He looked frail, but he was healthy, thriving, writing every day, driving even. He and my mother loved to travel, but he hadn't been out of New England in the five years since she'd died. Bill and I had been planning to take him on a surprise road trip to Skaneateles that summer. That also probably wouldn't have happened. By the end of March spring break, my schools had postponed reopening and then remained shuttered, and I took my classes online.

    In the five and half years since my mother died, my father and I spent hundreds of days together. I have a mountain of emails we sent back and forth. Three of our children got married and the fourth got engaged. My father attended two of those weddings (one had been in Houston; he hadn't wanted to go there and who could blame him?). He had been in our living room while our eldest son Will recounted the awkward but romantic story of his marriage proposal, down on one knee on a damp hillside in England, racing to get the words out and head back to town before the sun went down. (They eloped a year later.) Our daughters gave birth to his first two great-grandsons in 2019 and that spring and fall, I took care of one of them at the house twice a week. Theo always cried when I handed him to my father who had never been good with babies, even his own.

My father and Theo, his first great-grandson

After he moved in with us, we still ventured out on weekends to bookstores and library sales, antiquarian book fairs and restaurants, only now I didn't have to drive an hour to get him. He spent his days reorganizing, reading, browsing his books, and writing. Blue was happy to have someone to hang out with all day. On nice days my father spent hours in the hammock under the rowan tree, composing limericks and palindromes in

POSTSCRIPT

his head no doubt, often falling asleep as the shadows deepened. In the evenings we enjoyed Bill's fancy dinners, watched movies, and drank wine together. He rarely missed a Sunday morning Bible and Breakfast at Christ Church. He went out to lunch a few times with some old Gordon colleagues he'd reconnected (or reconciled) with. Our friend Russ came to visit, as did another old friend, Jeanette, when she was visiting from the west coast. He kept in touch with his pastor Chris from Middle Street Baptist Church who also visited occasionally, and with his friend Marge via landline. Tuesday nights became our designated movie night during which he usually nodded off, a glass of wine in his hand. He was here for the Thanksgiving wine tasting my husband organized and orchestrated, with wine that was far, *far* superior to my father's usual two-for-twelve-buck bottles. Two weeks before he died, January 5, during our second Christmas celebration after Will had returned from England, his girlfriend, now a fiancé, Bill's sister took our annual family New Year's photo, eleven of us crowded together on the couch in the living room. Renée in Houston had just had a baby who was too young to travel, so we left some space in the photo behind my father and me, and her husband later photoshopped their new family into the space behind the couch. My father, somehow now smaller than me—when had *that* happened?—is jammed against the end of the couch, grinning goofily and sheepishly it seems to me now. My left arm is draped around his shoulders.

Two days later, January 7, was Tuesday, movie night, although I don't remember what we watched. According to my moleskin planner, we drove up to the Book Barn in Lee, New Hampshire, on January 11. My father and I brought bags of books, most of which Vince gave us credit for. I'm sure we chatted with Vince and left with bags of different books. At Dante's we ate a late pasta lunch while the sun went down. We talked about Mike and his new wife Miranda, who were in Houston that weekend, the week of Renée's birthday, in order to meet their new nephew for the first time. On the drive home, it grew darker, and my father nodded off, his chin bobbing against his chest. One week later, "something bad happened." I picked up the New Year's cards from the printers a week after he died, so he never got to see them. He also didn't have to do his taxes. That job fell to me.

As for the result of the 2020 election, I can't be *absolutely* sure because we assiduously avoided talk about politics, so I will refrain from hazarding a guess as to what his reaction would have been. Whether or not he deployed a Hail Mary or two on his deathbed, I can't be sure, but if he did, I'm sure it didn't hurt.

New Year's Card 2020

43

PPS

NOT LONG BEFORE HE died, my father said to me, "I think the secret to a long life is curiosity." He was endlessly curious, at least in certain fields. Over forty years ago, in his sabbatical report of 1977–78, he wrote:

> If I had a couple more lifetimes, I would try for a PhD in linguistics, learn Arabic and modern Hebrew, live in Palestine or Jordan, learn to distinguish pottery types and be at least a part-time archaeologist. It is frustrating but also exciting to be reminded again how much there is to learn and how wide our horizons can be.

In his email inbox, dated Sunday, January 12, six days before he "croaked," I found an email he sent to Robin D. who headed up the aforementioned Bible and Breakfast, the one he'd been hoping to go to on January 19. The time stamp is 10:31 a.m., so he would have sent it soon after he returned from the meeting:

> Hi Robin,
> Enjoyed David Tam immensely. Also, your opening little anecdote. Not only have I heard it, I've told it myself a few times, only not involving men of the cloth. Hilarious.
>   Another one you can use sometime, if you haven't already. It's probably even true. A young couple applied for a class in how to speak Chinese. The instructor asked them why they wanted to take the class. Were they planning a trip to China? No, they said. We've just adopted a Chinese baby, and when he starts talking

we want to be able to understand him. You can have that for free [smiley face].

And thanks for the card and the angel. I need all the angels I can get. I'll pass the card along to Carolyn and Bill.
Cheers,
Ramsey.

I don't remember anything about a card, but I would be willing to bet he got all the angels he needed. *Gone home to glory.*

RENAISSANCE

Late afternoon's resplendent glow
Was all around me and I stood alone
On some hillside,
Alone on the brown earth
Under a flushed and dying sun.
The heavy day pressed in upon me
And etched for me in sharp relief
A certain unity of sense without
And self within and deity.
I should have been content with god
And man and nature one
But quite unaccountably I began to run
Not knowing where I went or why.
Then my synthesis of thing and thought
Of time and space was shattered
And in its place
A million little pieces, a million heres and nows,
The jagged edges of the whys and hows.
These tormented me as not before.
A whirling multitude of doubts and pale negations
Replaced the oneness and the affirmations.
Yet through this shivered windowpane
I saw a world
In pangs of birth
Out of discontinuity, out of the dry brown earth.
                    J. R. Michaels 1952

Appendix

Selections from My Father's Anthology

LIMERICKS, *BY J. R. MICHAELS:*

Fenton John Anthony Hort,
If he took Bishop Westcott to court,
Might have changed the marquee, which now reads as you see,
"Greek New Testament: Westcott and Hort."

Fenton John Anthony Hort
Gave the ending of Mark no support.
When Dean Burgon heard this, he said with a hiss,
"My dear Fenton, your Bible's too short!"

Fenton John Anthony Hort,
When he heard that his Bible was short,
Replied to the Dean, "Let's add 'God save the Queen,'
Or my project will surely abort."

Fenton John Anthony Hort,
When told that the Synod of Dort
Ruled the Bible inerrant to be quite apparent,
Said "So much for the Synod of Dort."

APPENDIX

Fenton John Anthony Hort
Left three works undone, they report:
Peter, James, Revelation. Ah, procrastination!
Poor Fenton John Anthony Hort!

Edna St. Vincent Millay
Was poetry's queen for a day.
Her candle so bright burned at both ends all night.
Poor Edna St. Vincent Millay!

A learned professor named Funk
Said the Gospel tradition was bunk,
And that Jesus was cryptic, not apocalyptic,
And other such similar junk.

An Englishman, N. Thomas Wright,
Once challenged Bob Funk to a fight.
With a Jesus not cryptic, but apocalyptic,
Tom said that the Gospels were right.

The eminent Dr. Nicole
Said "Theology's good for the soul.
From predestination to propitiation
It's best if you swallow it whole."

Edwin Abbott Abbott
Had a habit habit habit
Of reducing three dimensions to a plane.
In his Flatland universe, what could be a greater curse
Than something round hurled through his windowpane?

QUOTATIONS

G. K. Chesterton, at the end of his book entitled *Orthodoxy*: "Joy, which was the small publicity of the pagan, is the gigantic secret of the Christian. And as I close this chaotic volume I open again the small, strange book from which all Christianity comes; and I am again haunted by a kind of confirmation. The tremendous figure which fills the Gospels towers in this respect, as in every other, above all the thinkers who ever thought themselves tall. His pathos was natural, almost casual. The Stoics, ancient and modern, were proud of concealing their tears. He never concealed His tears. He showed them plainly on his open face at any daily sight, such as the far sight of His native city. Yet He concealed something. Solemn supermen and imperial diplomats are proud of restraining their anger. He never restrained His anger. He flung furniture down the steps of the Temple, and asked men how they expected to escape the damnation of Hell. Yet He restrained something. I say it with reverence; there was in that shattering personality a thread that must be called shyness. There was something that He hid from all men when He went up a mountain to pray. There was something that He covered up constantly by abrupt silence or impetuous isolation. There was some one thing that was too great for God to show us when He walked upon our earth; and I have sometimes fancied that it was His mirth."

F. J. A. Hort, in a letter to his children on the occasion of his father's death in 1873:
"Many children look forward hopefully to the time when they will be their own masters, without anyone over them. Well, let me tell you this. I have been a grown man for many years, for more than half my life; yet to me now one of the bitterest pangs is the feeling that I have no longer any one above me in my own family to look up to, and that I am now its oldest and highest member. I can hardly expect you now to understand quite what I mean, but if you keep this letter, and sometimes look at it in after years, perhaps you will understand better. Then you will know that one great blessing of our being children of the Heavenly Father is that it keeps us in childhood all our life long" (*Life and Letters of Fenton John Anthony Hort* 2:199).

The Serenity Prayer

by Reinhold Niebuhr (1892–1971), Complete, Unabridged, Original Version.
God, give us grace to accept with serenity
the things that cannot be changed,
Courage to change the things
which should be changed,

and the Wisdom to distinguish
the one from the other.
Living one day at a time,
Enjoying one moment at a time,
Accepting hardship as a pathway to peace,
Taking, as Jesus did,
This sinful world as it is,
Not as I would have it,
Trusting that You will make all things right,
If I surrender to Your will,
So that I may be reasonably happy in this life,
And supremely happy with You forever in the next.
Amen.

Palindromes by "Ye Smart Ramsey":

Campus motto: Bottoms up, Mac!
Deliver no evil gnostic illicit song. Live on, reviled!
Did a Toyota draw an award? A Toyota did.
Did a Toyota peep? A Toyota did.
Dogma: I am God.
Stressed diapers repaid desserts.
Distressed diapers repaid dessert, Sid!
Zeus, god, a dog, a plan, a canal, pagoda dog, Suez.
Eire, a plan, a canal, Pa., Erie
Flesh? Self!
God-pal? Deified lapdog!
He knits for odor of gnu dung. For odor of stink, eh?
Lonely Tylenol.
Onondaga? Gad, no. NO!
Oprah won red roses. Order now, Harpo!
Name now one man's sensuousness! Name now one man!
Regale me, lager!
To old Dallas, we Jews all add loot.
Wonks know!
Yamaha may draw an award? Yamaha may.

Selections from My Father's Anthology

Burma Shave: *(mine too)*

Watch the road.
Hang up the phone.
The life you save
May be your own.

PERSONAL REMINISCENCES

A couple of cameo scenes from our sabbatical in Cambridge, England, 1991. The first was at Heathrow Airport seeing my wife Betty off on a brief trip back to America for the birth of our grandson, Mikey. After I got her safely on the plane, I noticed a group of people among the crowd waiting for incoming passengers from the USA. They seemed to be a family, four or five people at least, British, anxiously waiting for some one person to come through customs. "What's keeping him?" I heard, and "It takes a while to get through, but he should be here any minute!" Then a cry of sheer joy, "Here he comes!" It was as if they were expecting the Messiah coming on the clouds: "And every eye shall see him." I felt a little left out. I knew nothing of their expectation, and consequently nothing of their joy. I was only an observer. Who was it they were expecting with such anticipation? Then I saw him coming. A pleasant well-dressed young man with Down syndrome, beaming, pushing an enormous baggage cart, obviously pleased as punch with himself for having made the flight alone, retrieving his baggage, and clearing customs. A Messiah indeed. What a magic moment! What a joy to be welcomed by those who loved him and wanted him, welcomed into the world, and now welcomed to Heathrow and to England.

The second scene was on St. Andrews Street in Cambridge that same year, the day before we were to go home to America. I was standing by a shop waiting for Betty and looking across the street at a fashionable women's boutique. In the window were three six-foot mannikins dressed in high fashion, long sweeping gowns reaching to the floor. Faceless mannikins they were, their heads resembling huge white eggs. Positively surreal. An English matron, fifty-ish, stopped by the window. She looked like any respectable English matron except that she was a dwarf. She could not have been more than three, three-and-a-half feet tall (about one meter as the Brits would say). She stared and stared at the three tall mannikins in the window for the longest time. It caught my attention. What was she thinking? What could be going through her mind? Finally, the dwarf lady made her move. After long deliberation, she turned and faced the door of the boutique head-on and walked determinedly into the store. From there on I was on my own. I could only imagine what she might have said. Perhaps, "Do you suppose I could have these shortened?" She has always been a reminder to me of the indomitable human spirit, human ingenuity, human aspiration. That's how God made us.

Yet another scene was in Grand Rapids, Michigan, summer of 2012, at the farmers market in that city. I was there with my wife Betty and her sister Lucy, they shopping and me mostly killing time after rushing through the market ahead of them in about five minutes. It was a very hot day, and I found a seat at the other end of the long single aisle, reading a book, and enjoying a cold bottle of water from a stand nearby. I noticed a tall man, maybe about sixty, in a broad-brimmed hat, standing facing the long aisle, carrying a homemade sign that said on one side "Sinners will be destroyed" and on the other "Repent and live." I was not exactly offended, but I was a little embarrassed. This, I thought, was no way to witness for Christianity. Not my style. His sign did not even mention God or Jesus by name. I kept on reading, ignoring the gentleman, who said nothing and just continued to wield his sign, turning it around every once in a while. Most other people ignored him as well. No heckling or protesting. This was Grand Rapids, after all, perhaps the northernmost of several buckles of the Bible Belt in the USA. Then something inside me told me, "Get up and buy a bottle of water and take it over to him." I did not want to do this. I was a Christian, but surely not that kind, and I really did not want to be implicated in his kind of Christian testimony. I had pretty much decided not to listen to this voice, but the next thing I knew I was on my feet and halfway over to the bottled water stand digging in my billfold for a dollar. I had absolutely no choice in this move. Nothing approaching free will. Irresistible grace for sure. I had been recruited, whether by his prayers or simply by the initiative of a sovereign God. I handed him the bottle of water, and said, "I thought you might need this," or something to that effect. He smiled and took it, said thank you, and that was it. No big deal, it seemed. I went back to my seat, my book and what was left of my own bottle of water, now lukewarm.

Bibliography

Atwood, Craig D. *Community of the Cross: Moravian Piety in Colonial Bethlehem.* University Park: Pennsylvania State University Press, 2004.
Baker, Eleanor. "Death to Book Thieves!" *Literary Review* 535 (2024) 64.
Banks, Louis Albert. *Immortal Hymns and Their Story.* Cleveland: Burrows Brothers, 1898.
Basbane, Nicholas A. *A Gentle Madness: Bibliophiles, Bibliomanes, and the Eternal Passion for Books.* New York: Henry Holt & Company, 1995.
Belsham, Thomas. *The New Testament in an Improved Version, upon the basis of Archbishop Newcome's New Translation.* Boston: Thomas B. Wait and Company, 1809.
Bierce, Ambrose. *The Collected Writings of Ambrose Bierce.* New York: Citadel, 1947.
Burgess, Gelett. *Goops and How to Be Them: A Manual of Manners for Polite Infants.* Bedford, MA: Applewood, 2004.
Byrom, John. *The Private Journal and Literary Remains of John Byrom.* Manchester: Chetham Society, 1856.
Chesterton, G. K. "A Second Childhood." In *The Ballad of St. Barbara and Other Verses*, 40–41. North Haven, CT: Leopold Classic Library, 2025.
Daniell, David. *The Bible in English.* New Haven, CT: Yale University Press, 2003.
Diabagio, Julie, and Sally Holben. *Skaneateles Through Time.* United Kingdom: Fonthill, 2015.
Didion, Joan. *The Year of Magical Thinking.* New York: Alfred A. Knopf, 2005.
Donner, Robert [Richard Gilman]. "She Writes Powerful Fiction." In *Conversations with Flannery O'Connor*, edited by Rosemary M. Magee, 44–57. Jackson, MS: University Press of Mississippi, 1987.
Dunning, John. *Booked to Die.* New York: Pocket Star, 1992.
Fadiman, Anne. *Ex Libris: Confessions of a Common Reader.* New York: Farrar, Straus and Giroux, 1998.
———. *The Wine Lover's Daughter.* New York: Farrar, Straus and Giroux, 2017.
Farrand, Max, ed. *Benjamin Franklin's Memoirs: Parallel Text Edition.* Berkeley: University of California Press, 1949.
Ferrara, Susan. *The Family of the Wizard: The Baums of Syracuse.* Bloomington, IN: Xlibris, 2000.
Fleetwood, John. *The Christian's Dictionary: or, Sure Guide to Divine Knowledge. Containing a Full and Familiar Explanation of all the Remarkable Words made Use of, in the Holy Scriptures, and in the Writings of the most eminent and pious Divines, whether ancient or modern.* London: J. Cooke, in Pater-Noster-Row, 1775.

Bibliography

Frost, Joseph. *Divine Songs of the Muggletonians, in grateful praise to the only true God, the Lord Jesus Christ*. London: R. Brown, 1829.

Gaustad, Edwin. *Baptist History Celebration 2007: A Symposium of Our History, Theology and Hymnody*. Springfield, MO: Particular Baptist, 2008.

Greenaway, Kate. *Under The Window: Pictures & Rhymes for Children*. New York: Routledge & Sons, 1880.

Grossman, Walter. "Gruber on the Discernment of True and False Inspiration." *Harvard Theological Review* 81 (1988) 363–87.

Gutjahr, Paul C. *An American Bible: A History of the Good Book in the United States, 1777–1880*. Stanford: Stanford University Press, 1990.

Hamilton, Gail. *Gail Hamilton's Life in Letters*. Vol. 1. Edited by H. Augusta Dodge. Boston: Lee and Shepard, 1901.

———. *A Washington Bible Class*. New York: D. Appleton and Company, 1891.

———. *Women's Wrongs: A Counter-Irritant*. Boston: Ticknor and Fields, 1868.

———. *X-Rays*. Hamilton, MA: n.p., 1896.

Herbert, A. S. *Historical Catalogue of Printed Editions of the English Bible, 1525–1961*. New York: American Bible Society, 1968.

Hoffman, Clare. *Sister, Sinner: The Miraculous Life and Mysterious Disappearance of Aimee Semple McPherson*. New York: Farrar, Straus and Giroux, 2025.

Hostetler, John A. *Amish Society*. Baltimore: Johns Hopkins University Press, 1963.

Keay, Julia. *Alexander the Corrector: The Tormented Genius Whose Cruden's Concordance Unwrote the Bible*. New York: Overlook, 2005.

Kerr, Carolyn Michaels. "Survival of a Favorite." *Flannery O'Connor Review* 18 (2018) 70–75.

Kipling, Rudyard. *The Holy War*. First Published in 1917.

Knox, R. A. *Enthusiasm, A Chapter in the History of Religion with special reference to the XVII and XVIII centuries*, Oxford: Clarendon, 1950.

Metz, Christian. Quoted in "The Journey Begins," translated by Helen Rind and Henrietta Ruff. Amana: Amana Church, 1992.

Michaels, J. Ramsey. "Atonement in John's Gospel and Epistles." In *The Glory of the Atonement*, edited by Charles E. Hill and Frank A. James III, 106–18. Downers Grove, IL: InterVarsity, 2004.

———. "Charles Thomson and the First American New Testament." *Harvard Theological Review* 104.3 (2011) 349–65.

———. "A Flannery O'Connor Christmas Card." *Flannery O'Connor Review* 13 (2015) 160–66.

———. "Four Cords and an Anchor." In *I (Still) Believe: Leading Bible Scholars Share Their Stories of Faith and Scholarship*, edited by John Byron and Joel N. Lohr, 173–85. Grand Rapids: Zondervan, 2015.

———. *The Gospel of John*. Edited by Ned Stonehouse et al. New International Commentary on the New Testament. Grand Rapids: Eerdmans, 2010.

———. *Revelation*. Edited by D. Stuart Briscoe and Haddon Robinson. The IVP New Testament Commentary Series 20. Downers Grove, IL: InterVarsity, 1997.

———. Review of *Horses Can See in the Dark* by Marietta Ball. Amazon, October 14, 2014. amazon.com/Horses-Can-Dark-Marietta-Ball/dp/1468030221.

———. Review of *Suitable Accommodations* by J. F. Powers. *Flannery O'Connor Review* 12 (2014) 139–40.

———. *Servant and Son: Jesus in Parable and Gospel*. Eugene, OR: Wipf & Stock, 2017.

Bibliography

———. "*A Washington Bible Class*: The Bloodless Piety of Gail Hamilton." In *Strangely Familiar: Protofeminist Interpretations of Patriarchal Biblical Texts*, edited by Nancy Calvert-Koyzis and Heather Weir, 191–202. Atlanta: Society of Biblical Literature, 2009.

———. "A 'World with Devils Filled': The Hawkes-O'Connor Debate Revisited." *Flannery O'Connor Review* 6 (2008) 119–34.

Michaels, J. Ramsey, ed. *The Spirit of Prophecy Defended*. Leiden: Brill, 2003.

Miller, William. *Evidence from Scripture and History of the Second Coming of Christ about the Year 1843, exhibited in a course of lectures*. Troy: Kemble & Hooper, 1836.

Newell, Peter. *The Hole Book*. New York: Harper & Brothers, 1908.

———. *The Slant Book*. Rutland, VT: Charles E. Tuttle, 1967.

Nicole, Roger. *Standing Forth: Collected Writings of Roger Nicole*. Fearn, Ross-shire: Mentor, 2002.

Notes on Scripture (Designed for Young Inquirers). Edinburgh: Waugh & Innes, 1832.

Oates, Joyce Carol. *A Widow's Story*. New York: HarperCollins, 2011.

O'Connor, Flannery. *Collected Works*. New York: Library of America, 1988.

———. *The Habit of Being: Letters Edited and with an Introduction by Sally Fitzgerald*. New York: Farrar, Straus and Giroux, 1979.

———. *Mystery and Manners*. New York: Farrar, Straus and Giroux, 1962.

Ribuffo, Leo P. *The Old Christian Right: The Protestant Far Right from the Great Depression to the Cold War*. Philadelphia: Temple University Press, 1983.

Robinson, Robert. *A Plea for the Divinity of Our Lord Jesus Christ, in a Pastoral Letter Addressed to a Congregation of Protestant Dissenters at Cambridge*. Cambridge: Francis Hudson, 1780.

Roberts, David. *The Holy Land, Syria, Idumea, Arabia, Egypt, & Nubia. From Drawings Made on the Spot by David Roberts, R. A. with Historical Descriptions by the Revd. George Croly, L. L. D. Lithographed by Louis Haghe*. London: Day & Sons, 1855.

"Run from Rabbit." Review of *Rabbit, Run*, by John Updike. *America* 19 (1960) 257–58.

Schwartz, Hillel. *The French Prophets: The History of a Millenarian Group in Eighteenth-Century England*. Los Angeles: University of California Press, 1980.

Scott, R. Neil, and Irwin Steight, eds. *Flannery O'Connor: The Contemporary Reviews*. New York: Cambridge University Press, 2009.

Simms, P. Marion. *The Bible in America*. New York: Wilson-Erickson, 1936.

Smith, Wilbur. *Before I Forget*. Chicago: Moody, 1971.

Tureng. "Wirkungsgeschichte." https://tureng.com/en/german-english/wirkungsgeschichte.

Twain, Mark. *The Adventures of Huckleberry Finn*. New York: Harper & Brothers, 1912.

Updike, John. "The Child Within." In *Just Looking: Essays on Art*, 33–41. New York: Knopf, 1989.

———. *Rabbit, Run*. New York: Knopf, 1960.

Wakefield, Gilbert. *A Translation of the New Testament*. Boston: Harvard University Press, 1820.

Woolley, Edward A. *Prospect Cooperative Club: A Great Social Experiment*. Nantucket: Sheepfold, 2006.

Wortis, Joseph. *Tricky Dick and His Pals*. New York: The New York Times, 1974.

www.ingramcontent.com/pod-product-compliance
Lightning Source LLC
Chambersburg PA
CBHW071715160426
43195CB00012B/1688